THE PRIMARY CURRICULUM:

A Process Approach to Curriculum Planning

THE PRIMARY CURRICULUM:
A Process Approach to Curriculum Planning

Second Edition

Geva M. Blenkin and A. V. Kelly

P·C·P
Paul Chapman
Publishing Ltd

First published 1987
by Harper & Row Ltd
London

Reprinted 1988
by Paul Chapman Publishing Ltd
London

British Library Cataloguing in Publication Data
Blenkin, Geva M.
    The primary curriculum: a process approach
to curriculum planning.——2nd ed.
    1. Education, Elementary——Great Britain
    ——Curricula
    I. Title   II. Kelly, A. V.
    372.19′0941   LB1564.G7

ISBN 1 85396 027 6

Typeset by Inforum Ltd, Portsmouth
Printed and bound by Butler & Tanner Ltd, Frome and London

CONTENTS

'The primary school has its own canons of excellence and criteria of success; it must have the courage to stand by them.'

The Hadow Report, 1931

INTRODUCTION TO THE SECOND EDITION

The first edition of *The Primary Curriculum* was written with the deliberate intention of reasserting that view of education which had been suggested as the most appropriate for the Primary sector of schooling by both the Hadow (1931) and the Plowden (1967) Reports, of identifying the implications for that view of subsequent developments in curriculum theory and of demonstrating some of the misunderstandings displayed in many of the criticisms which have been directed at it. It also attempted to show that the form of recent and current political intervention in the curriculum reveals similar levels and kinds of misconception. This was done not to press a particular ideology of education on Primary teachers, as has been suggested by some critics, but rather to articulate a view of education which we believe most Primary teachers embrace but which they themselves have not always been able to articulate clearly, and thus to protect from external attack and misinformed criticism.

Two significant things have happened since the publication of that book. First, the level of external political intervention has increased, without any change in its form or quality, so that the only change in its impact is that it has – at least in some areas – become a good deal greater. Secondly, there has been a developing awareness of the essential elements and the crucial distinctiveness of the approach to curriculum which that book outlined, an awareness which has been followed and fostered by several other books devoted to an examination of Primary education which have subsequently emerged, so that teachers are both more alive to what is implied by the idea of education as process or development and more conscious of the educational inadequacies of the other approaches which are being foisted on them. Thus the tension which we noted in 1981 as existing between the perception of the teacher's task taken by most teachers themselves and that of those external to the schools whose views are being thrust upon them has, if anything, increased.

The Introduction to the first edition has been reproduced and follows this new Introduction. It sets out the main purposes of that book and these continue to be fundamental. Two further things need to be done, however, to illuminate what this second edition is additionally attempting. The major points of change need to be identified, since these are of great significance not only in illustrating how the educational climate has changed since 1981, but also in highlighting some major developments in our own thinking. First, however, we must endeavour to put right what we see as a serious misunderstanding of the position we adopted and tried to outline in 1981. This in itself may be further evidence of the tone and tenor of subsequent developments.

In 1981, our main aim was to articulate the essentials of 'progressivism' in a way we felt had not been done before. No real attempt, in our view, had been made prior to that to establish for this kind of 'progressive' philosophy any real basis in a genuine curriculum theory; and there was no evidence that its deeper curriculum implications had been understood or appreciated nor that it was based on a curricular analysis of any degree of sophistication. Indeed, we tried to show that there was much evidence that quite the opposite was the case. At that time such an analysis and articulation were necessary. In offering them, however, our aim was to take the debate a good deal further and, in particular, to develop the notion of education as process, a notion which we see as being much more complex and sophisticated than that of mere 'progressivism'.

We, therefore, wish to disclaim the title of 'Romantics' which some have given us as a result of the publication of that book, and particularly its connotations of starry-eyed idealism. We see that as reflecting a serious misapprehension of what that book was attempting, and a failure to recognize its intention (if not its effect) of providing a more rigorously argued base for this kind of view. It was not intended as a mere restatement of 'progressivism' nor of the Hadow/Plowden philosophy. Certainly, their starting point is ours and their basic tenets are ours, as our Chapter 1 continues to reveal, but the notion of education as process seems to us to go far beyond anything encapsulated in the term 'progressivism', certainly in the sense in which that has often been interpreted by both its supporters and its critics, and in particular to include a level of theoretical analysis that most statements of 'progressivism' have conspicuously lacked. It was that that we attempted to articulate.

For much has happened since the publication of the Plowden Report in 1967 to increase our understanding both of curriculum and of how children's educational development can best be promoted, and perhaps especially our appreciation of the interaction of the two. The work of people like Lawrence Stenhouse in the field of curriculum and of people such as Jerome Bruner,

Margaret Donaldson and Eliot Eisner in that of child development, and, indeed, in the interface of these two areas, has done much to promote the emergence of an understanding of education and curriculum to which the term 'progressivism' does scant justice. For their work has provided a base for a more closely argued and more deeply analytical exploration of this general approach to education, and thus demands that it be acknowledged as a far more complex matter than many discussions of it, by both theorists and political agencies, have either allowed or recognized. It is a gross misunderstanding of the thrust of our first edition to see it as merely restating a romantic 'progressivism'. We hope this second edition will make that completely clear in a way that the first edition clearly failed to do.

There is some reason to hope for this too. It is possible that the misunderstanding of the position we were concerned to explicate in 1981 was due to our articulation of it. Certainly, at that time, a reassertion of the basic ideals of 'progressivism' was needed, and, if we achieved no more than that, we are reasonably content. Since then, however, the cause has been taken up by many others. Many teachers have found a voice. And there has been that subsequent increase in publications supporting or exploring this general view to which we referred earlier. The reassertion of basic principles has thus been made. It should now be easier to take these further and to make it clear that we are taking them further. It is that which is the main concern of this revised edition.

It may be of interest – especially to those who received our first edition so well – if we briefly outline the major changes we have felt it appropriate to make for this new edition with that general aim we have just outlined especially in mind. For these reveal not only the movement in our own thinking but – more importantly – developments which have taken place in the intervening period, changes in the attitudes and perceptions of teachers, changes in the climate within which we all work and advances which have occurred in our understanding of education, of curriculum and, most importantly, of children. They are all of them modifications and amendments which have been prompted not only by our own perceptions of what has been happening since 1981, but also those of the many people who, in making welcoming and supportive noises about the book, have also offered much constructive advice and helpful comment on where and how it might be improved, and what developments a new edition might attempt to reflect.

First, we have endeavoured to take fuller cognizance of those recent advances in development psychology and related fields which have done so much not only to underline the need for this kind of approach to education but also to identify some of its most important features. We claimed in the first edition that there was much support in the work of developmental psychologists for this approach; that support seems to us to have increased immeasurably as a result of recent work in that field and in certain related fields such as that of the study of human language and other forms of symbolization.

Secondly, and perhaps as a result of this, we have felt able to reduce somewhat the scale of the rather massive attack we mounted in the first edition on the behavioural objectives approach to curriculum planning. We are still aware how easily teachers slip into this simplistic form of planning, primarily because it is so simplistic, but we are also of the view that teachers in general, especially those in Primary schools, are now much more conscious of the inadequacies of this approach – would that the same could be said of the Inspectorate and the authors of those 'definitive' statements on curriculum we continue to receive from political sources – and that what they now need is not so much a parading of the arguments against that approach as a clearer exposition of how they might avoid sliding into it – or being forced into it by external pressures. We have attempted, therefore, to offer a fuller explanation and elucidation of what it means to plan the curriculum in terms of developmental processes and, further, what such a curriculum looks like in practice.

We have felt if necessary, on the other hand, to develop further our arguments against content-based planning, and our reasons for claiming that this too is incompatible with a process-based approach. For content is the other current obsession of our political masters, and we need to be just as clear about what this form of curriculum planning entails as about the implications of product-based or objectives-based planning. This concern with content as the prime factor in curriculum planning is being manifested particularly in what is happening currently in the field of teacher education, so that that too will loom larger in this edition than it did in our first.

For this reason, we have felt it further necessary to point up, rather more than we did in 1981, the contrast between the view of education as process, to which we believe most teachers in Primary schools are basically committed, and the general tenor of the political climate and consequent external pressures to which we all, as teachers, are increasingly exposed. For, if we are right in suggesting that teachers' thinking has moved some way towards a clearer view of, and thus a deeper commitment to, the idea of education as process, we have also to acknowledge that the political view, as evinced in both policy and discussion documents emerging from the Department of Education and Science, has moved at least as much in the other direction.

We have also become increasingly conscious that this latter, and somewhat limited, view has often been reinforced in its limitations by the 'findings' of some ill-conceived and somewhat superficial 'researches' into education in the Primary sector, and, since the impact of some of these has been out of all proportion to their value, or indeed validity, we have felt it appropriate in this new edition to devote a little time to a consideration of that impact and the question of their validity.

Finally, we have been taken to task since the publication of that first edition, especially by some like-minded colleagues in the Secondary field, for appearing to appropriate this form of education for the Primary sector of schooling. They have rightly pointed out to us that there are many teachers in Secondary schools, especially in particular curriculum areas such as Craft, Design and Technology, who are attempting to work in precisely this way, who could benefit from the kind of analysis we are attempting here, but who may not do so because of our apparent concentration on the Primary school. It was for this reason that we included a section in the follow-up text to the first edition, *The Primary Curriculum in Action*, which took the reader 'Beyond the Primary School'.

In this second edition we have broadened our scope slightly in order to allow for this. There is a further reason for attempting to do so. A feature of the educational scene in the last few years has been the increased interest in the Primary/Secondary divide, a growing concern to smooth the process of Primary/Secondary transfer and a desire to improve the quality of Primary/Secondary liaison. The policy of discouraging the continuation of Middle schools has increased the need for developments of this kind. The prime consideration, however, from the point of view of those of us who are committed to the approach to education outlined here, must be with the question of whether this will enhance or diminish the influence of that view, whether it will lead to an extension of that approach into further areas of the Secondary school curriculum or its contraction in the Primary school under the pressure of the more content-based practices which Secondary schools in general tend to favour. Again we must recognize that the tone and tenor of current political initiatives would suggest that the latter is likely to be the outcome. Again, therefore, there is a clear need to keep this aspect of the current scene in mind, and this is something else we have attempted to do in this second edition.

All these issues, then, seem to us to have grown in significance since 1981, and we have been concerned to give greater prominence to all of them in this revised edition.

Lastly, we have been flattered, if somewhat disturbed, to discover that in many places, both institutions of teacher education and centres for their in-service and continuing education, our book has been used as a textbook. We have not heard of any cases where it is read, or chanted, in unison, or learnt by rote, but we do know of many situations in which groups have systematically studied and analysed its themes chapter by chapter.

We have tried, therefore, to respond to the many requests we have had to organize it in a form and style which would support this kind of use. We have, for example, tried to equalize the lengths of the individual chapters to ensure regular and even proportions of 'homework', although again we have not been able to achieve this with Chapter 6; and we have offered at the end of each chapter a short bibliography listing the books we feel it might be appropriate to read in order to explore further and develop the ideas we have offered. We hope these will aid those who wish to use the book in this way, but at the same time we hope that tutors will ensure that it promotes the critical powers of their students and encourages them to their own critical analysis of what is offered and that it does not become an alternative to such personal exploration. For it is pesonal development through first-hand engagement with ideas that is at the root of the view of education we are concerned to promote, and this is at least as important for teachers themselves as it is for their pupils.

This last reflection on the way in which the book has been used since its publication in 1981 leads us to the final point we wish to make in the Introduction. The response we have had to the first edition has been immensely gratifying. We have received favourable and supportive comments from many different quarters. We have been invited to talk to groups of teachers, student-teachers, advisers and others in many parts of the country. And everywhere we have been welcomed and given every encouragement to continue to develop and press this view of what education can be. It is clear that we were right to claim, as we did in 1981, that there are many teachers, especially in Primary schools, who embrace this philosopy and whose lack hitherto has been not of the will to work in this way but of the help they need to do so effectively. We are pleased, gratified, even flattered, at being regarded as offering this kind of help. We have been delighted to discover how widespread support for this kind of view is. We take it as encouraging evidence that there is hope for education yet, despite the depressing lack of vision displayed by those who are currently attempting to control and direct it. We hope that those who received the first edition so warmly will not be disappointed in this second edition, and that it will encourage them further to develop their own thinking and their own practice along lines which can only lead to enhanced experiences and improved prospects of genuine educational growth for their pupils.

INTRODUCTION TO THE FIRST EDITION

A great deal of attention has been directed in recent years towards the theory and practice of curriculum development. This has brought a necessary and welcome rigour to curriculum study and, indeed, to the study of Education itself and has resulted in the emergence of a body of theory that, while drawing on other contributory disciplines, has nevertheless begun to develop its own unique focus on the educational process itself.

For a number of reasons, however, the predominant flavour of the work that has been done in this field hitherto, certainly in the United Kingdom, has been that of post-Primary education, the education of the 11–18 age-group. For most of those who have been engaged in research or responsible for publications in curriculum theory have been people whose own first-hand experience of teaching has been at the Secondary or even the Tertiary level. Most of the curriculum development that has been undertaken in a formal way has gone on within subject areas and has thus seemed to be more clearly relevant to the subject-based curriculum of post-Primary institutions than to the holistic, undifferentiated approach associated with the traditions of the British Primary school. And finally, as a result of this, most, although by no means all, of the curriculum projects sponsored by such bodies as the Schools Council have been firmly directed at the development of particular subjects at the Secondary level.

On the other hand, a lot of what has been written about the Primary school has lacked the rigour necessary for a proper analysis of both its theory and its practice. Intuition and inspiration have their place as much in education as in any other creative activity, but the measures they lead to must at some stage be examined and evaluated with some degree of care and objectivity, so that what is of value in them can be identified and described. Other material too that has been written about the Primary school has tended to concentrate unduly on method to the exclusion of other, more fundamental, aspects of curriculum planning and development. And, lastly, there has also been a tendency, especially evident in some of the more formally constituted projects in the Primary field, to approach some of the issues of the Primary curriculum from a Secondary perspective.

However, until the recent establishment in some areas of Middle schools, catering for pupils between the ages of 8 and 12 or 9 and 13, a change of educational milieu at the age of 11+ was a major feature of the English system and common to every child, and, on either side of this almost watertight divide, two quite different educational traditions have developed. The term 'Primary school', therefore, a generic term for Nursery schools, Infant schools, First schools and Junior schools, as well as those schools which cater for the whole of this age-range, conjures up thoughts of a distinctive approach to educational practice, an approach which has been adopted also by some, although by no means all, of the newly established Middle schools.

As a result, the Primary curriculum has many features that make it worthy of a proper study by the curriculum theorist in its own right. It has developed, especially in relation to the education of the very young child, in a manner largely free from the external constraints imposed on the curriculum of other institutions by such things as public examinations and from the internal constraints of a structure based on distinct subject departments. It has also, until recently, been free for the most part from the demands of politicians, industrialists and other 'consumers' for a concentration on the teaching of certain kinds of subject and certain skills. This has enabled it to develop steadily over a long period of time, so that the concept of curriculum planning, development and innovation at this level of education long predates the establishment of bodies such as the Schools Council whose task it has been to promote such changes nationally. For the same reason, it has also been able to adopt a largely non-instrumental approach to curriculum planning, has been using for some time what has only recently on its arrival in the Secondary school become recognized as a 'process model' of curriculum and may thus be considered to be rather nearer to achieving a truly educational curriculum than most types of institution. In short, it has developed its own unique ethos, the essence of which is an emphasis on the development of the child, on learning for its own sake and, as a corollary of these, a largely undifferentiated approach to curriculum content and curriculum planning. It is this feature of the English Primary school that has attracted the attention, the interest and the admiration of educationists throughout the world.

However, it is clear that this approach to education is not everywhere reflected in practice. For here, as in every other sphere of human activity, there is much variety and the gap between the ideal and the reality, between theory and practice and even between particular theories and practices is one that must be acknowledged. Many schools continue in their practice to display either an allegiance to the older 'elementary school' or even the 'preparatory school' traditions (Blyth 1965) or to reveal a failure to appreciate all that is entailed by the acceptance of the newer 'progressive' view. We would not wish to be understood, therefore, as suggesting that the view of the curriculum we are about to examine is to be seen in the work of every Primary school or of every Primary teacher.

Some Primary schools, however, and some Primary teachers have for a long time been employing a particular approach to the planning, the execution and the recording of their work. It is possible also to find some teachers in certain areas of Secondary education who have been attempting to do the same. There are notable examples of this approach to education to be found too in the private school sector. Although these may be a few in number, what they have been doing is worthy of consideration in its own right.

What we do hope to show, therefore, is that a different and unique educational tradition has emerged from the development of the English Primary school, a tradition which, while not being manifest in the practice of all schools, is certainly apparent in that of some, particularly those concerned with the education of younger children, and has become enshrined in the theory of Primary education through the approaches that have been adopted to the preparation of teachers for this level, through the work of many local authority advisers and through the official pronouncements of the two major government reports in this area, those of the Hadow Committee (1931) and the Plowden Committee (1967).

It is this 'progressive' tradition that we intend to examine here, partly because it has this kind of official sanction, but especially because we regard it as providing a valuable and important model for educational planning and one that, in our view, is currently at risk, not only from external pressures on schools but also because of a lack of clarity among some teachers and educationists over what it entails.

For recent demands for a monitoring of standards and the greater public accountability of teachers threaten to apply criteria of measurement and a style of evaluation to the Primary curriculum that derive from other, different sources and are likely, therefore, to be unsuitable for the task. They are thus likely to introduce distortion rather than rigour, to cut across the natural development of a good many years and to lead to losses rather than gains in educational terms. The Primary curriculum, like that of any other type of educational insitution, must be evaluated, but it must be evaluated in its own terms, so that techniques and procedures appropriate to it must be developed for the purpose. The principles that have underpinned curriculum development at the Primary level must be examined in their own proper context, and we must not allow them to be perverted by the application of criteria of a different and inappropriate kind to their continuing development.

Furthermore, there is evidence of an increasing interest in curriculum development among treachers in Primary schools, an interest that has been fostered by many local advisers and others in an attempt to promote in teachers the kind of reflection on and understanding of their work that will enable them to appreciate its basic principles and thus to respond appropriately to these growing external demands. Again, this is a process which can only be successful if it begins from a familiarity with those ideas that have emerged from the long tradition of thinking about Primary education.

Finally, there is reason to hope that such an examination may reveal a good deal that will be of value to curriculum theory generally. If we are right to claim that the Primary curriculum has been less subject to external constraints and thus less prone to pressures towards planning of an instrumental kind, it may have more to offer to those who are seeking a genuinely educational rationale for curriculum planning than the curriculum at any other level of education. This would constitute, then, a further reason not only for studying it but also for preserving it from the dangers of distortion that come with attempts to bend it to fit other, unsuitable models.

The exploration undertaken here of the Primary curriculum, then, is prompted primarily by a conviction that it is an important, valuable and unique form of curriculum which has developed in a different manner and in a different context from that to be seen in other educational institutions. Furthermore, there are three particular reasons why it is felt important to attempt an analysis of it at this point in time. Firstly, we must examine the implications and dangers of current demands that we evaluate it from a perspective that may not be appropriate to it. Secondly, we must try to help teachers to develop the kind of understanding of the principles that may lie behind their work that will enable them to make a proper assessment of proposals for change, whether initiated from inside or from outside the school. And, thirdly, we must seek for those lessons that are to be learnt about curriculum generally once we are prepared to accept and examine the Primary curriculum on its own terms and to recognize it as valid in its own right.

It is to all three of these purposes that this book will address its attention.

CHAPTER 1

THE THEORETICAL BASES OF THE PRIMARY CURRICULUM

'God makes all things good; man meddles with them and they become evil.' When Jean Jacques Rousseau began his *Emile* with those words, he articulated a totally new conception of education which has continued to grow both in influence and sophistication ever since. For the works of those major exponents of what has come to be called 'progressive' education in two subsequent centuries, people such as Pestalozzi, Herbart, Froebel, Montessori and even John Dewey, have been but footnotes to that of Rousseau, refinements and developments of the view of education first propounded by him. And it is in the pursuit of the same philosophy of education that a number of schools, and indeed their heads, have become household names. People like J.H. Badley at Bedales School, A.S. Neill at Summerhill, Susan Isaacs at Malting House and Kurt Hahn at Salem School and later at Gordonstoun, who have come to be regarded as the pioneers of 'progressivism' in educational practice, have all in their different styles been endeavouring to translate into reality ideas first proposed by Rousseau.

Recent developments in curriculum theory have taken these views a good deal further and have led in particular to the emergence of the view of education as process, or as a series of processes of development. This view has also, and especially, been promoted by studies of children's learning undertaken by those working in the field of developmental psychology. It is this developed version of this approach to education which now needs to be articulated.

In the public sector of education, the influence of this movement has been greatest on the English Primary school. There are at least two reasons for this. The first of these is the relative weakness of external constraints on the curriculum of the Primary school. Whereas at Secondary level the demands of public examinations and the pressures of parents and employers have had the effect of inhibiting curriculum development, the Primary school, certainly since the demise of the 11+ but even during its lifetime, has been largely free to adopt a form of education whose end-products cannot be so readily measured.

Secondly, both the theory and the practice of the Primary school has been greatly influenced in the present century by the work of those developmental psychologists who have been concerned, again like Rousseau, to persuade us of the necessity of fitting our educational provision to the development level of the individual child. This approach has, in our view wrongly, been regarded as being primarily of relevance to the education of young children. And its main effect has been to reinforce the development of the curriculum of the Primary school along the lines we are describing.

Thus there has emerged a distinctive 'philosophy' of Primary education in England, which most practitioners at that level would acknowledge in theory even if they do not always aspire to it in practice, and a view of the curriculum which is distinctive not so much in content and method as in the very conception of education upon which it is based. The influence of this view of education is now beginning to be felt at other levels of education; much of what is currently being regarded as new in our approach to the curriculum of the Secondary school, for example, has long been accepted as an integral part of that of the Primary school. And it is for this reason as much as for any other that its main features need to be identified and critically analysed.

This process must begin with a discussion of the two related sources of those principles that can be identified as fundamental to the theory and practice of Primary education – the ideas of the 'progressive' movement in education and the theories of the developmental psychologists. The major characteristics of each of these influences we must now examine.

The influence of 'progressive' theories of education

Although there is evidence of educational innovations along these lines before Rousseau's time (Stewart and McCann 1967), as we suggested at the beginning of this chapter, any discussion of that view of education that has come to be described as 'progressive' must begin with the theories of Jean Jacques Rousseau, since it is here that they are first articulated. In social philosophy generally, his work marks the transition from the theories of the Renaissance to those of modern political theorists. Renaissance theories were rooted in medieval and, indeed, in classical thought, the concepts of which the theorists of the Renaissance had not only inherited but also transformed. Rousseau performed the same service in turn for their theories; he is thus both the last of a long line of Renaissance theorists and the first of the modern political theorists. His contribution to education theory has a comparable significance. He was a 'born revolutionary' who 'had no respect for existing institutions or conventions' (Lester-Smith 1958, p.36). He was one of the first to recognize that a fresh start was needed and to provide the springboard from which it could be made.

The view of education which he inherited from his predecessors was in essence that of Plato, to which people had found it necessary to make few modifications. It is a view that is still very much with us today and provides the theoretical basis for that other kind of curriculum that we suggested earlier has continued to predominate at the post-Primary level of education. There are several features of this view that need to be picked out here, since they were a source of particular concern to Rousseau and continue to be to many modern educationists.

The theory of knowledge which one embraces is fundamental to the view one takes of the curriculum and must provide the starting-point for curriculum planning. We must begin by noting, then, that this view is firmly rooted in a rationalist epistemology (Kelly 1986), since it regards knowledge as having a status that is largely independent of human experience, as 'God-given' and thus as absolute and, for the most part, unchanging. As a result, it sees knowledge as the most important factor in the educational equation, views the development of the intellect as the supreme function of education, believes that adults know best and are thus entitled to impose their views on children and regards the child as a 'man-in-the-making' and education as a preparation for life. When it descends from its lofty intellectual peaks to view education in a social context, it regards the needs of society as taking precedence over those of the individual. In general, therefore, it adopts a product ideology, an instrumental, means–end view of the educational process as centrally concerned to attain a particular kind of end-result.

It is worth noting that this view of education, which, as we suggested, is essentially that of Plato, fitted well with Christian theology, particularly as expressed by such philosophers as St. Thomas Aquinas, with its view of knowledge as revealed by God to man and thus as quite literally God-given, and, consequently, of values as absolute and unquestionable. Indeed, its notion of 'original sin' provides a useful gloss on the whole theory, since it suggests that whatever the child himself brings into the educational situation can be ignored, discarded or even positively crushed as inevitably worthless.

It was this view that Rousseau was concerned to refute in every detail. His rejection of the notion of original sin and adoption of the contrary view is apparent from the opening words of his *Emile* which we have already quoted: 'God makes all things good; man meddles with them and they become evil.' This kind of romanticism has never been far away from 'progressive' theories of education nor has the optimism about human nature that such a view entails. It is worth noting in passing, however, that it is not essential to the view of education as process. His total dissatisfaction with education as practised in his own day had already been expressed quite unequivocally in the Preface to that work. 'I shall say very little about the value of a good education, nor shall I stop to prove that the customary method of education is bad; this has been done again and again, and I do not wish to fill my books with things which everyone knows. I will merely state that, go as far back as you will, you will find a continual outcry against the established method, but no attempt to suggest a better.' The theory of education which follows reveals all the essential elements of 'progressive' theories of education, and thus the basic features of the process view, and we must look at each of these briefly in turn.

The first of them is a new and completely different epistemological basis. In other words, it starts from a different view of what knowledge is and of what constitutes our grounds for claiming that we know something (Kelly 1986). This is not well worked out in Rousseau's writings and certainly not clearly enunciated, since, although scoring highly on ideas, he does not earn many points for his expertise or craft as a producer of painstakingly reasoned philosophical arguments, but its influence is apparent and it is certainly a key feature of educational 'progressivism'.

One of the major developments in philosophy itself at this period is the emergence of an empiricist epistemology, albeit of a somewhat primitive kind. The earliest clear statement of this is that of John Locke, whose claim that 'everything that comes into the mind enters through the gates of sense' commenced the challenge to the dominant rationalist theory of knowledge that, as we have seen, regards the intellect as supreme and as capable of apprehending knowledge unaided, and indeed preferably untrammelled, by the senses. David Hume, with whom Rousseau lived for some time during his exile in England, had developed this view to the point where knowledge appeared not only to be no longer God-given and absolute but in fact to be highly tentative and uncertain, indeed to a point where the very possibility of our knowing anything with any degree of certainty seemed itself to be questionable.

The implications of such a view for education are wide-reaching. For, in the first place, to accept such a theory of knowledge, or even merely to acknowledge that it has claims to acceptance, requires that we be less positive, less certain and, indeed, less dogmatic in making decisions about what kinds of knowledge are valuable and can with justification be imposed on others. It also leads to a recognition that the acquisition of knowledge is not just a matter of the application of the intellect but requires a wider form of personal experience. It is this kind of epistemology that is fundamental to this view of education, as we shall see more clearly when we consider the more developed theories of John Dewey.

This in turn leads to several other key characteristics of this view of education. For, if it is difficult to justify imposition on children, if, in fact, this is that very 'meddling' that Rousseau complains of, it can only be replaced by a process of natural growth in which we pursue a policy of non-interference or, rather, of interfering only to promote a natural growth and to protect the growing child from the corrupting influences of the adult world. 'Tender, anxious mother,' says Rousseau, 'I appeal to you. You can remove this young tree from the highway and shield it from the crushing force of social conventions. . . . From the outset raise a wall round your child's soul.'

The more positive aspect of this policy is the creation of conditions in which the child can learn from experience. 'Give your scholar no verbal lessons, he should be taught by experience alone.' 'Put the problems before him and let him solve them himself. Let him know nothing because you have told him, but because he has learnt it for himself. Let him not be taught science, let him discover it.' In this Rousseau is clearly revealing his indebtedness to Locke who had claimed that since, as we saw above, 'everything that comes into the mind enters through the gates of sense, man's first reason is a reason of sense experience'. Education, then, as Rousseau tells us, 'is a question of guidance rather than instruction'.

Next, we must note the essential individualism of this approach to education. This again is a characteristic feature of that movement that has been called the 'Enlightenment' of which Rousseau was a part. It is particularly opposed, therefore, to that aspect of the traditional approach to education that regards knowledge as the central element in the educational process and thus defines that process in terms of its content or its end-product rather than the individual who is the object of it. It leads, therefore, to a view of education as child-centred: the individual child himself or herself rather than knowledge becomes the focus of the process. The child is not seen as a 'man-in-the-making' but as an individual already possessing his/her own embryonic personality and unique characteristics. Rousseau complains that educationists 'are always looking for the man in the child, without considering what he is before he becomes a man.'

Finally, we must note that this prompted the emergence of that psychological dimension that has always been an important feature of 'progressivism' in education. What we have been considering here is essentially a philosophical tradition, but it is clear that from the first this new psychological dimension is an important feature of that tradition and this is one reason why, as we shall see, the advent of the developmental theories of the present century has given added impetus to the movement. For if we are to argue, as Rousseau did, that education should take greater account of child nature, then we must accept the corollary that we must pay more attention to the study of the psychology of the child and in particular, as Rousseau's own words show, to developmental aspects of this. 'We know nothing of childhood; and with our mistaken notions the further we advance the further we go astray. The wisest writers devote themselves to what a man ought to know, without asking what a child is capable of learning.' We must turn our attention, then, away from the end-product of the educative process and from its content and concentrate it on the individuals who are the objects of that process. This is what the notion of child-centredness fundamentally implies.

There is contained in the work of Rousseau, then, all the major features of what was later to be called 'progressive' education. All of these features can also be seen, in one form or another, in the work of the 'great educators' of the nineteenth century. Pestalozzi, for example, stresses the need for education to begin with concrete experiences and advises us to delay the introduction of verbal lessons, and especially those remote from the child's real interests, until the natural course of development renders them appropriate. 'His contribution to curriculum planning was concerned with the need to plan for each stage of development. In some respects he could be said to have anticipated Piaget' (Gordon and Lawton 1978, p.60). Herbart explicitly acknowledges the centrality of an empiricist theory of knowledge to his theory. He also emphasizes the importance of psychology to the study of education, suggesting that 'a large part of the enormous gaps in our pedagogical knowledge results from lack of psychology'; furthermore, in his own work in psychology he lays great stress on the important role played by subjective factors in human perception, thus reinforcing the individualism we have claimed is endemic to this view of education. Froebel restores the philosophical emphasis, but reaches similar conclusions concerning the notion of education as development from within, as the unfolding of the child's – inherently good – spiritual nature in an environment protected as far as possible from those external influences that might mar it. A major vehicle for this kind of development in Froebel's view is play, 'the characteristic activity of childhood' (Rusk 1957, p.251), which to be truly educative must be guided and directed, since, as he tells us, 'without law-abiding guidance there is no free development'. Finally, Maria Montessori stresses the centrality of the right kind of environment to education and emphasizes the role of first-hand experience and the important of providing help at the right psychological moment in the child's development, to adapt instruction to the child's stage of development, if that development is to be forwarded. Thus the major themes in the work of all these educationists are developments and refinements of those to be found in that of Rousseau.

The greatest and clearest statement of this view of education, however, is to be found in the writings of John Dewey, who refashioned its foundations by placing it in the context of a social philosophy expressly designed for the twentieth century. In many ways his work is the culmination of the theories we have been discussing and its full impact is only now beginning to be appreciated.

Dewey's epistemological position is also empiricist but it is an empiricism that has an important additional ingredient. The concept of evolution which dominated the thinking of the second half of the nineteenth century is seen by him as offering the key to an understanding not only of the development of living organisms, nor even just of the growth of society, but of the development of knowledge itself (Kelly 1986). For he sees knowledge as in a state of continuous evolution and truth as a matter of 'what works' or, more accurately, what particular set of hypotheses best explains current human experience. In short, his model for all human knowledge is that of scientific knowledge – hypothetical, subject to constant modification and revision in the light of the emergence of new data from new experiences but at the same time enjoying current, if temporary, acceptance and agreement, especially among those best qualified to judge. Such a view does not make knowledge subjective at the personal, individual level, as many have thought and as, indeed, some proponents of pragmatism, such as William James, have claimed. But it does deny to it the kind of objectivity that we saw the rationalist claiming for it. Knowledge is not God-given; it is 'man'-made; but it is made by 'men' acting collectively as social beings not by individuals acting on their own.

Several important things follow for education from this basic epistemological position. In the first place, if this is what knowledge is, then it can only be acquired through experience, so that again experience is seen as the focus of the educative process. To know that something is the case, on this view, is not to have been told by someone that it is; it is to have discovered and established for oneself that the particular hypothesis or set of hypotheses under examination provides the best available explanation of what has been experienced or observed. The basic method of education, therefore, is problem-solving, the framing and testing of hypotheses, since this is the method by which all knowledge is built up into a coherent whole and by which it continues to evolve through constant modification. Each individual must build up and keep under constant review his/her own coherent body of knowledge of the world of his/her own experiences. For the same reason, the division of knowledge into 'subjects' is only justified if it contributes to this process and if it is based on criteria that the individual recognizes as relevant to the organization of his/her own knowledge and experience.

Secondly, education on this view is again a process of growth or development. If education is the means by which we help the individual to structure his/her experience in this way, then it must start from within rather than being imposed from the outside. To see education as the imposition of knowledge from without is either to fail to recognize the evolutionary nature of knowledge or to seek to impose one's own values or the values of adult society on the next generation. Either way it is a process of indoctrination rather than education, since it does not allow the individual, or, indeed, society itself, to develop its own knowledge based on its own, ever-new and changing experiences. In fact, it does not allow knowledge itself to develop and evolve, since it results in a hardening of that knowledge which is based on past human experience. It is not only wrong for the individual, therefore; it is wrong for human society as a whole, since its effect must be to slow down and inhibit the process of human evolution. Education cannot be adequately defined in terms of its content, it must be recognized as a process, or a series of processes.

This does not mean, however, as we hope to show in greater detail in Chapter 2, that the teacher must pursue a policy of non-interference. To say that s/he must not impose is not to say that s/he has no positive role to play in the educative process. That role for Dewey, as for his predecessors, is summed up in the word 'guidance'. The teacher is there to guide the child in the development of his/her experiences and of the ability to build those experiences into a coherent body of knowledge and understanding. The criterion by which s/he is to guide the child is what Dewey called the 'experiential continuum' – those experiences are to be promoted that are most likely to be productive of further experiences and vice versa. The principle again is that of the continuous development of knowledge and experience.

Lastly, we must note that such a view of education does not restrict it to what goes on during the years of schooling. What is being described here is a continuous lifelong process of learning from experience, developing and modifying one's knowledge in the light of ever-new experiences. Education, then, is not a preparation for life; it is life itself. 'The educational process has no end beyond itself: it is its own end. . . . Since in reality there is nothing to which growth is relative save more growth, there is nothing to which education is subordinate save more education' (Dewey 1916, pp.49–51). Again, therefore, we see that on this view education is defined as a process rather than in terms of its end-product or end-result or of its content.

Many of those who have contributed to the development of this view of education, including Dewey himself, were also practitioners of education and the changes that they and others were endeavouring to introduce into educational practice throughout this time, although inevitably less 'pure', reflect these basic theoretical positions. For in their methods and approach they attempt to be child-centred and to take full account of an ever-growing knowledge of child psychology; they reveal an unwillingness to impose on children; they adopt a looser attitude towards discipline; they encourage informal methods which place the emphasis on providing children with first-hand experiences, often through play; they stress the learning of the child rather than the teaching of the teacher; and they evince a willingness to experiment with the content of the curriculum and, in particular, to introduce subjects of a practical kind. In short, in their practice too, they display a concern with education as a process rather than with its content or its products and this is the essence of the new and distinctive concept of education and of curriculum that they have both introduced and adopted.

It is important to be clear, however, that this approach to education has not been adopted only by those schools and teachers who have been described as 'progressive' and have often even been regarded as cranks or eccentrics. For it is this approach that has come to be characteristic of English Primary education. It is not of course manifest in the practice of all Primary schools, as we pointed out in our Introduction, and it will emerge from our later discussions that its practice often does not match the educational principles described here; but we hope to show that it is central to the thinking about Primary education that is reflected in the language of teachers of this age-range and the principles upon which their courses of preparation are based, in fact that these principles are now enshrined in the folklore of Primary education. Indeed, a major purpose of this book is to reveal to teachers the practical implications of principles to which some pay only lip-service. To say, then, that the influence of the 'progressives' on Primary education has been significant is not to claim that all Primary education is 'progressive; it is, however, to suggest that much of our practice and all of our thinking about it are characterized by those features we have just identified and, furthermore, that the connections between our theory and our practice need to be pointed up, and indeed brought closer to each other.

These features are also such as to render the view of curriculum that this approach leads to distinctive in its total conception and quite different from that view that has tended to dominate discussion of the curriculum of the Secondary school.

It could be argued that the work of Dewey has been a watershed from which has flowed much of the work of others who have influenced the development of thinking along these lines since his day. It might even be argued that this is especially true of the work of the developmental psychologists which has been particularly influential in recent years. However, we have noted that a recognition of the importance of the study of child psychology has been a vital feature of this movement from the beginning, since, in fact, Rousseau himself stressed the need for us to discover and understand 'what a child is capable of learning', and that it has been a clearly identifiable element within it at least since the time of Herbart. And so it may be wiser to regard the growing influence of developmental psychology merely as a change of emphasis within a continuing tradition.

However this may be, there is no denying that the work of the major figures in the field of developmental psychology in the last half century, and especially that of Jean Piaget and Jerome Bruner, has provided a major boost to the growth of this view of education and the curriculum, and has taken it a good way beyond what is encapsulated in the term 'progressivism'. It may even be the case that the curriculum of the Primary school has of late been influenced too much by considerations of a purely psychological kind and that other important dimensions have often been ignored. The influence of this work on the development of the view of curriculum we are endeavouring to describe has been very great and we must now look carefully at its major features.

The influence of developmental psychology

Before looking in some detail at the main features of the work that has been done in this field, we must first pick out its most significant general implications for our understanding of education. For the main impact of this work has been that it has not offered merely useful advice on methodological questions but has provided insights of a kind which have resulted in the emergence of a completely new concept of education. It is perhaps the most important single factor in the development of 'progressivism' into the concept of a process-based curriculum.

This is best understood if we contrast the approach which has been adopted by those working in this field with that of the behavioural psychologists. For, when we do so, we immediately notice two fundamental differences. Not only do the developmentalists wish to assert a crucial distinction between animal learning and human learning, they also wish, within the latter, to claim that there are important qualitative differences between the thinking of the child and that of the mature adult, and thus important parallel differences in their modes and ways of learning. Let us consider these points further.

Within behavioural psychology the key concepts are connectionism, associationism and reinforcement (both positive and negative). Learning is a matter of behavioural changes resulting from the making of connections between experiences as a result of the association of those experiences with each other, and especially the association of them with experiences of reward (positive reinforcement) or punishment (negative reinforcement). Thus, having shown that dogs can be taught to salivate by the association of certain kinds of experience with the production of meat, cats to learn to operate escape mechanisms from boxes for the reward of food and pigeons to dance or play 'ping-pong' by similar devices, behavioural psychologists have gone on to claim that children, and indeed all humans, can be taught what we wish to teach them by the use of similar connectionist or associationist techniques. Thus some of them, such as B.F. Skinner, have even gone so far as to argue that teachers are, or should be, superfluous to this kind of teaching programme, since they are inevitably less efficient than the teaching machines which might be developed to replace them.

There are many points in this kind of theory which we might wish to explore and debate further. Two are particularly relevant to our discussion here. The first of these is that this kind of analysis of human learning offers us, as teachers and educationists, advice on methodology only. Even if we accept its validity, it tells us only how we might promote children's learning; it can offer no guidance on what kinds of learning we might feel it appropriate to promote. It is for this reason that those who have attempted to apply this form of psychological theory in the field of curriculum planning, like, for example, those major advocates of the behavioural objectives model, have claimed to be value-neutral, to be offering in their taxonomies not advice on what we *ought* to be setting out to teach but merely on how we might do it most efficiently once we have decided *on other grounds* what we want to teach (Bloom 1956). It was the adoption of this kind of view of psychology, therefore, that led Denis Lawton (1975) to see its role in educational planning in purely methodological terms. Indeed, if this is the only kind of psychology one acknowledges, then this can be its only role in educational planning.

The first general point to be made about the perspective, and the contribution, of developmental psychology is that it goes far beyond this. It offers us a new concept of learning and thus invites us to consider whether that new concept is not what we ought to be addressing our attention to. For it adopts a view of learning not as that kind of passive response to externally provided stimuli that is the whole of the behaviourist view, but as an active, dynamic process which can only occur if there is genuine interaction between the learner and his/her experiences, a genuine involvement of the learner with those experiences. The notion of 'active learning', then, which has emerged from work in this field is crucial not only to an understanding of what has been its major preoccupation but also to an appreciation of the distinctive view of learning, and thus, consequently, of teaching and of education, that this work has promoted. True education, it claims, is not 'mere learning'; it is far more than that; it is the development of the individual's capacities which results from a properly active engagement with the wealth of experiences the sensitive teacher can provide.

A second major difference between this approach and that of behaviourism is its consequent recognition of the fact that there is more than one form of learning. In particular, not only has it rejected the notion that human learning is indistinguishable from that of animals, it has also wished to maintain, as we suggested earlier, that the learning of children is different from that of the mature adult, because the styles and modes of thinking available to them are different. It has thus wished to maintain that there are stages of intellectual development through which children must pass, or different modes of thinking which they must be helped to develop, before they have available to them all the intellectual apparatus which might be employed by the mature, educated adult. What is crucial here of course is that these modes of thinking, these developed forms of intellectual apparatus, are only available to the individual whose educational experiences have promoted the development of them. It is this that is central to the view of education we are exploring here. And it is this that is an essential component of the notion of education as process, or as a series of processes of development.

The major focus of this work, then, has been its concern with understanding the development of childen's thought processes and the variables that effect them. The most profound influence on this movement has been that of the developmental theory of Jean Piaget and it is that we must consider first.

When examining the influence of Piaget's work on the development of the Primary school curriculum, we must stress from the outset that his work has been largely descriptive in nature. He sets out to describe development and not to propose what makes development possible or how it can be promoted. For, as Jerome Bruner (1968) points out, Piaget's principal mission is not psychology; his work has focused on a strong and continuing interest in philosophy, particularly in epistemology, the grounds for and nature of knowledge, and in logic, the process of reasoning.

His early training in biology led him to focus on an understanding of the nature of knowledge through a close study of how humans come to know, an approach which he calls 'genetic epistemology'. He rejected the two main theoretical views of how the infant comes to understand – one arguing that it is a matter of genetic inheritance, the other that the environment is all-important. He set out rather, through close observation of a small number of children, to study the origin and development of concepts of space, time, logic, mathematics and causality. From his description of these he postulates that both genetic and environmental factors shape the development of the human infant. In essence, the child is neither pre-programmed nor shaped by his/her environment; s/he acts upon his/her environment so that shaping it and being shaped by it are both central to his/her development (Patterson 1977).

From his earliest work he has insisted that the individual is an active participant in his/her own development and not a passive organism acted upon by the environment, as is clear from what he says about interaction and opportunities for active learning. Such positive intelligent actions he sees as mainly overt in the infant and young child and becoming more covert, in the form of mental operations, as the child matures.

Piaget's studies of children, which span more than fifty years and have been concerned at various stages with children's thinking and reasoning, the development of language, judgement and their conceptions of time, space, number and morals, are complex and difficult. Indeed, one of the main criticisms of his work is that his writing about theories which are in themselves complex is obscure and almost incomprehensible (Flavell 1963). Fortunately, there have been many attempts to interpret, summarize and develop his ideas (Beard 1969; Furth 1970; Donaldson 1978) and it is through these interpretations that the main influences on Primary education have come.

We should also note in the setting of this discussion that there have been two main periods of influence. The first began in the 1930s at the time of the development of a rationale for early childhood education; the second in the curriculum reforms of the 1960s, especially in approaches to the teaching of science and mathematics in the early years of schooling.

When his early work was published in the 1930s, it was seized upon by the 'progressive' educationists, especially those in the United Kingdom who were concerned with the education of very young children, who saw its significance in offering a scientific justification of their 'progressive' ideology. Susan Isaacs, for example, who was already developing a system of detailed observations of young children in her work at the experimental Malting House School in an attempt to develop a more scientifically based theory of infant education (the child study movement), showed particular interest in his early work, although she was critical of his methods and saw him as too doctrinaire in some of his conclusions (Whitbread 1972). Together with other educationists, she did, however, help to ensure that his findings were disseminated to the teacher training colleges of the time and in this way his views began to have some impact on the Nursery and Infant schools of the 1930s and 1940s.

Two features of his early work were incorporated into the study of child development in training institutions if not into the classroom practice of the time and were profoundly influential, since they were features that transformed both the view of how children think and that of how intelligent behaviour develops. These were, first, his insistence upon the active nature of intelligence and his explanation of why intellectual development is an active process, and, second, his view that the child's thinking is qualitatively different from that of the intelligent adult. Both of these features of his theory merit a closer examination here not only because they came to be central to his explanation of knowledge but also because they are similarly central to an understanding of the development of that view of education which we are suggesting began when Rousseau made similar claims about child nature.

Piaget has always regarded human intelligence as positive and creative so that in his view the human infant can never be seen as an 'empty bucket' to be filled. This, R.A. Hodgkin (1976) argues, is his fundamental insight and a recurring theme throughout his long life. He equates cognition with action. In his theory of intelligence, the child's intellectual development is equivalent in his/her structuring and restructuring of his/her perception of his/her environment through his/her manipulation of that environment. This activity manifests itself as observable motor activity during infancy, as the young child physically manipulates objects in his/her environment. Gradually it becomes less overt and thus less obvious, as the activity comes to take the form of mental operations and its structures become more complex. These covert mental operations, however, are equally active in nature. Furthermore, he claims that the overt actions are necessary precursors of the covert mental actions and thus the essential foundations for more complex thought; in short, that the stages of intellectual development are invariant. Thus, although the resolutions of a problem will differ according to the stage of development, this active feature of thought processes is unaffected by changes in the style of cognitive functioning and remains unchanged as the individual develops.

As was stated above, Piaget accepts neither the genetic nor the environmental explanations of intelligence but, paradoxically, he incorportates both into his explanation of active learning. He describes two process, assimilation and accommodation, which occur simultaneously as the individual fluctuates between the two in what he calls the process of equilibration. Again, these two processes can be observed at every level of development. Johanna Turner offers a useful analogy to illustrate this point when she shows how the cognitive system, in Piaget's description, can be seen to operate in a similar way to the digestive system. 'The organism has a cognitive system which is an organized system as the digestive system is an organized system; the environment is analogous to the food taken in, which both affects the organism and is affected by it; the final cognitive structures are like the final state of the body, that is they are a result both of the invariant functions (digestive processes) and environmental influences (the food)' (Turner 1975, p.13). Neither environmental factors nor inherited potential alone, therefore, can adequately explain intellectual development.

In this way, from his earliest work, Piaget's theory of intelligence can be set outside the nature/nurture controversy. For, although assimilation processes are prompted from within, accommodation processes are shaped by factors, both physical and social, that are external to the individual and, in the process of equilibration, both are transformed as the individual strives for adaptation or balance between the two (Downey and Kelly 1979). Thus he offers us a new and different concept of intelligence.

The function of the intellect according to Piaget is this striving for balance and the process is always dynamic. Equilibrium is never achieved, as external stimuli and internal demands cause constant alterations or interruptions in the process. Further than this, the process of adaptation or cognitive development cannot occur if the stimuli can be assimilated without alteration to the individual's existing structure; nor can it occur if the demands of the stimuli are too overwhelming and too far beyond the individual's ability to accommodate them. In other words, the situation can be either too undemanding or too demanding for the learner to develop intellectually. Piaget argues that cognitive development occurs only when the discrepancy between the learner's existing structures and the demands of what is presented to him/her is such that his/her interest is aroused and s/he seeks to resolve the conflict. This is the situation that he describes as one of optimal discrepancy. This cognitive conflict or optimal discrepancy can be equated with a kind of intrinsic motivation and again his explanation of motivation is based on action and self-regulation.

One further important point needs to be added and that is the distinction he draws between intellectual development and learning. On his account, the term 'learning' is used to describe the acquisition of information or knowledge. Learning can certainly take place, therefore, when the learner remains passive and is fed information. When this occurs, however, Piaget argues that no fundamental development has taken place unless the learner recognizes a contradiction in his/her existing understanding. If the learner comes to see this contradiction for himself/herself, then the processes of equilibration begin (Donaldson 1978). Thus cognitive development, as opposed to learning, can only occur when the individual is active. The role of action, then, in intellectual development is for Piaget the most critical factor.

Thus he has from his earliest writings proposed that opportunities for acting upon the environment must be provided if intellectual development and not simply narrow learning is to be encouraged, since learning is subordinate to the learner's level of development. Returning to this theme in a more recent work, he states that active methods of education must 'give broad scope to the spontaneous research of the child or adolescent and require that every new truth to be learned be rediscovered or at least reconstructed by the student, and not simply imparted to him' (Piaget 1973, pp.15–16). And again, 'To understand is to discover or reconstruct by discovery, and such conditions must be complied with if future individuals are to be formed who are capable of production and creativity and not simply repetition' (Piaget 1973, p.20).

Having defined intelligence as a process of active adaptation to the physical and social environment and having seen all intelligent acts as dependent on some underlying structures that develop in an organized and interrelated manner, Piaget also identifies four major stages of intellectual development, each of which, he argues, produces qualitatively different modes of thinking and problem-solving. These are (1) the Sensori-motor stage, (2) the Pre-operational stage, (3) the stage of Concrete Operations and (4) the stage of Formal Operations. An understanding of these stages is fundamental to his work, since they provide an explanation of the different preoccupations of the learner which occur at various stages of maturity. The different preoccupations produce different kinds of resolution to problems, although the intellectual process is the same, being fundamentally that of equilibration which we described above.

During the sensori-motor stage the main tendencies are to seek out novel objects and events, to try to make these interesting events endure, thus revealing what Piaget calls 'intentionality', and, in this way, to develop the concept of permanence, that objects have an existence outside of oneself, independently of one's actions and perceptions. The example usually cited as evidence that this change is occurring is the behaviour of a baby when an object with which s/he is playing is hidden from him/her. 'Up to the age of six months or so, he makes no attempt to recover the object. . . . The argument then is that his gradual progress in constructing such a concept is reflected in his increasing skill in working out where an object has gone' (Donaldson 1978, p.135).

During the second period, that of pre-operational thought, Piaget asserts that a new stage of development begins as the child acquires the ability to represent objects and events with symbols and is thus able to go beyond the immediate. However, he identifies 'irreversibility' as the most important characteristic of pre-operational thought, i.e., an inability to 'retrace' one's thinking in order to make judgements about one's environment. A three-year-old, for example, will become puzzled at the apparent disappearance of some of his/her bricks if s/he changes his/her building from a tall tower to a squat garage and uses the same bricks for both structures. Pre-operational thought, therefore, could be defined as pre-logical. For, athough symbols, including language, broaden the scope for thought, the mechanisms of logical reasoning, even in the concrete, are being prepared for but are not yet part of the functioning intellect.

Concrete operational thought is characterized by the developing ability to 'reverse', so that genuine 'operations' become possible when this stage is reached. Examples of this stage are usually taken from the child's approach to numerical problems. 'When a child reasons, for instance, that the number of a set of objects must remain the same although its arrangement in space has been altered, he is said to do this by understanding that the original arrangement could be reached again merely by reversing the movements that changed it' (Donaldson 1978, pp.135–136). At this stage, then, his/her bricks are not so mysteriously 'lost'. The structures of the period of concrete operations are referred to by Piaget as 'logico-mathematical' in nature; they are still rooted in the concrete of objects and events but display a limited ability to hypothesize. The concrete operational thinker is capable of manipulating things, whether s/he does so in a practical situation or in his/her mind, but, in either case, it is necessary for him/her to be able to relate it to his/her own concrete experiences. To illustrate this point, Donaldson quotes the problem:

Edith is fairer than Susan.
Edith is darker than Lily.
Who is the darkest

and notes that, 'This problem gives considerable difficulty to many children of ten. Yet if it were a question of arranging three dolls in serial order, the task would be easy for them' (Donaldson 1978, p.139).

It is when the learner is no longer dependent on the manipulation of things and is able to manipulate propositions or ideas that his/her thinking can be said to have reached that of the intelligent adult. The final stage of formal thought, according to Piaget, is characterized by the ability to deal with all possible combinations of objects and events within a cognitive system and thus demonstrates the emergence of hypothetico-deductive reasoning.

The aspect of Piaget's theory which explains conceptual development through stages has attracted most attention from teachers and has had most influence on their attempts to translate his ideas into practice, as we will see in later chapters, particularly Chapter 6. For it is clear that, if this theory of development is accepted and if the teacher is to be effective in promoting the child's conceptual development, then the material and experiences that are planned must take account of the child's stage of conceptual understanding. It is also clear that, if the conceptual demands of curriculum content are to be matched effectively to the child's level of understanding, the teacher must be able to diagnose the level, must, in other words, be an expert in child development. The practical implications of both of these points – the conceptual demands of knowledge and the diagnostic abilities of the teacher – will be discussed more thoroughly later.

One product of the attempts to translate these ideas into practice is worthy of note here, however, and that is that, although the description is linked to chronological stages in childhood, the assumption cannot be made that all young people of fourteen will have developed through all the stages nor can it be assumed that all adults will have done so, or, even if they have once attained that goal, that they will maintain it; least of all can it be assumed that the intellectual development of younger children can be measured merely by reference to their chronological ages.

Although the age of development from one stage to the next and the extent to which individual young people and adults are able to employ deductive reasoning are both open to fierce debate, it is now generally accepted, as a result of Piaget's theory, that the developing thought processes of children in Primary schools are dependent on some reference to practical situations. They are, in other words, unable to reason and understand in an abstract and theoretical way. Their reasoning is linked to either the handling of real objects and real situations or reflection upon concrete reality. Cognitive development occurs only when the young child acts upon and reorganizes his/her perception of reality. The implications of this explanation of cognitive development offer support both for the practical and exploratory work engaged in with children in Primary schools and for the stress placed on discovery methods of teaching. Teachers have also been encouraged, as a result of Piagetian theory, to think of intelligence as more than an innate mental faculty which simply matures as the child grows up. In summary, the work of Piaget has had an increasing influence on the ideology of Primary education and his creative leadership in the field of developmental psychology has transformed the view of how children think and hence how they can best learn.

As was said earlier, however, his work is descriptive in nature and this has led many to claim that a knowledge of his work is of little use to the teacher, as it offers no explanation of how teachers can directly support and promote intellectual development (Foss 1969; Dearden 1976). Further than this, a cursory study of his explanation of intellectual development can be counter-productive, as his studies focus on the development of the individual child whether s/he is in school or not and can be interpreted as an invitation for the teacher to set up a challenging classroom environment and then to stand back and allow development to occur unhindered by adult intervention. It is at this point, therefore, that a consideration of the work of Jerome Bruner becomes important, especially the work he undertook in the 1960s.

Bruner was concerned that a theory of cognitive development should influence and be influenced by both a theory of knowledge and a theory of instruction. He argued that, unless developmental psychologists approached problems in this interdependent manner, their developmental theories would be 'doomed to trivality' (Bruner 1968, p.21). He set out, therefore, to prescribe – not describe – a theory of instruction which would promote both the child's development and the child's active learning of the most appropriate features of skills, processes and knowledge within the confines of his/her culture.

One important element in Bruner's theory of cognitive development is that it is a process by which human beings increase their mastery in achieving and using knowledge. The learner's actions will be purposive, therefore, and will be directed at resolving problems presented by the environment and hence to the structuring and restructuring of his own view of the world. It is because of this explanation that Bruner has been described as a phenomenological psychologist, for he argues that reality for the learner has no existence outside his own perception of or creation of reality (Patterson 1977). It also led him to the prescription of a key feature in his theory of instruction.

For he argues that the learner is constantly employing strategies in order to understand and thereby reduce the complexities of the world. By studying the employment of these strategies or modes, the teacher can suggest or encourage the selection of an appropriate one – appropriate both to the learner's level of understanding and to the knowledge or skill to be learned. He identifies three modes by which the learner can represent the world. The first is through action (the enactive mode), the second is through visual or other sensory organization (the iconic mode) and the third is through words or language (the symbolic mode). He suggests that, although the three modes emerge sequentially and will in turn have a powerful influence on mental activity at different ages, each mode continues to function and interact with the other two modes throughout intellectual activity.

There are clear implications for education in this characterization of intellec-tual activity, and these have been elaborated upon in recent years by Eliot Eisner. He, like Bruner, argues that an ability to understand and to employ different modes of representation is not something that an individual acquires simply by getting older. Indeed, his main concern is that the opposite is more likely to be true in Western cultures at present. For he claims that schooling systems, by overemphasizing experiences which lead to discursive and numerical forms of thinking and knowing, reduce the opportunities of representing a wide range of sensory experience, thus reducing also the ways in which individuals will be able to conceptualize this experience and narrowing cognitive development (Eisner 1982).

Eisner argues for a more sophisticated view of human development and one which does not separate the affective from the cognitive. For his view highlights the central role of the senses in what he calls the twin processes of human conceptualization and expression, and, like Bruner, he asserts that 'forms of representation are the devices that humans use to make public conceptions that are privately held. They are the vehicles through which concepts that are visual, auditory, kinesthetic, olfactory, gustatory, and tactile are given public status' (op. cit., p.47). Also like Bruner, he sees the process as dynamic and therefore argues that 'the choice of a form of representation is a choice in the way the world will be conceived, as well as choice in the way it will be publicly represented' (op. cit., p.50).

He emphasizes how different sensory experiences (visual, auditory etc.) will find expression in different forms and hence will shape both the meanings that can be held and those that can be conveyed. In this way he shows that it is sensory experience and the expression of this that play a fundamental role in concept formation.

Eisner develops this view further by arguing that the form of representation which is adopted is one of two important considerations in the process of conceptualization. For each form of representing experience can be treated in one of three modes (his use of the term is different from Bruner's). Experience can be represented as a replica (mimetically), as an expression of the deep structure underlying the experience (expressively) or in a manner which conforms to the meaning assigned within a particular culture (conventionally).

In this analysis Eisner provides us with a more detailed image of how cognitive development proceeds, and a more elaborate framework for a theory of instruction which will support this development. He argues that 'to exploit the power of human conception, to tap and employ its versatility in the interests of disclosure, deliberation, and understanding, seems to me to be a virtue we should seek' (op. cit., p.91).

The contribution of Bruner and Eisner, therefore, is to suggest the link between the learner's active cognitive development and the role the teacher can play in promoting this development. To the stages of development are added the modes of learning which are defined either by the learner's level of mastery or by the nature of the material to be understood. They see a main function of the teacher as being to aid the growth of the learner by enabling him/her to recode experiences into increasingly powerful representational systems. 'It is this,' writes Bruner (1968, p.21), 'that leads me to think that the heart of the educational process consists of providing aids and dialogues for translating experience into more powerful systems of notation and ordering' – a point that has led him and other developmental psychologists in recent years to an increased interest in language and other forms of communication.

Through this work, therefore, we see added to the description of the nature of cognitive development an analysis of the kind of teaching which will enable development and growth to occur. And we must note too the suggestion that different kinds of thinking are to be seen not so much as stages through which children may pass on the road to intellectual maturity as modes of handling experience which persist into mature adulthood, different pieces of intellectual equipment, different capacities, which continue to be available to us for dealing with subsequent experience and converting it into further knowledge.

This line of thinking has not only been pursued and developed by Bruner and Eisner but has also been amplified by other recent work in developmental psychology such as that of Margaret Donaldson (Donaldson 1978; Donaldson, Grieve and Pratt 1983). We must return to this in Chapter 4 when we explore in greater detail what is meant by a process-based approach to education and curriculum planning.

It will now be apparent that the main effect of the work of developmental psychology has been to support and develop the views of those theorists and practitioners whose work we discussed in the first section of this chapter. For they empahsize the same features of the process of education that we noted there. They begin with the assumption that we cannot hope to educate children unless we have some understanding of the processes of cognitive development. This in turn suggests that we have to regard education as a process of growth and that in this process of growth the developing experience of each individual child is crucial. They also emphasize the need for the child to be active in the process. Thus the key concepts are again those of development, growth, experience, activity, individualism and, in general, child-centredness. They thus form a second part or strand of the growing tradition we have been endeavouring to describe that has led to the emergence of what we are also claiming to be a distinctive conception of education and the curriculum as a process or series of processes of development.

What we hope to be able to demonstrate now is that it is this conception of education that is fundamental to an understanding of the curriculum of the English Primary school.

The curriculum of the English Primary school

We claimed earlier that the absence of those external constraints, such as the pressures of external examination syllabuses and the demands of parents and employers for vocational preparation, that have inhibited curriculum development in the Secondary school, has allowed the Primary school to respond more readily and more extensively to the theories of educational thinkers and to the innovations of educational practitioners. We have also been attempting to demonstrate that the main sources of such influences have been the 'progressive' or child-centred movement and the work of the developmental psychologists to which it gave rise, and this has led to the emergence of a curriculum that is different not only in its content but in its very conception.

That this has been the underlying philosophy of the English Primary school since its inception is apparent from even the most cursory examination of the two major public statements of official policy in Primary education, the report of the Hadow Committee in 1931 and that of the Plowden Committee in 1967.

The Hadow Report on Primary Education (1931) gave public utterance to a profound change of attitudes to education and represented the major landmark in the shift from an Elementary to a Primary school philosophy, that is from a philosophy that saw the education of the young child as a preparation for something that was to come later to a philosophy that insisted on viewing it as a process in its own right. As such it reflects all of the main features of that 'progressive' view of education that we have been attempting to outline, and, albeit in embryonic form, of the view of curriculum as process.

For it draws attention to the fact that the education of young children had at one time been concerned almost solely 'to secure that children acquired a minimum standard of proficiency in reading, writing and arithmetic, subjects in which their attainments were annually assessed by quantitative standards' (Board of Education 1931, Introduction) – shades of present-day demands for a monitoring of standards in 'the basic skills' – but that 'today it . . . handles the curriculum, not only as consisting of lessons to be mastered, but as providing fields of new and interesting experience to be explored; it appeals less to passive obedience and more to the sympathy, social spirit and imagination of the children, relies less on mass instruction and more on the encouragement of individual and group work, and treats the school, in short, not as the antithesis of life, but as its complement and commentary' (ibid.).

It claims that the planning of the curriculum must be based on the experiences of the pupils and that if that principle is adopted 'knowledge will be aquired in the process, not, indeed, without effort, but by an effort whose value will be enhanced by the fact that its purpose and significance can be appreciated, at least in part, by the children themselves' (ibid.). It argues further that in order to do this we must adopt methods 'which take as the starting-point of the work of the primary school the experience, the curiosity, and the awakening powers and interests of the childen themselves' (ibid.).

The Report then goes on to justify these claims by stressing the need to relate educational provision to the developmental stage of the pupil since 'life is a process of growth in which there are successive stages, each with its own specific character and needs' (Board of Education 1931, p.92). It also empha-sizes its recommendations by drawing attention to the fact that since the basis of social life has been transformed by industrialization – a claim that would seem to have even more force now than it had in 1931 – the practice of the schools is no longer merely to teach pupils those things that they cannot be taught at home such as 'reading, writing and cyphering' (op.cit., p.93) but to provide them with much more than that, 'to broaden their aims until it might now be said that they have to teach children how to live' (ibid.).

In fact, the Report's commitment to that philosophy of education that we have been describing is summed up in its most often quoted words: 'Applying these considerations to the problem before us, we see that the curriculum is to be thought of in terms of activity and experience rather than of knowledge to be acquired and facts to be stored. Its aim should be to develop in a child the fundamental human powers and to awaken him to the fundamental interests of civilized life so far as these powers and interests lie within the compass of childhood' (Board of Education 1931, p.93). These words represent the first public and official statement of what has recently come to be called a 'process' model of curriculum.

That this has continued to be the essence of the philosophy of the English Primary school and that this is the model which is officially regarded as offering the most appropriate base for its curriculum is apparent from a similarly cursory examination of the view of curriculum, both implicit and explicit, in the Plowden Report on Primary Education (1967) which has thus added to that official credence and sanction first given to it by the Hadow Committee. For, in spite of the inevitable fact that the practice of some schools and some teachers continues to reveal a lack of understanding, or even of acceptance, of those basic principles that we have tried to pick out, those principles are clearly fundamental to the declared policy of Primary education as set out by the Plowden Committee.

The Report itself attempts to summarize this philosophy of education and we can do no better than to quote at length its own summary.

A school is not merely a teaching shop, it must transmit values and attitudes. It is a community in which children learn to live first and foremost as children and not as future adults. In family life children learn to live with people of all ages. The school sets out deliberately to devise the right environment for children, to allow them to be themselves and to develop in the way and at the pace appropriate to them. It tries to equalise opportunities and to compensate for handicaps. It lays special stress on individual discovery, on first hand experience and on opportunities for creative work. It insists that knowledge does not fall into neatly separate compartments and that work and play are not opposite but complementary. A child brought up in such an atmosphere at all stages of his education has some hope of becoming a balanced and mature adult and of being able to live in, to contribute to, and to look critically at the society of which he forms a part. Not all primary schools correspond to this picture, but it does represent a general and quickening trend (CACE 1967, pp.187–188).

All the main characteristics of 'progressive' education, and even of the notion of education as process, that we have tried to pick out in this chapter are contained in that summary – the attempt to treat the child as a child, the emphasis on education through experience and learning by discovery, the view of knowledge as integrated or at least as not compartmentalized, the attention to developmental stages and the definition of education and curriculum in terms of processes.

This approach to education is emphasized in a negative sense in the list the Report also gives of what it calls 'danger signs, which would indicate that something has gone wrong in a school' (p.187). These it lists as 'fragmented knowledge, no changes in past decade, creative work very limited, much time spent on teaching, few questions from children, too many exercises, too many rules, frequent punishments, and concentration on tests' (ibid.). Furthermore, the Report's commitment to a 'process' model of curriculum is clear from its recommendation not only that class teachers should be encouraged 'to look critically at their day to day work' (p.187), but that they should be urged to do this by 'relating it to guiding principles and not simply to short term objectives (ibid.).

Again we must make it clear that we are not suggesting that the practice of schools and teachers evinced an immediate response to the ideals expressed by either the Hadow Report or that of Plowden. In fact, the survey of Primary education recently conducted by HM Inspectorate (DES 1978), which we will consider in greater detail in Chapter 6, and the work of the ORACLE research team (Galton, Simon and Croll 1980) revealed that 'progressivism' is not as widespread in Primary schools as has often been believed. The evidence of both these studies was of course derived from an examination of the curricula provided for 7-, 9- and 11-year-olds and it may be conjectured that similar studies of Nursery and Infant schools may have revealed a more extensive commitment to 'progressive' principles.

However, it would seem clear from this brief glimpse at the philosophy of education propounded by both the Hadow and the Plowden Committees that, although the practice of many schools continues to fall short of these ideals, wherever and whenever the curriculum of the Primary school is subjected to any kind of proper scrutiny, it is considered from the perspective not only of that view of education that has come to be called 'progressive' but also of that now being described as process-based, the major features of which this chapter has endeavoured to identify. It would thus seem reasonable to assume that we have described most of the salient features of what is, in theory if not always in practice, the philosophy of the English Primary school.

Summary and conclusions

We have attempted in this opening chapter to trace, albeit briefly, the development of a new view of education and model of the curriculum from the time of Rousseau through to the present day. We have argued that the essential characteristics of this model have been present from the very beginning but that they have been developed and refined through the theory and the practice of people such as Pestalozzi, Herbart, Froebel, Montessori and, especially, John Dewey. We have also tried to show that this movement has gained further impetus in recent years through the work of developmental psychologists such as Jean Piaget, Jerome Bruner and those others currently working in this field.

The characteristics that we considered to be the essential features of this approach to education and the curriculum were several. In the first place, we noted that it is based on an epistemology that is fundamentally empiricist. This we tried to trace from the influence on Rousseau of the empiricist philosophy of John Locke and David Hume to the more sophisticated pragmatism of John Dewey. This we suggested leads in turn to a tentative and undogmatic view of knowledge and thus to an unwillingness to define education too closely in terms of a content that can justifiably be imposed on children. On the contrary, we saw that it leads to an emphasis on experience as the only source of true learning and to a view of education as the guiding of this experience into productive channels. A corollary of this view is the concern to tailor education-al provision to the needs of individual pupils which we saw was a major feature of the work of some of the theorists and practitioners whose ideas we considered. Lastly, we noted that from the very outset there has been a strong emphasis on the need to study child psychology, to understand how children think, learn and develop cognitively, an emphasis that we suggested had led to that surge of interest in the study of intellectual development that has been a significant factor in the study of education in the last half-century. In general, we tried to show that what this view of education essentially involves is the recognition that education is a process that must be considered on its own terms and not from the point of view of any extrinsic goals or results it may be said to have; that, in the words of John Dewey, 'there is nothing to which education is subordinate save more education'. It is a process by which children are helped to acquire those capacities which will enable them to continue to learn and develop, by broadening both their horizons and their scope to explore beyond those horizons.

We then tried to show through an examination of the philosophy, both implicit and explicit, of the Hadow Report (1931) and the Plowden Report (1967) that this movement has had a major influence on the development of our thinking about and, albeit to a lesser degree, our practice of Primary education. We suggested that this influence is largely due to the absence of those external constraints that have inhibited curriculum development at other levels of education. However, we were also concerned to show that this in itself may suggest that the curriculum model that has emerged in this way leads us closer to what we might be prepared to regard as education as such, simply because it is further from those utilitarian demands and pressures that are prone to turn schooling into a form of training, a preparation for something else, and thus to encourage a means–end or instrumental model of the curriculum, a product ideology. For it is a model whose focus is the process of education itself rather than its end-products or end-results.

We must not appear, however, to be claiming that this approach to education is peculiar to the Primary school, and especially not that it only has applicability there. It is a form of education which seems to us to be the only acceptable form at any level, the notions of active learning and of development through genuine experience being, for us, essential ingredients in any process that is to be worthy of description as education. And, furthermore, in practical terms, it is a form of education which can be seen in some Secondary schools or in some areas of Secondary schools, and even, sometimes, in Further and Higher Education. It can also be identified as a significant feature of much that is coming to be called continuing education.

What we are wishing to stress in our conclusion to this chapter is, first, that it is a model of education and curriculum which must be recognized as distinctive and evaluated on its own terms and in its own right; second, that, if we wish to do this we can do no better at the present time than examine it in the context of the Primary school where it has been longer established and somewhat better worked out, at least in theoretical terms; and, thirdly, that its distinctive features need especially to be understood by teachers at a time when there is so much pressure on them to move away from this approach. This is particularly important when the attempts to smooth the transition from the Primary to the Secondary school, to ease transfer at that stage and to improve liaison between those two sectors of education are raising crucial questions as to whether the largely content-based or product-based approaches of much of Secondary schooling should dominate or whether the process-based philosophy which we have suggested is at the root of much of the thinking about Primary education should be encouraged to extend upwards. For, in our view, the educational merits of the view of education and curriculum as process are such as to render its attractions irresistible at every level of educational provision.

We must not be understood, however, as wishing to claim that it should be adopted uncritically. Certainly, a good many searching questions can and should be asked about it and we are, on the contrary, asserting that a rigorous and critical analysis of it is long overdue. It is also the case that currently there are pressures for change in the opposite direction – towards introducing an instrumental model into the planning of the curriculum of the Primary school. For this reason, as much as for any other, the present is an appropriate time to consider critically the theoretical bases and practical implications of this tradition. It is to this that we must, therefore, turn in our next chapter.

Suggested further reading

Rusk, R.R. (1957) *The Doctrines of the Great Educators*. London: Macmillan, Chs. VIII–XIII.
Kelly, A.V. (1986) *Knowledge and Curriculum Planning*. London: Harper & Row.
Bruner, J. (1968) *Towards a Theory of Instruction*. New York: Vintage.
Donaldson, M. (1978) *Children's Minds*. Glasgow: Fontana, Collins.
Eisner, E.W. (1982) *Cognition and the Curriculum: A Basis for Deciding What to Teach*. New York and London: Longman.

CHAPTER 2

A CRITIQUE OF PRIMARY EDUCATION

In our first chapter we attempted to pick out the major features of the curriculum of the Primary school, but we made it clear that we were not to be understood as suggesting that the model upon which it is based should be accepted without further criticism. It is not the only model that is available and it has certainly not been without its critics, since the time when the Archbishop of Paris ordered Rousseau's *Emile* to be torn and burnt in Paris by the Public Executioner. In fact, on many the word 'progressive', when used in the context of education, has had the effect of causing them, like Mussolini on hearing the word 'democracy', to reach for a gun. It is vital, therefore, that we analyse these ideas and consider them carefully and critically. This is particularly necessary, too, if we are right in claiming both that their influence is spreading and that, as a result, the pressures against them are mounting.

However, it is equally important that we set about this task in the right way or, rather, that we avoid tackling it in an appropriate way. It is not worthwhile, for example, to consider those objections to it that are raised by those who take the essentially conservative view that all change must be wrong and traditional methods and approaches to education necessarily right. Such a view does not help not only because it is fundamentally silly and nonsensical but because, since more than two hundred years have passed since the publication of *Emile*, it is difficult to argue that 'progressivism' does not itself have the support of a considerable tradition. Those who speak of this approach as involving 'new and untried methods', therefore, are displaying a considerable ignorance of the history of educational ideas.

It is equally inappropriate, however, to approach an evaluation of this view of education and the curriculum by asking if it works or, worse, by claiming that it does not. To do that is to beg many questions. At best, it is to misunderstand the essential nature of this view; at worst, it is to be guilty of a total illogicality. For, as we tried to show in Chapter 1, this view of education is based on the notion that education is an activity engaged in for its own sake; it is a 'process' model not a product model of curriculum; and so there is a fundamental contradiction involved in any attempt to evaluate it in terms of predetermined results. We will see later that this is a fundamental flaw in many attempts that have been made at research in Primary education.

Thirdly, it is not acceptable to criticize it merely by pressing the claims of an alternative theory of education or of the nature of knowledge, or, worse, by evaluating it in the terms of a different theory of knowledge or education. To do that is like attempting to criticize poetry by the rules of prose. Rather we must attempt to weigh these alternative theories against each other and to assess the relative merits of each.

The only productive form of evaluation and critical analysis of this view is one that examines its conceptual bases, the central elements of the theory on which it is founded, and then considers the problems of its implementation in practice. It is this kind of critique that we shall attempt in this chapter.

In doing so, we shall find that there are several main areas that we must look closely at. In the first place, a major criticism of this approach to education has been that it is conceptually confused, that its philosophical bases are unsound. This in turn leads to two kinds of issue that we would do well to consider separately – questions about the validity of the theory of knowledge upon which it is based and questions about the theory of education that this gives rise to. These are two areas we need to examine in some detail. Thirdly, we need to consider some of the criticisms that have been directed at the methods of teaching that it has given rise or support to. It has, of course, been accused of being over-concerned with method, 'strong on method, weak on aims', and this charge we must examine. But the methods themselves, in particular the notion of learning by discovery, have been severely attacked and this problem we must look at also. Lastly, the practical implementation of this view of education has often left much to be desired even by its advocates so that inevitably criticisms have derived from this and it has been described as 'fine in theory but impossible in practice'.

All of these kinds of criticism we must consider very carefully if we are to work out a proper rationale for this approach to education. In doing so, we will find that there is considerable overlap between them, but for clarity's sake we will attempt to consider them under three headings – the underlying theory of knowledge, the central elements of the resultant theory of education and the associated methods of teaching.

An empiricist theory of knowledge

We pointed out in Chapter 1 that the underlying philosopy of this view of education is an empiricist theory of knowledge. We noted to, some of the major features of this kind of theory. In particular we saw that, since its basic tenet is that all knowledge derives from experience, it must reject the notion that some knowledge transcends human experience and is derived from some other source. This in turn leads to a questioning of the possibility of our obtaining knowledge that might be regarded as universally valid, if by this we mean valid for all time and independently of developing human experience (Kelly 1986). In its primitive form, as expressed by such philosophers as David Hume, this led to the claim that none of our knowledge could be regarded as possessing any kind of validity. 'If we believe that fire warms or water refreshes 'tis only because it costs us too much pains to think otherwise.' However, the influence of later versions of rationalist theories of knowledge, such as those of Kant and Hegel, has led to the emergence of a modified version of empiricism. This claims, as we also noted in Chapter 1, not that we cannot have universal knowledge at all or that all our knowledge must for ever remain at the level of subjective experience, but merely that we must recognize that such universal knowledge as we do have is temporary and hypothetical, subject to regular and continuous modification and revision; it is universal in the sense that it is universally accepted only at this point in the evolution of mankind. This is the essence of that version of empiricism that was fundamental to the work of John Dewey, which in turn, again as we suggested in Chapter 1, has had an important influence on the theory of education we are discussing.

Inevitably this is a theory that is attacked by those who take a contrary view of knowledge. For there are still those who wish to press a rationalist view – not perhaps in the primitive form in which it was offered by philosophers such as Plato, but in the more advanced version of such philosophers as Kant, and, more recently, such educationists as Richard Peters (1966). The essence of their view is that some kinds of knowledge do have a status that is independent of the knower or at least independent of human experience, that is in fact *a priori*. To some extent the knowledge they are referring to is that whose validity derives from certain logical relationships between concepts and this few empiricists would want to deny. But a rationalist epistemology goes far beyond this in its claims about the validity of knowledge and the extent to which this kind of analysis of knowledge can take us (Kelly 1986).

What is fundamentally at issue is the meaning to be attached to the word 'truth'. For the empiricist, truth is a matter of correspondence; to be true an assertion must somehow correspond with the observed 'facts' of the case, with one's own experience or with that of everyone, or at least it must explain those 'facts' better than any other available theory. Thus the truth of, say, Archimedes' principle is based on its ability to explain certain phenomena and consequently to provide us with a basis for sensible action, so that, for example, none of us fills the bath to the brim before stepping into it and some of us can build metal ships to sail across the oceans of the world. It is this that the pragmatist means when he defines truth as 'what works'. On this analysis, too, let us note, truth is temporary and hypothetical and we cannot be dogmatic in any sphere.

For the rationalist, however, there is more to truth than this, there are more areas in which we can claim to have valid knowledge and the degree of our certainty is much higher. For s/he will argue that rationality itself can provide us with certain universal truths whose validity depends not on their correspondence with observed phenomena nor on purely utilitarian considerations of their pragmatic effectiveness but on their logical coherence or, rather, on the illogicality and incoherence of denying them. Such truths may be few in number but they provide us, it is argued, with certain 'first order principles' from which very much more can be derived or deduced. In this way, it is argued, we can demonstrate the validity of certain 'truths' about morals, about aesthetics and about knowledge itself. We can recognize, for example, the central value of rationality itself, without which no kind of discussion or debate would be possible, and see that that in itself sets up certain standards for human knowledge.

Few people, of course, would wish to deny the importance of rationality and its centrality to human discourse. The questions are how one defines 'rationality' and how far one thinks it takes us. What the rationalist wishes to argue is that the universal validity even of moral and aesthetic 'truths', in fact of all judgements of value, can be shown to derive entirely from their coherence, their rationality, their logic, or rather from the incoherence, irrationality and illogicality of denying them. Thus, to return for a moment to the field of education, the rationalist believes that the inclusion of certain subjects in the curriculum can be justified, or, rather, that their inclusion can be shown to be essential, either in terms of their effectiveness in promoting the development of rationality itself or of their demonstrably superior and intrinsic value. In other words, s/he believes that we can identify with assurance those human activities and those areas or even bodies of human knowledge that are intrinsically worthwhile and which must, as a result, comprise the core of the curriculum. One of his/her major criticisms of 'progressivism' then is that, since it does not accept this analysis of knowledge, it does not accept the right of certain subjects to be included in the curriculum regardless of how individual pupils react to them.

It will be clear, therefore, that the conflict is not just between different views of knowledge; it is also crucially between different views of values, of what constitutes our justification for pressing particular value assertions (Kelly 1986). It is not just a matter of the philosophical stance we take over the basis of human knowledge; it is, more importantly, a question of what resultant justification we feel we have for making judgements of value. Thus the rationalist will argue not only for a higher level and wider degree of certainty in human knowledge: s/he will also have a firmer view of what is valuable and thus of what should be taught to children in school. The empiricist, and the pragmatist in particular, will take a much more tentative view of knowledge and will see dangers in any attempt to be too firmly positive and directive about what we teach children in schools. S/he will argue, with John Dewey, that no such thing as imposition of truth from without is possible and, further, that to impose the values of the present generation on the next in this way is a form of indoctrination rather than education.

This, in turn, creates problems for the 'progressive' and the process views of education. For, if it makes us tentative over the content of our teaching, it also, as a consequence, raises important questions about the criteria upon which we can make any decisions in this area. That is a problem we must face if we accept this particular view of knowledge as the basis for our approach to education and it is one we must consider later. The quesion we must ask here, however, concerns the relative merits of these alternative views. What grounds are there for taking one view rather than the other?

The first point that should be made is that the empiricist theory of knowledge, especially in the form the pragmatist gives it, is a better character- ization of knowledge and has proved a better model for those areas of human knowledge that have seen the most dramatic advances in recent time. There can be little doubt that the progress that has been made in science and technology has been very largely due to the adoption of a theory of knowledge that is more suited to research in these spheres and that science only began to advance when the purely intellectual, rationalist approach to its study, which was inherited from the Greeks, was replaced by a model which emphasized experimentation and empirical research (Kilpatrick 1951). It is this that has led John Dewey and others to suggest that we should adopt and recognize the validity of the same model in other spheres where advance has been less marked and, one might also say, less successful, in order to facilitate progress there. Notable among these areas, of course, are those of human values and social living, of which education is an important part.

One might argue further that the evidence grows daily in support of the view that such values have to be held at least as tentatively as our knowledge in the scientific sphere, that their hypothetical nature has to be acknowledged and that the need for constant change and modification has to be recognized. The basis of the rationalist universal has crumbled considerably in recent times. Rapid social change has brought an awareness of the fact that moral and aesthetic values do change; the pluralism, both moral and cultural, of modern advanced industrial societies draws attention to the fact that different views, moral, aesthetic and cultural, must be tolerated and have equal claims to validity; and the result of this is a good deal of support for the pragmatist's basic principle of the evolutionary nature of all human knowledge. Conversely, it offers no kind of support for the acceptance of the validity of rationalist universals.

The counter-argument, of course, might be that society has got it wrong, that the change we can see represents merely progress towards the attainment of certain moral, aesthetic and cultural ideals, as Hegel would argue, or that it represents, as Plato would claim, a degeneration from such ideals. In short, the rationalist point of view in itself denies the relevance of observations of what is actually happening to the question of the validity of the ideals, the universal standards, it wishes to uphold. It is also true that rationalist epistemology is not concerned to deny the validity of empiricism in certain spheres of human knowledge, such as that of the empirical sciences; its claim is merely that there are other spheres, notably those areas where values are involved, to which the empiricist model is unsuited. In short, its case is that empiricism is not the only model of human knowledge, that it is not a model that appropriately characterizes all forms of human knowledge and understanding.

There are further problems, however, concerning the validity of this kind of theory even in those very areas in which it claims to have a special contribution to make or be able to shed particular light and clarity. Firstly, the precise basis upon which it makes these claims is obscure and somewhat confused. For, while it is not possible to deny that rational interchange and discourse between rational beings requires a level of logical coherence, there are no grounds for arguing that this also requires of them an unquestioning agreement on and acceptance of certain values, moral, aesthetic or cultural (Kelly 1986). The argument that such values do have some kind of objective existence independent of human experience is a metaphysical, one might almost say mystical, one and its bases are, to say the least, highly problematic. The very notion of absolute value is a difficult one, as is that of intrinsic value. The idea that value, like moral worth or aesthetic beauty, inheres in objects and activities rather than in the eye of the valuer is equally difficult to comprehend.

And it must be recognized that to hold a different view of what is valuable in any of these spheres is not always to be guilty of irrationality or incoherence. If it were otherwise, pluralism would not be possible and could be shown to be irrational and thus wrong.

One might argue, of course, that it is not a pluralism of ultimate beliefs that characterizes modern societies but rather a pluralism of interpretations of these ultimates. The issues of interpretation is important but it creates more problems for the rationalist than it solves. For it draws attention to the fact that, even if one were to accept that such universal values exist, it would be impossible to know what they are or to reach agreement over them at any level except that of such extreme generality that they would offer no guides for action. Higher order principles need to be interpreted and applied and they can in themselves offer no criteria of interpretation. Thus it might be accepted, for example, on rationalist arguments that truth-telling is an important and fundamental value, but a moment's thought will reveal the variety of practical interpretations that then become possible. For few but the most inflexible bigots would claim that there will never be an occasion when one might feel it right to modify this principle, or that it is not open to a wide range of interpretation. The same is true of all values, moral, social or aesthetic, even those that one might concede have a universal acceptance, if not a universal validity.

We are thus faced with the inevitability of a plurality of value positions. If this is not at the level of ultimate universals, its existence must certainly be recognized at the level of practical interpretation and implementation. And so a rationalist epistemology, even if valid, offers little help in practice, and this has particular relevance and importance for education. For it means we must accept the inevitability of disagreement over what rationality is, over what kinds of subject areas will promote it and over which subjects might have intrinsic value and thus a right to be included for their own sakes in the curriculum. This is why those who wish to promote this kind of approach to educational planning have come up with such strange arguments to support it.

Even if we accept, therefore, that the concept of intrinsic value is meaningful, in spite of its mystical flavour, it will not help us with the practicalities of educational planning. It might, however, appear to do so, as it clearly has to some, and it is in this respect that it can be dangerously misleading, not least because its main effect is to emphasize and draw our attention to questions about the knowledge that is to be acquired in the process of education rather than those about its effects on the pupils who are to acquire it.

In the last analysis, then, at the level of practical educational decisions, as in any other practical sphere, we must accept the inevitability of a pragmatic view and it is this that is giving strength to that approach to education we have seen described as 'progressive', since that is its essence. An examination of rationalist epistemology reveals serious weakneses especially at the level of practicalities; the pragmatic view, on the other hand, displays some corresponding strengths. Both of these have implications for education since they result in similarly 'conflicting' views here. We must now turn to a consideration of the main points of this conflict.

The 'progressive' and 'process' theories of education

The rationalist view of the nature of knowledge, as we have seen, has a number of serious weaknesses and thus creates a number of serious problems for any theory of education that is based upon it. A theory of education that is based on an empiricist view of knowledge, however, will present its own problems and difficulties and these have attracted the attention of the critics of the 'progressive' theory of education. It is to a consideration of them that we now turn.

We saw in the last section that an empiricist view of knowledge leads to a greater degree of uncertainty about knowledge and especially about the nature and validity of value assertions. A major target for the critics of this view of education, then, has been its inability to provide hard and fast value criteria and the problems and difficulties that this gives rise to. This inability is acknowledged by the proponents of the view but both the inability itself and solutions offered to it have attracted criticism.

There are three possible criteria that one can use in making decisions about the curriculum, three possible sources of answers to the fundamental questions that need to be faced. One can look, as we have already seen, to analyses of the nature of the knowledge and the claims that might be said to derive from these; one can turn to sociological, or even political, views of the nature of society and consider society's demands; or one can put into the central position the child himself or herself.

These positions are not by any means mutually exclusive but the empiricist base of 'progressivism' in education must lead to a rejection of any approach to curriculum planning that is concerned solely or primarily with a consideration of the bodies of knowledge that are to form its content. For it is centrally opposed to rationalism and its view of knowledge as 'out-there' or 'God-given', as we saw in Chapter 1, and, as a result, it cannot agree that the selection of that knowledge that is to be part of education is to be made on the assumption that certain bodies of knowledge are intrinsically worthwhile, in a way independent of the manner in which we view them. This must be recognized as the essence of an empiricist and especially a pragmatic approach to education and thus of that 'progressive' theory of education that it has spawned.

Difficulties are also presented for this theory of education by an undue emphasis in curriculum planning on the nature or the 'demands' of society. For to plan the curriculum on the basis of what society may be said to be or to need, to attempt to use education to fit pupils into society, is to adopt an approach to education that is essentially utilitarian or instrumental and this too we have seen is rejected by the 'progressive' educational philosophy we are examining here. It is also to ignore the continuously evolving and developing nature of society which may be said itself to require that the emphasis in education be placed on the development of the child.

Thus, as we have seen, this view of education regards it as of central importance that the choice of educational experience be made by reference to the child as the recipient of those experiences. And the essence of the process view of education and curriculum as opposed to the merely 'progressive', is that we see education and plan our curricular provision by reference to the processes of development those experiences may promote. In pursuance of this, it has been argued, therefore, that the choice must be based on the needs of children or on their interests, a view that we saw was implicit in all such theories from that of Rousseau and has been made explicit in the works of John Dewey and, more recently, by such people as Pat Wilson (1971).

However, both the notion of needs and that of interests as the basis for educational decision-making have been challenged on several grounds. It has been pointed out by several writers that 'needs' is a value term and thus cannot provide us with a firm criterion of choice. There can be many views and opinions as to what children need or what any particular child needs, ranging from those of the child himself to those of the politicians responsible for the public funding of the educational system. Each individual or group will assess such needs in terms of further criteria that will derive from a particular view of the goals and purposes of the activity. In short, the notion of needs in itself will not resolve our problem since some further basis is required upon which we can evaluate the different interpretations that will be offered.

Similar problems arise over the notion of 'interests'. In the first place, the use of this term, it is said (Dearden 1968), creates a certain unhelpful ambiguity, since there is likely to be conflict between what a child is interested in and what is in his/her interests. This conflict is, of course, identical with that we have just noted as arising from the attempt to use needs as our guideline.

A further and rather different problem arises, however, when one faces the issue of how to make choices among the many interests that children will undoubtedly have. The idea that one should discover what children are interested in and develop that, rather than deciding what they ought to be interested in and imposing that willy-nilly upon them, is an important one and certainly reflects to a large extent the approach to education that Dewey and others have advocated. But children are interested in many things and a choice has to be made as to which of their many interests should be encouraged and promoted; further choices need to be made, too, concerning the ways in which, even the directions in which, they are to be promoted. The child we always hear about in this context, although we seldom have the fortune to meet him/her, is the one whose abiding interest, we are told, is in pulling legs off insects. But what criteria do we justify discouraging the pursuit of this interest, since clearly it cannot be by appeal to the notion of interests itself?

Indeed, it has been argued (Hollins 1964) that there is a fundamental inconsistency in this approach to education in that in its practice teachers and educators can be seen to be appealing to certain moral and aesthetic standards while at the same time denying that such standards have any validity. It is further claimed (Darling 1978) that this 'pedagogical megalomania' leads to a form of manipulation and thus of social control every bit as serious, or even more so because of its insidious nature, as any direct attempt to impose certain bodies of predetermined curriculum content.

Again, therefore, the value question is raised and again it is clear that some further criteria of choice and decision must be found.

One major criticism of this view, then, focuses on the inadequacy of notions like 'needs' and 'interests' as a basis for decisions about curriculum content. For there are many different interpretations that can be placed on these notions, and further criteria are required upon which we can evaluate the needs and the interests themselves.

The same kinds of criticism are levelled at the idea of education as a form of growth of the child, the unfolding of the inner potential of the child, which is another version of this theory, another suggested source of guidelines for educational decision-making. We have no basis for deciding what the aims of education should be, it is argued, no grounds for treating education as a means to an end. As Dewey puts it, education can have no ends outside itself, it is its own end. It can only be viewed, then, as a continuous and life-long process of growth.

This view, which has called been the 'horticultural' model of curriculum planning (Hirst 1975), not least because it is often illustrated by the use of similes such as that of the acorn growing into the oak tree, has been attacked on a number of grounds (Dearden 1967, 1968, 1976). The first of these is that it presents us with identical problems to those we have just seen as deriving from the use of notions such as 'needs' and 'interests'. For 'growth' is also a value term. Certainly, when it is used in contexts other than those of physical growth, it brings with it notions of approval for certain kinds of growth or for growth in certain directions. At the very least, it raises questions about the direction of growth and introduces problems of choice which it cannot of itself resolve. As any horticulturalist knows, growth can either be allowed to occur unhindered or it can be controlled and directed in a countless variety of ways. Similarly, if growth is to be interpreted as self-realization or as the unfolding of inner potential, questions must be asked about the kind of self that is to be realized and the kinds of potential that are to be allowed or encouraged to unfold. The alternative is to regard the notion of growth as implying a complete determinism, a process over which no control can or should be exercised. Such a process would be more properly described as maturation than education for the very reason that it lacks that element of control that the notion of education would seem to entail.

If education is to be more than maturation, then, if there are important conceptual distinctions to be made between these two notions, it must concern itself with decisions about the direction or at least the manner in which children are to be assisted to grow and these decisions are again of a kind that the notion of growth itself cannot resolve for us.

It is this that has led to a further major criticism of this approach to the curriculum of the Primary school and, especially, of what has been seen as the underlying philosophy of the Plowden Report (CACE 1967). For, in that Report, much time was devoted to the child and his/her patterns of learning in school and very little to the overall direction that education should take. The chapter devoted to aims (CACE 1967, ch.15) is, in fact, very brief, tentative and somewhat unsatisfactory, and it almost suggests that aims are hardly worth discussion at all.

A cautionary note about such neglect has come from Richard Peters (1969) who quite rightly shows that the value judgements concealed in apparently descriptive passages of the Plowden Report are 'a much more subtle and insidious way of influencing peoples' attitudes than an open discussion of aims would be. Aims invite discussion because they are abstracted to guide action' (op. cit., p.2).

As a development of this point, it has been argued that it is logically impossible for the 'progressive, child-centred theory to be 'strong on methods but weak on aims' as it is commonly accused of being (Dearden 1976), so that it is unwise of its adherents to try to avoid making aims more explicit. However implicit and unstated they may be, a set of aims is certainly implied by the value-judgements that guide the selection of materials, the arrangement of the school environment, the questions asked and the possible lines of development that are envisaged.

Dearden argues that, in the 'progressive' Primary school, teachers certainly avoid making aims that are 'prescriptive of content' by concerning themselves only with what he terms 'relational aims', that is, aims that focus on the child's development of a positive attitude to learning. He goes on to claim that 'these relational aims can be conveniently grouped under three main headings: (i) intrinsic interest (eagerness, curiosity, learning to learn, absorption, etc.); (ii) self-expression (expressing one's own individuality, being oneself, etc.); (iii) autonomy (making independent judgements, choosing with confidence, self-direction, learning by discovery, etc.)' (Dearden 1976, p.54). These 'relational aims', although essential for setting the context within which truly educational activities can occur, offer no guidance, he argues, for the direction that this education should take. Dearden wishes to preserve these important 'relational aims' but he also wishes to give direction to educational activities. This he attempts to do by suggesting the formulation of aims which are made explicit and acted upon by teachers through their work of initiating children into the main forms of knowledge and understanding which have historically developed (op. cit. p.55) and by ensuring that content and skills have 'future usefulness, whether for the later stages of education itself or by way of 'preparation for life' (ibid.).

It is clear that this view reflects the tensions and conflict between the process and product approaches to educational planning, which we shall explore more fully in Chapter 3. It is also clear, however, that it exacerbates rather than resolves those tensions and that conflict, because it reduces the 'relational aims' to the status of means and makes the end-product again the main focus of educational planning. It is thus a good example of an attempt to both have the cake and to eat it and, as a suggested solution, by appearing to solve the problem, it merely serves to distract attention from the real point at issue.

Furthermore, it does not take proper cognizance of the way in which some teachers have set about the problem. For, in protecting their implicitly held view of education as process, some Primary teachers have been understandably reticent about stating directional aims. But this is not to say that they have been unconcerned either with the direction that intellectual development will take or with the selection and promotion of certain kinds of activity and content in preference to others. The evidence suggests, however, that their way of resolving this difficult problem has been rather different from that suggested by Dearden. For they have sought a solution not by looking to views about the nature of knowledge but, in a manner consonant with the general position implicit in their approach, by turning first of all to theories about the nature of the child.

It is for this reason that this approach to education has both stimulated and been itself advanced by that new view of intelligence and the associated developmental approach to educational psychology which we argued in Chapter 1 has been the second and more recent factor in its growth. For it is to the work of developmental psychologists and psycho-linguists, especially those who have pursued and extended the ideas of Jean Piaget, that teachers have turned for an answer to questions about what the process of education should consist of.

Again, therefore, we are forced to recognize the need for a different set of criteria by which decisions of this kind can be made.

A further criticism which has been levelled at this approach to educational planning, however, has drawn attention to the fact that rather random forms of learning may well result if we make decisions about what children should be encouraged to learn by reference to their needs, their interests or the growth of their potentialities. For it has been argued (Dearden 1976) that we cannot ensure that in pursuing their interests children will acquire knowledge across that range of areas that some feel to be desirable, whether this is interpreted as meaning a grounding in the 'basic skills' or initiation into discrete forms of understanding or realms of meaning. Nor can we ensure a 'balance of spread of activities over a period of time, not necessarily daily, or perhaps even weekly, but within a manageable period over which the teacher can keep steadily in view where the educational process is going' (Dearden 1976, p.54).

Another aspect of this same problem reveals itself when we begin to ask questions about the origins of pupils' interests or to stress that, if a problem-solving approach is to be adopted, the problems we ask pupils to tackle should be genuine problems that are their own in a real sense. For it has been pointed out (Hollins 1964) that children must possess some knowledge before they can recognize the existence of a problem and, although this distinction between knowledge and problem-solving is drawn somewhat naïvely, this line of criticism has the merit of drawing attention to their interrelatedness. Similarly, children must have some experiences before interests can be aroused, so that again we need to note the importance of experiences that are provided as well as those that are a response to interests that are already established. Furthermore, we are adopting naïve notions both of experience and of what will constitute an educational environment if we do not recognize that without help children will not be able to acquire the concepts necessary to understand their experiences or to pick out the important and relevant elements of that environment.

All of these criticisms would be completely damning if non-interventionism were an essential element in this form of education and, indeed, they are completely damning of those theories that take that view. More sophisticated adherents of 'progressivism', however, and especially those who now adopt a view of education as process, have long recognized that intervention by teachers in the development of their pupils is both necessary and justified. It is necessary if problems of the kind just outlined are to be avoided, and justified, if by nothing else, at least by the notion of education itself. For education becomes impossible, as indeed does curriculum planning, without some notion of deliberate attempts to control children's growth and development; we have maturation only, no role at all for the teacher and no acknowledgement of the importance of his/her knowledge and skills. Thus all such theorists speak of education as guidance and they recognize that it is the task of teachers to intervene in order to obviate many of the difficulties that have been listed – to make choices concerning the kinds of interest to be encouraged and the ways in which they might be developed, to evaluate pupils' experiences, to decide what constitutes needs and which needs shall be met, to decide on the kinds of growth and development to be promoted.

In so far as these criticisms are based on the assumption that the point at issue is whether teachers should intervene or not, then they carry little weight and, indeed, represent a rather disturbing failure to appreciate what has been going on for a long time in both the theory and the practice of education. However, in so far as they draw our attention to questions about the nature and the basis of such intervention, their effect is a salutary one. For these are questions that need to be asked and explored.

In exploring them, however, we must beware of making the kinds of tacit assumption that seem to underlie these criticisms themselves. For they appear to make certain assumptions which it is the purpose of this book to argue are fallacious.

In the first place, they appear to take too readily for granted that, while it is a difficult and value-laden question that we face when we attempt to make decisions about the curriculum by references to the needs and interests of children, the same difficulty does not emerge when we turn instead to the needs and interests of society, when, for example, we begin to define 'basic skills' and areas of knowledge that everyone should be introduced to by reference to social and economic needs. In fact, the same difficulty is met there. For, once we reject those criteria that derive from a rationalist perspective on knowledge, there is nowhere to which we can turn to find a similarly objective base for curricular decisions.

Secondly, they make that mistake because they assume that the search is for criteria of curriculum content. For those who make this kind of criticism of the 'progressive' and of the process approaches to education, even if they do not do so in the belief that certain bodies of knowledge have a right to be taught because of some intrinsic value that they possess or because they act as gateways to certain forms of thought, nevertheless assume that the search is for some alternative basis for choices of content. If they do not go that far, they assume that ultimate educational choices are concerned with aims and thus criticize this view because it has problems in stating its aims or the directions of the process of growth and development it is concerned with. They thus imply that we should make educational evaluations by reference to content or to aims. It is here that they go seriously awry.

It is our contention that while such criticisms have drawn attention to the need to find suitable criteria of choice in educational decision-making, they have seriously misled us as to the direction in which we should be looking for such criteria. The questions they are asking must indeed be asked but the answers to them are not of the kind they envisage. For the questions are not about content or direction, they are about processes, and the criteria we are seeking will be found only by exploring those processes that are fundamental and integral to education. In short, the criteria of choice, the basic values of this approach to education, are those that derive from the concept of education itself, so that the ultimate value is the intellectual development of the individual (Kohlberg and Mayer 1972). It is this that constitutes the essence of the process approach to curriculum planning and the awareness of this is one of the major factors that has taken this view well beyond that of mere 'progressivism'.

To discover what this involves is the central purpose of this book and we shall begin to focus more closely on this in later chapters. We may be able to do so more effectively, however, if we first complete our critique of Primary education by considering some of the criticisms that have been made of the kinds of educational practice that it has been felt to require.

The practical implications of this view

The view of education that we are currently examining has inevitably led to major changes in teaching method and these in turn have brought out the critics. To some extent, of course, their criticisms are directed more properly at the underlying theory of education rather than its practice, since to a large degree, once that theory is accepted, certain implications for methodology unavoidably follow. To some extent too the criticisms have been based on a failure to understand the impact of these changes or, as we suggested at the beginning of this chapter, an attempt to evaluate them by appeal to unsuitable and inappropriate criteria. However, serious criticisms have been offered of 'Primary methods' and no critique of this form of education would be complete without some discussion of them.

Active learning

The one essential practical demand made by a view of education that lays stress on the superiority and, indeed, the centrality of first-hand learning through personal and individual experience is that the learner should be active in the educational process. This we have seen is a central feature of the theories of those philosophers and educationists who have supported this view and it is reinforced, as we have also seen, by the researches of the developmental psychologists. Learning, if it is not to be 'inert (Whitehead 1932) and if it is to be part of a wider process that can properly be described as education, must be active. The learner must not be merely a passive recipient of what is taught, s/he must be him-/herself involved in the process. Education, on this view, is a good deal more than mere learning. This means that we must acquire a new and more sophisticated view of teaching as not merely, and perhaps not ever, 'telling' but rather as facilitating learning and promoting development, helping pupils to learn for themselves.

There are two major practical results of adopting this view, each of which we must consider in turn. For, in the first place this view of teaching has led to a stress on what have sometimes been called 'activity methods', the attempt to implement the recommendation of the Hadow Report (1931) that the curriculum be thought of 'in terms of activity and experience', and, secondly, it has prompted the emergence of the notion of 'learning by discovery'. Both have had their critics and both we must examine.

There is no doubt that the idea of education as activity has resulted in some practices that it would be difficult to justify on any grounds. The belief that, if children are not engaged in busily – and often noisily – doing something that involves movement about the classroom, then they are not learning properly is, to say the least, naïve. So too is the converse, that when children are so engaged they are necessarily enjoying profitable and productive experiences. Nevertheless, the practice of some teachers has appeared to reflect some such simplistic view and has rightly, therefore, attracted criticism. We should not however, see such criticism as merited by the notion of 'active learning', but recognize that it is properly directed only at examples of its inept implementation. Once we do this, we realize that effort should be more profitably directed at helping such teachers to acquire a clearer concept of what they are doing than at attempts to persuade them that they ought to be doing something quite different.

The problem is not eased, however, when theorists, in criticizing this approach to education, adopt a similarly naïve view of what is meant by 'activity'. For again the assumption is that what is being argued is that children can only learn by being physically active and, while this is a theory that is deserving of criticism, it must be stressed that it is not the view that is being propounded by most of the advocates of the process approach. Rather it is a caricature of their view.

There are two ways in which such an interpretation does violence to the notion of active learning or at least leads to a gross misinterpretation of that notion. In the first place, if we take the naïve view that suggests that children must be seen to be in gross physical motion if we are to claim they are learning actively, we are led to the view that all forms of teaching by the teacher are to be excluded from the process. Secondly, if, in order to avoid that conclusion, we accept a definition of activity that includes other kinds of pupil activity, such as sitting at a desk or table and reading or writing or even copying material from a book or from the blackboard, we find the critics asking whether as a result there is anything to the notion of 'active learning' at all, whether it is any different from traditional methods, since 'are not copying blackboard notes, reading round the class and doing "comprehension" exercises activities?' (Dearden 1968, p.137).

The error of both of these interpretations is the failure to recognize that the essential feature of the notion of 'active learning' is not a demand for physical activity of any kind but for the direct personal, intellectual or 'mental' involvement of the pupil in the learning process. In other words, the claim is not just that there should be activity in the classroom but 'that there should be a special kind of activity' (Dearden 1968, p.138).

Furthermore, it is important to note that the special nature of this kind of activity is not to be found in any aspect of its physical manifestations nor in any particular methodological device. It is to be sought rather in the kind of mental 'set' that accompanies the activity. All human activity is 'mental' in the sense that it is always conscious (Ayer 1964; Dearden 1968) and it is to this conscious aspect of activity that we must look in order to achieve a proper understanding of what is meant by 'active learning' and 'activity methods'. For the central point that is being made is that pupils should not be seen as passive recipients of whatever information is meted out to them by their teachers but should be actively involved in the learning process in such a way that what they learn becomes truly a part of them and is not merely plastered on in the form of those 'inert ideas' (Whitehead 1932) to which we referred earlier. The contrast is between active and inert forms of learning, rather than between physical activity and relative inertia. In short, what are often referred to as 'activity methods' are no more and no less than those methods that are adopted in order to foster education through experience in order in turn to promote what is seen as the proper kind of intellectual development in pupils.

Once we appreciate this and recognize the kind of concept of active learning that is held by most of its proponents, the force of many of the criticisms of it is diminished. Furthermore, we immediately become aware of some additional arguments in support of it, since it becomes clear that what is at its heart is a concept of education as essentially concerned with intellectual development and with the acquisition of conceptual understanding rather than mere knowledge or rote-learning.

Unless we disagree with that kind of concept of education, therefore, the only basis upon which we might criticize 'activity methods' is that they are not the most efficient way of promoting such a form of education. Such a claim would be difficult either to prove or to disprove. Any attempt to deal with the issue at this level, however, would have the merit of facing up to the right kinds of question rather than attempting to evaluate the effectiveness of these methods by reference to some highly subjective, and seldom acknowledged or made explicit, view of what it might mean for them to 'work', a view, for example, such as one derived from their effectiveness in promoting the acquisition of the 'basic skills'. For it would reveal clearly that it is with the promotion of education itself we are concerned and not only with one particular aspect of it.

Furthermore, there is at least a *prima facie* case for arguing that pupils are more likely to develop in the ways that this kind of concept of education entails if they are encouraged to become active participants in the process rather than passive recipients of the direct activities of their teachers. It would appear to make the teachers's task unnecessarily difficult to require him/her to promote this kind of learning by adopting methods in which teacher-activity dominates and pupil–activity is kept to a minimum.

There is also a further indication of the probable effectiveness of activity learning even of the overt and physical kind that may be particularly relevant to the education of pupils in the Primary age-range, but which we ought perhaps not to ignore in considering the needs of older pupils too. For it is clear from the work of the developmental psychologists, as we saw in Chapter 1, that intellectual development must pass through a stage at which concepts can only be grasped through concrete examples or through action, when the learner represents his/her world in the enactive mode. Furthermore, this is not a stage of development that is passed and left behind. It is quite clear that many adults have never got beyond it and equally clear that even those whose intellectual development has gone very far still find the enactive mode of representation a most useful device in many contexts. This would suggest both that active methods of teaching and learning are likely to be effective at any stage of intellectual development and that they are likely to be particularly apposite to the education of young children. This, again as we saw in Chapter 1, has been the main thrust of the influence of developmental psychology on the development of the philosophy of Primary education. We can see now that it leads us almost inevitably to embrace 'activity methods' as a corollary of the acceptance of that philosophy.

A commitment to 'activity methods', then, implies no more, and indeed no less, than an attempt to seek the best ways of promoting active learning. Any more simplistic interpretation of it, therefore, is inadequate and misleading in respect both of its theoretical justification and its practical implementation. It is thus not a proper target for those critics who wish to attack the concept but only for those whose concern is with the inadequacies of its practice.

Learning by discovery

The same is broadly true of the related notion of 'discovery learning' to which we now turn. There is an important sense in which all learning is discovery and we would do well not to lose sight of that in any discussion of the criticisms of discovery learning. For by definition we can only learn things that we did not know before, so that all learning is the discovery of something that is new to us. Those critics, therefore, who direct their attacks at the idea that children might be thought to be breaking the barriers of human knowledge are adopting a view of discovery that is mistaken as well as naïve. There is nothing in the meaning of the term discovery that implies that my discoveries have to be unique and new to mankind. That is why when I discovered a new 'pub' last night I did not plant a Union Jack in its saloon bar and inform the press. This kind of criticism of discovery learning is like similar criticisms that have been made of the notion of creativity in education and is based on similar conceptual confusions. All learning is discovery. The important questions are what kind of discovery it is, how it supports educational development and how it can best be promoted.

However, there is a more serious aspect of the claim that discovery learning is impossible that we must consider, not least because it throws light on those questions. It is sometimes argued, in a manner reminiscent of the sophists' argument put by Socrates in Plato's dialogue, *Meno*, and sometimes with explicit references to that argument, that you cannot discover anything because, if you already know it, logically you cannot discover it and, if you do not already know it, you will not recognize it when you do come across it. The argument as put in the *Meno* was intended, of course, to show the impossibility of all learning and Socrates' answer to it was to demonstrate, by skilful questioning of an ignorant slave which elicited a remarkable 'knowledge' of mathematics, that all learning is in fact remembering (*anamnesis*). Few, if any, would today wish to propound a similar solution; yet some criticisms of discovery learning are reminiscent of this view and reflect a similar conceptual confusion to that which lies at the root of all those paradoxes that the sophists wrestled with.

This kind of argument, especially by its appeal to the case Plato makes in the *Meno*, should alert us to the fact that we have here, yet again, an example of a criticism of this form of teaching mounted from the perspective of a rationalist view of knowledge, in spite of the fact that it is an approach to education which we have seen is based on an empiricist epistemology and thus cannot rationally or logically be attacked from such a perspective. For the assumptions behind this line of criticism are that there exists some body or bodies of knowledge to be discovered and that the learning process, however it is structured, must be directed towards the acquisition of this knowledge. Not only, therefore, does it impose an incompatible rationalist perspective on the discussion; it also relegates the notion of learning by discovery to being merely a form of methodology, and attempts to evaluate it only in terms of its effectiveness in bringing about learning of this kind, learning as the acquisition of predetermined knowledge.

Several points must be made in response to this. First, the notion of discovery learning, for the advocates of 'progressivism' or of a process-based curriculum, is not a mere method of instruction; it reflects that essentially different approach to education we have been concerned to elucidate, and which is encapsulated in the idea of active learning. It is for this reason, secondly, that we would favour the use of the term 'enquiry learning', since the most important ingredient is that of pupil enquiry not that of the discovery of knowledge. For what is crucial to this notion is that the knowledge acquired should result from genuine experience and that this can best be achieved by engaging pupils in meaningful enquiries, in seeking knowledge and experience for themselves through explorations they can see the point of. Thirdly, it does not make sense in this kind of context to be asking whether pupils will in this manner acquire all the knowledge they ought to be acquiring in schools. For to ask that is to miss the point entirely and to introduce a completely different and incompatible view of education into the debate. It is a view which is irrelevant in the context of the very different approach to education and curriculum we are exploring.

The essential element in the notion of discovery- or enquiry-learning is to be sought, and found not by considering the nature of knowledge, and what it is assumed education should be concerned to transmit, but by exploring the process of learning and development which this view of education is suggesting should be promoted. Criticisms framed in terms of the former, then, are not merely invalid; they are irrelevant. What is being claimed is that children's development can best be promoted by providing them with opportunities to explore, to enquire, to find out for themselves. The only valid criticism of this approach, within the context of this view of education, therefore, is one which might set out to show that there are other better ways of encouraging development of the kind we are seeking.

However, the claim that discovery is not possible unless one knows what one is discovering – not a problem incidentally that caused Columbus too many sleepless nights – does draw our attention to an important aspect of the notion of learning by discovery. For it is important to realize that the questions one can ask are limited by the knowledge one already possesses and that prior knowledge is needed if one is to recognize the importance of what one discovers (Dearden 1968). It is also the case that discovery is what Ryle has called an 'achievement' word and 'carries an implication of the *truth* of what is put forward' (Dearden 1967, p.141), or at least of its significance, so that one must know how to establish its truth or its significance. It is further the case that education, especially when it is seen as development, involves the acquisition of theoretical concepts and that these are 'interconnected in elaborate and carefully constructed systems' (Dearden 1968, p.123), or at least must be so structured in his/her own mind by the individual child.

In short, we must recognize that learning by discovery, or enquiry, in the context of education cannot be a random collecting of disconnected 'facts' (even if such an unstructured form of learning is possible in any context) but necessitates the active participation and guidance of the teacher at all stages. In the often quoted words of Jerome Bruner, 'discovery, like surprise, favours the well prepared mind' (1971). The teacher's task, then, is to prepare the child for his/her explorations and to help him/her to appreciate, to interpret, to understand and to structure what those explorations reveal to him/her.

Those criticisms that are directed at haphazard learning by discovery, then, are entirely justified. They often arise, however, from a naïve view of what is meant by the term or the simplistic polarization of this approach to learning and the idea of instruction or even of teaching itself. For many, it would seem, the question is should we teach by instructing or should we stand back and let children find out for themselves. The answer is that just as the term instruction itself does not necessarily imply the use of didactic methods so the idea of learning by discovery does not rule out the possibility of teacher-guidance. As so often, it is the polarization itself that creates the difficulty and the confusion. The only sensible concept of learning by discovery is one which recognizes the essential contribution of the guidance that the teacher can and should provide.

We might consider the different forms that such guidance might take, for example by distinguishing the structuring of the educational environment from more direct forms of intervention, and thus propose different models of discovery learning (Dearden 1967). Essentially, however, the distinction is between intervention and non-intervention. It thus reflects a more general criticism that has been directed at this approach to education, since from the beginning there has been a notable lack of clarity over this question of whether teachers should or should not interfere in the development of children. It is to a consideration of this issue that we now turn.

Teacher-intervention

We have already referred to the negative approach to education that derived from Rousseau's view that children should be allowed to develop naturally, the optimistic view that he took of human nature leading him to claim that we should not meddle with the child's natural goodness but rather protect him/her from the corrupting influences of society. Others who followed, such as Friedrich Froebel and Maria Montessori, propounded similar views.

There, is, however, a fundamental inconsistency in such views that emerges in both the theory and the practice of these theorists themselves. For Rousseau advises a good deal of active interference in Emile's education at adolescence. Froebel often adopts a mandatory stance in relation to education, especially in its later stages, and Montessori's careful structuring of the environment is a form of interference which, although subtle, is every bit as effective, and perhaps even more so, than intervention of a direct and more overt kind. Furthermore, we have already noted on several occasions that the message of developmental psychology is that children's intellectual development will only proceed if they receive the right kind of help, support and guidance.

Again this leads us to the same conclusion. Non-intervention is not possible and attempts to argue for it are rightly open to the kinds of criticism that have been offered. Most of these criticisms, however, lose their validity when one recognizes the greater complexities of the approach to education that is being advocated and particularly the important interventionist role of the teacher in it. It is not intervention itself that should be under debate, it is the most appropriate form of intervention that is the concern.

The case, then, is that the most appropriate, indeed the only suitable and effective, form of teacher-intervention in pupil's learning is that of guiding their discoveries rather than informing or telling them of ours. This is, of course, in harmony with the basic premises of this view of learning, which we have already examined in detail, since its concern is with the child as a learner rather than with the 'facts' to be learned, with the structures the child can be helped to give to his/her own knowledge rather than with a structure inherent in the knowledge itself and, in short, again with the idea of education as the development of understanding rather than as the acquisition of knowledge. It is the manner of learning that is crucial rather than the method. It is this that is the most effective and cogent answer to that further criticism of the practice of discovery learning: that it is uneconomical, that it requires too much time and energy. For the case made here is that, whatever time and energy are necessary, it is the only way in which effective learning can occur. And there is much supporting, if negative, evidence for this claim in the manifest ineffectiveness of more didactic forms of teaching in promoting learning and intellectual development of the kind it is being claimed here is educationally desirable. If development is our concern, we must adopt whatever means and measures will be conducive to its promotion. It is only when our concern is with the knowledge to be transmitted and acquired that the claim that discovery learning is uneconomical has any force.

In general, then, the criticisms offered have been directed at somewhat naïve views of 'activity methods' or 'discovery learning' or non-interventionism and lose much of their force when these notions are more clearly explicated. It must be said in conclusion, however, that they may have more strength when directed at the practices of some teachers purporting to implement these approaches, since these practices often themselves evince the confusions we have attempted to identify and reveal the kind of lack of clarity in thinking about this view of education that we are claiming needs to be rectified.

They also, of course, alert us to the fact that some of the inadequacies of this kind of education will be due not so much to conceptual confusions in the minds of teachers as to the practical problems it creates for them and to factors which exacerbate these problems. For it will be clear that to attempt to guide and support children in their own explorations will make greater demands on the teacher's expertise than the provision of pre-planned and pre-packaged material and that the individualized approach that becomes essential when one tries to assist and promote the intellectual development of each pupil will create problems of classroom organization and control that will be much more complex than those presented by most forms of class-teaching. It will also be apparent that the teacher's success here will depend not only on his/her own expertise and understanding, it will depend equally on the context provided for him/her by his/her employers, on the size of the class, for example, on the kinds of resource material available, on the geography of the school and classroom, on the school's general climate and so on.

Many criticisms of this kind of teaching, then, take the form of assertions that while it might be fine in theory it is impracticable in classes of thirty or more pupils. One can only answer that kind of criticism by pointing out the obvious, that if it is fine in theory it has to be made practicable and that, since there clearly are teachers who can and do enjoy enormous success even in these conditions (Blenkin and Kelly 1983), all teachers must be encouraged to develop their professional expertise to the same level. In short, criticisms must be directed at the underlying theory and not at inadequacies of practice. If that is felt to be sound, the practices must be made to work and criticisms of them must be limited to their effectiveness and not extrapolated to include their theoretical bases. The fact that some people play football or violins very badly does not in any way negate the value of sport or music; the fact that some doctors are incompetent does not mean that the practice of medicine should be abolished; the inadequacies of some teachers, therefore, should not be seen as invalidating the theories they purport to embrace. The only valid criticisms are those directed at the theories themselves or at those factors beyond the teachers' control that may be corrected or adjusted to facilitate their work.

Summary and conclusions

We have tried in this chapter to examine in some detail the major criticisms that have been made of that approach to education which in Chaper 1 we argued was the basic philosophy of Primary education. We have looked at these criticisms under three headings, considering, firstly, those that have been directed at its epistemological assumptions, then those concerned with its central tenets as a theory of education and, lastly, those that reflect some of the dissatisfactions felt at the kinds of educational practice it has led to.

Our main conclusion is that most of the criticisms have either been launched from a different epistemological base or that they misunderstand the essential principles of this view of education and fail to appreciate its nuances and complexities. In particular, they appear to lack a full understanding of what is involved in an approach to educational planning that concerns itself primarily with processes rather than with products or content, that regards questions of what education is and of what its essential components are as logically prior to questions about its directions or its subject-matter.

The remaining chapters of this book will attempt to elucidate some of the things that this approach implies as well as to produce further arguments in support of the view that it is the only approach to education that in the last analysis is tenable.

Suggested further reading

Dewey, J. (1938) *Experience and Education*. New York: Collier (first Collier Books edition 1963).

Dearden, R.F. (1968) *The Philosophy of Primary Education*. London: Routledge & Kegan Paul.

Kohlberg, L. and Mayer, R. (1972) Development as the aim of education. *Harvard Educational Review* 4, pp. 449–496.

Bruner, J. (1971) *The Relevance of Education*. Harmondsworth: Penguin (first Penguin Books edition 1974).

CHAPTER 3

CURRICULUM PLANNING IN THE PRIMARY SCHOOL 1 – SOME INCOMPATIBLE MODELS

It has been suggested several times in the previous two chapters that the view of education we have tried to describe and analyse and which we have claimed is fundamental to the philosophy of the Primary school leads to or necessitates the adoption of a particular model of curriculum planning. We now turn to an examination of the main features of that model and first, in this chapter, to a consideration of the inadequacies of the alternative models which are, increasingly, and in our view, mistakenly, being pressed upon teachers for their use in curriculum planning.

Before we do so, it may be worth devoting a little attention to the question of what we mean by a curriculum model. The term 'model' has at least four different meanings in common usage. It is perhaps most often used to denote small-scale replicas of any kind of concrete object, as when we speak of model railways, model ships or model soldiers. We also employ the term when we wish to distinguish different brands or versions of the same kind of product, especially in the realm of transport – cars, bicycles and so on. Thus, to ask someone what model of car s/he drives is not to suggest that racing scale-model cars is one of his/her hobbies. Thirdly, the term is used, in a prescriptive sense, to connote perfection or at least a high level of achivement in a particular sphere. It is in this sense that we hear of model farms, model dairies, model bakeries and so on. A builder who assures us that his/her new housing estate consists of model homes is not attempting to sell us dolls' houses (as a glance at the prices s/he is asking will quickly reveal). Lastly, a direct derivation of this is the use of the term to suggest that this degree of perfection or achievement should be regarded as offering a blueprint for others, a 'model' for them to copy, an example for them to 'model' themselves on. This kind of usage is perhaps most often figurative, since it is this sense of the term that is being used when we describe people as 'models' of patience or good humour or self-control or any other quality that is regarded as desirable and praiseworthy and thus to be emulated.

Clearly there are connections between all of these uses. Clearly too, elements of all of them are present when we use the term in the context of curriculum planning, or indeed in any area of the social sciences. However, it is the elements highlighted in the last two uses of the term that we have identified that are especially to the fore here and it is important to be aware of what each of them implies. For while one implication is that we are referring to blueprints for planning, plans for action or at least particular versions of such plans or blueprints, there is also the added connotation, never very far away, that the particular version we favour reflects a degree of near-perfection, that it represents a 'model' form of curriculum planning, and that it is for that reason that we favour it.

When we speak of curriculum models, then, we are not usually speaking of alternative and equally satisfactory approaches to curriculum planning. We are acknowledging that there are alternative approaches but we are also recognizing that there have to be grounds for selecting between them and, usually, committing ourselves to a particular approach to that task of selection. In short, every curriculum model is based on a particular view of education, a particular set of educational values, and to adopt or advocate any one model is to be committed to its view and its values and, conversely, opposed to those that underpin alternative models. The criteria of selection are derived from fundamental principles and not from methodological considerations of simple effectiveness.

Thus it is here. For we are arguing that commitment to the view of education we have described entails commitment to a particular model of curriculum planning and, further, that we can best demonstrate and delineate the strengths of that model by first exposing the weaknesses of the major alternatives.

The essence of the approach to education we are concerned to explicate here is its conviction that education must be viewed as a process, and thus must be defined and planned in terms of that process. It must also be evaluated in the same terms. It is, therefore, a view which is at odds with, is positively incompatible with and is thus not reducible to the other two approaches to education and curriculum planning which one finds commonly advocated, that which sees it and thus sets about the planning of it in terms of its content, and that which starts from a concern with its products, with statements of its 'aims and objectives'.

Both of these approaches can be discerned in discussions of education from the time of Plato onwards. They are also very much to the fore in the current educational debate, especially as it is conducted by politicians, and they are the favoured approaches in most of the documentation that has emerged in recent times from the Department of Education and Science. For, in so far as one can identify any clear view of curriculum in that documentation, it is its joint concern with content and with objectives that shines through. There is little to be seen there that can be interpreted as reflecting a view of education as process, except in a highly muddled way from time to time when it is felt that some concern with children ought to be envinced.

These two approaches are not always clearly distinguished from each other. In fact, as in the recent official documents, they are usually to be found being run together in both theory and practice. This is also true of Plato's view, and it may reflect as well as anything else the fundamental confusions which are to be seen in both of these views of education and approaches to curriculum planning. For our purposes here, however, they must be considered separately, since each is in conflict with our notion of education as process in different ways, so that the concern they give us is somewhat different too and each needs to be explored and explained in its own right.

Broadly, our case is that education can be planned and the curriculum framed from three different perspectives – that of the knowledge to be transmitted (content), that of the aims and objectives to be attained (product) or that of the children to be educated and the development of those children (process). These perspectives are designated by Alan Blyth (1984) as those of 'forms of understanding and endeavour', 'social imperatives' and 'process' respectively. It will be our concern in this chapter and the next, first to list what we see as the major inadequacies of the first two of these approaches and then, in Chapter 4, to explore in detail the implications of the third.

Furthermore, it will be our intention throughout both chapters to establish the mutual incompatibility of the process approach with either or both of the other two. It is true that many dichotomies within educational theory in the past have been less than helpful – traditionalism v. progressivism, instruction v. discovery, interventionism v. non-interventionism and so on. And there are those, such as the Inner London Education Authority's 'Thomas Report' (ILEA 1985) and others (e.g. Barnes 1982) who would currently advise us that it is acceptable to base our curricula on an amalgam of views or models, mixing together a concern with content, a concern with products and a concern with processes, or, perhaps worse, using one approach in one context and another in another. It will be our concern here to establish that such an approach is untenable, that it is in plain fact muddled and that the acceptance of such a position in theory must lead to a perpetuation of the kind of muddled practice one too often sees. Indeed, it is not going too far to argue that it is precisely this kind of muddled thinking, and the confusions of practice it has given rise to, that has been a major factor in the discrediting of 'progressivism' to which we have already referred. These three approaches, as we indicated just now, are based on quite different value positions, and it is necessary to decide which of these value positions one favours in order to be absolutely clear about what kind of approach to curriculum planning follows from that. This is a point we will return to later.

Curriculum as content

In arguing against the idea that curriculum planning must begin from considerations of content, we must not be interpreted as wishing to claim that curriculum content is not important or, worse, that it is not necessary. Clearly, there has to be a content to education. Our concern is to criticize those views which would put that content first and make it the prime criterion in curriculum planning.

And that is one of the salient features of current official policy in education. As we suggested just now, there is an assumption underlying most of the recent official publications on curriculum, especially the *Curriculum Matters* series (DES 1984; 1985 a,b,c,d; 1986a), that the main requirement of a curriculum document (apart perhaps from a statement of 'aims and objectives') is a delineation of the proposed content of the curriculum, the knowledge that is to be transmitted. A corollary of this is the assumption that the major ingredient in the preparation of teachers, the most important requirement for being a teacher, is knowledge of some form of relevant subject content (the only other significant requirement being the skills that are needed to transmit the content efficiently and effectively). This is the first principle upon which current 'reforms' in teacher education are being based. For an increasing number of teachers for all sectors of schooling, including Infant and Nursery schools, are being prepared by way of the 3+1 route, three years spent studying a subject or subjects 'relevant to the school curriculum', followed by one year of training for the task of teaching that subject or those subjects. And requirements have now been established that even those intending teachers who continue to offer themselves for a four-year (B.Ed.) course of preparation must spend at least two of those years studying a curriculum subject. The message is clear. Curriculum is content, and the prime concern of schooling is with *what* children ought to learn, what knowledge they must acquire during the period of their formal schooling. Furthermore, there are those around who *know* what this should be.

Such views abound and they take many forms and are based on many different kinds of justificatory arguments.

For some, of course, there are no such arguments. No justification is felt to be necessary. Sadly, one feels that this is the case with most of the current official pronouncements and much of the policy reflected there. It is another of those unquestioned assumptions with which educational theory, and too much of its practice, abounds. It is part of the folklore, the mythology. Traditionally, school curricula, especially at Secondary level, have been planned and framed solely in terms of subjects and their syllabuses. This is the only form of curriculum planning many people, especially those whose experience of teaching has been in Secondary schools, and often in the selective and elitist sectors at that, are familiar with, so that they do not begin to understand that there can be other kinds of approach to it. It is thus assumed that, at all levels of schooling, curriculum planning is the drawing up of subject lists and detailed syllabuses.

For others, it is not merely that they assume curriculum planning is about subjects; they recognize the need to justify that approach and are therefore prepared to offer such justification. There are, however, several forms of such justification, and it will be worthwhile considering each in turn.

Forms of justification

First, there is the overtly instrumental form of justification. Where current policy feels it appropriate to offer justification, it usually does so in these terms. There are certain kinds of knowledge which are – at least at the present time – useful, in that they are economically important, so that these ought to loom large in the school curriculum. This is the only explanation one can offer for the dramatic increase in the emphasis on the teaching of science and technology in schools, and, indeed, at all levels of education, which we have seen in the last ten years or so – and the corresponding demise of the Humanities subjects. In fact, it can be dated precisely from the speech made by James Callaghan, as Prime Minister, at Ruskin College, Oxford, in 1976, in which he roundly attacked teachers for encouraging, or at least permitting, too much study of the Humanities and thus too little of the science and technology vital to the economic health of society.

We will consider the problems created by this instrumental view of schooling a little later when we look at the notion of curriculum as product, since there is a clear overlap between the two. We must merely note here that one kind of justification for planning the curriculum in terms of its content is this kind of instrumental case – a concern with what schooling is felt to be *for*, defined in terms of the needs of society, rather than with what it is, defined in terms of the growth and development of the child.

The second major kind of argument for planning the curriculum in terms of its content is somewhat more sophisticated than this, and does attempt to allow for the fact that it is conceptually difficult to conceive of education in instrumental terms, in terms of goals and purposes extrinsic to it. This is the kind of view which begins from a conviction that there are certain kinds of knowledge which are superior to other kinds, and that education consists in providing children with access to knowledge of this superior kind.

Fundamentally, this is the view of Plato, whose curriculum is set out in clearly defined subject terms and whose choice of subjects for inclusion is obviously based on his view that the subjects chosen are superior to other kinds of knowledge which might have been chosen. One way in which he feels their superiority is displayed is that they are non-utilitarian – an early assertion that education cannot be planned on instrumental considerations. A second important way in which they are superior, however, is that they involve high levels of intellectual activity, their cognitive content, as it would now be called, is high, they demand great efforts of mind to master and to understand. We thus have human knowledge placed into a hierarchical structure, at the head of which are those branches or subjects which are non-utilitarian and highly abstract, and at the tail those which are practical and have a heavy affective or emotional dimension. Thus, for Plato, the supreme form of knowledge and of intellectual activity is philosophy, and, trailing a long way behind, come such subjects as art, craft and drama (to none of which would Plato even concede the term 'knowledge').

This kind of view is well embedded in the Western European educational tradition. It is almost certainly what underlies, if only implicitly, the current pressures towards content-based curriculum planning. It is a view which has recently been asserted in several forms in the work of that school of educational philosophers founded by Richard Peters in the 1960s and 1970s. Richard Peters' own view is in essence that of Plato. They may differ on the matter of the precise ordering of subjects within their respective hierarchies, but in essence they are both claiming that subjects are superior, first, if they can be shown to be non-utilitarian, justified for inclusion in the curriculum on the grounds that their value is intrinsic rather than extrinsic, what Richard Peters (1965, 1966) calls 'intrinsically worthwhile activities', and, second, if their cognitive content is high, if they can be seen to be intellectually demanding in the traditional sense.

Education is thus seen as the initiation of children into these forms of intellectual activity. Indeed, children have been depicted by Richard Peters as starting off 'in the position of the barbarian outside the gates' (1965, p.107). 'The problem is to get them inside the citadel of civilisation so that they will understand and love what they see when they get there' (ibid.). And the way to achieve this is to initiate them into those forms of knowledge which constitute human rationality, 'the activities and modes of thought and conduct which define a civilised form of life' (op. cit., pp.107–8).

Other members of the same school have come up with their own arguments to justify what is essentially an identical position. Thus John White (1973), for example, has argued that the curriculum should include, compulsorily for all pupils, certain subjects whose characteristic is that they cannot be understood without direct engagement in them. These are what he calls 'Category 1' activities which must be compulsory components of the curriculum because 'no understanding of X is logically possible without engaging in X' (op. cit., p.27). Inevitably, these activities are those whose cognitive content is regarded as being high. They are activities like mathematics, science and philosophy, not like art or physical education. Paul Hirst (1965, 1974) too has argued that the curriculum should consist of subjects which exemplify all the several different forms of rationality he feels able to identify. Education, he believes, is the development of the rational mind, its initiation into rationality, and, since, on his view, there are several forms of this, the curriculum must include subjects which will offer access to all these forms. Indeed, since most of the lists he offers contain seven such 'disciplines', what is being advocated is a kind of educational heptathlon.

All of this represents a point of view, and a well-established point of view. It is our concern to stress here, however, that it is only one point of view, that there are others and that it is at odds, in a very fundamental way, with the view of education and curriculum we are attempting to explicate in this book.

There are several reasons for claiming this, and several reasons why this view is not compatible with our view of education as process.

The incompatibility with the process view

In the first place, all of these arguments are mounted from the perspective of the knowledge to be transmitted through the curriculum and not that of the children to whom it is to be transmitted. They are all of them arguments built on analyses of the nature of knowledge and views both of what that nature is and of what constitutes superior kinds of knowledge. We have argued through-out that it is our prime and central concern to plan our curriculum provision by reference to the development of the child. And that implies that we must select the content of education by reference to what is likely to promote that development and not by reference to what constitutes knowledge or superior forms of knowledge.

It is quite clear, and there is much sociological evidence to confirm this, that curricula planned in this way, by reference only to the knowledge-content to be included in them, have been for many, even most, pupils the very opposite of educational. They have not succeeded in bringing them 'inside the citadel of civilization' and they have certainly not persuaded them 'to understand and love what they see when they get there'. They have not promoted development of any kind, and certainly not of the kind we have been attempting to define and the developmental psychologists to explore. They have proved to be alienating to large numbers of pupils, especially those from social and ethnic backgrounds which have their own notions of what constitutes civilization and where the point and purpose, the 'intrinsic value', of such subjects and activities have been far from self-evident. They have been regarded as irrelevant and meaningless. And their effect has often been positively anti-educational.

It is our view that, if education is to promote development, and especially if it is to have any hope of promoting the development of all pupils, and not merely those from 'privileged' backgrounds, then the curriculum must be planned by reference to the pupils themselves and their developmental needs, so that the choice of content becomes not the first consideration but secondary to consideration of the pupils themselves.

The second way in which this view of curriculum as content is at odds with our notion of curriculum as process is in the view of knowledge upon which it is built. Essentially, the only perspective from which one can mount a case for the notion that certain kinds of knowledge are intrinsically worthwhile or hold a superior position in the knowledge hierarchy, indeed the only pespective from which one can accept the idea of a justifiable subject hierarchy, is that of the kind of rationalist epistemology we discussed briefly in Chapters 1 and 2 (Kelly 1986). To argue that value somehow inheres in the knowledge itself rather than in 'the eye of the beholder' is to assume a status for human knowledge that only a rationalist epistemology can support.

We saw, however, that a major feature of the process or developmental view we are arguing for here is that it has rejected that view of knowledge and accepted a much more tentative view, a view of knowledge as itself subject to constant change, development, evolution. Such a view cannot support the idea that certain forms of knowledge have a natural superiority or a value which is intrinsic. Indeed, it regards no knowledge or body of knowledge as permanent enough to have claims of that kind made for it. Such ideas, then, are at odds with the very foundation of our process view.

The view that curriculum planning can or should begin from considerations of its knowledge-content, then, is based on beliefs and/or assumptions that it is of the very essence of the process view to challenge and reject.

The third point that needs to be made is in many ways the most interesting and the most revealing one. Closer analysis of the arguments we have just explored would suggest that their proponents are themselves fundamentally concerned not with the content or the knowledge that they seem to be obsessed with but rather with the forms of development they seem to assume that content, or those bodies of knowledge, will promote. Their concern may be narrowly with intellectual or cognitive development; nevertheless development does seem to be their main concern.

For Plato's main reason for advocating the kind of curriculum-content he proposes is that through exposure to that kind of knowledge the individual's intellect will develop to the point where it is functioning at maximum efficiency. And Richard Peters does not really believe that the simple possession of certain kinds of knowledge will be enough to get the barbarian pupils inside the citadel of civilization. He is convinced that exposure to those activities will affect the development of the individual to the point where s/he will become a different person, a more fully developed person. This comes out most clearly in the emphasis he wishes to place on the *manner* of education rather than its *matter*. The only point too in requiring pupils to engage in John White's 'Category '1 activities is that this will, in his view, promote the development of their rational capacities, a view that comes out perhaps more obviously in Paul Hirst's argument for access to all the several forms of rationality. For the concern there is not centrally with the forms themselves, but with what exposure to them will, it is assumed, do for the individual. We have even been informed recently by a member of Her Majesty's Inspectorate, from which source one might be entitled to expect greater clarity of thinking than this, that the current requirement for a massive emphasis on subject study in the preparation of teachers is designed to ensure a high academic standard within the teaching profession. Again, the assumption that things happen to people, that they develop, as a result of exposure to certain kinds of knowledge is plain.

The central concern, then, is with development, and thus with education as a process, or series of processes, of development. The limitations are, first, that it is only intellectual development that is the concern – indeed, from that kind of rationalist perspective it is not possible to generate a theory which can accommodate other forms of human development (Kelly 1986) – and, second, the related assumptions that exposure to certain kinds of knowledge only will bring about such development and that exposure to the same kinds of knowledge will achieve this for all pupils. A third difficulty is that, because the emphasis is on knowledge-content, insufficient attention is given to the anlaysis of the kinds of development we should be concerned to promote and the most effective ways of doing this.

It is these assumptions and their attendant difficulties that the process view is concerned to challenge and overcome. And it sets about this by suggesting that if the development of the pupil is the prime concern then it is the first thing we must explore, the first source of questions we must face. It must not take second place to the debate about knowledge nor must curriculum planning begin from statements about the knowledge-content that must be included.

The process approach offers us only one kind of justification for the content of our curriculum – the contribution it can be expected to make to the development of the pupil. And it must be recognized, and accepted, as a corollary of this that the same content will not necessarily work for all pupils. Indeed, given the great diversity of backgrounds from which pupils come – and, indeed, given the great diversity of human nature – it is highly unlikely to. What will be common is the kind of development we will be concerned to promote, or rather the principles underlying such development, and this we must explore in the next chapter.

Perhaps enough has now been said to illustrate why a content-based approach to curriculum planning is seen by us as unsatisfactory and as incompatible with the process-based approach we are advocating. It is time now to consider, perhaps in a little more detail, why the associated product-based model offers as many, if not more, difficulties.

Curriculum as product

There are two aspects of the instrumental approach to curriculum planning which, although they are clearly interrelated, we would do well to consider separately here. The first of these is that general form of instrumentalism, that approach to curriculum planning which starts by asking what it is for and looks towards some conceived or imagined end-product as the prime consideration. The second is that quite specific version of this, the 'aims and objectives' approach, that form of planning which was being urged on teachers in the USA in the early part of this century, which received its two classic statements in the work of Ralph Tyler in 1949 and of Benjamin Bloom and his associates in 1956, and which, despite the fact that education, like all other branches of human endeavour, has moved on considerably in the thiry years since then, seems only now to be reaching the consciousness of our political masters and those whose concern it is to press their views upon us.

Instrumental approaches

It is perfectly possible, and by no means illogical, to view schooling in instrumental terms, to see it as designed to prepare childen for work by providing them with skills of one kind or another, to train them up into certain forms of behaviour or even to condition or indoctrinate them into the acceptance of certain values and beliefs – moral, social, political or religious. Such forms of schooling are not uncommon, but they would normally be described as training, or, in those extreme cases, as conditioning or indoctrination. It is unusual to find them being called 'education', except when that term is being used very loosely and without real thought or when people wish to conceal from us the realities of what schooling is being used for. For, when we think about it clearly, we do tend to reserve the term 'education' for something that goes some way beyond these forms of training or conditioning. And one of the ways in which most people's concept of education does go beyond this is that it carries connotations of being somehow valuable in its own right, worth having for its own sake and not merely as a means to something else.

It is this that Richard Peters (1965, 1966) had in mind when, as we saw earlier, he claimed that the concept of education brings with it the notion of initiation into intrinsically worthwhile activities. If we avoid again entering into argument with him over the question of precisely what kinds of activity might satisfy that definition, we can recognize the value and the significance of that basic notion, that unless we are engaging pupils in something felt, by them and us, to be worth doing for its own sake, we are unlikely to be doing anything we could reasonably describe as educating them.

An educational activity, then, must be justified in its own right and on its own terms, and not by reference to some extrinsic purpose or goal. And it must be evaluated in this way too. The success of an educational experience or activity must be gauged by criteria intrinsic to it, by considerations of such things as the growth and development it has promoted and not by any extrinsic end-product. To take a concrete example, the educational success of a project in design and technology is to be judged not by the quality of the artefact(s) which may have been produced at the end of it but by the educational experiences of the pupil or pupils. To evaluate any activity by criteria other than this is to treat it not as a form of education, but as some form of training or even indoctrination. It is exactly this kind of thinking that has led so many teachers to see the public examination system of Secondary level as being, potentially at least, and usually in actuality, anti-educational.

It was this as much as any other feature of the traditional approach to education that encouraged Rousseau to revolt against it. A major objection he had to that traditional view of education which had derived from the work of Plato was that it was planned according to some blue-print of the end-product it was intended to produce, the kind of adults the education system should create. It was a kind of moulding process, designed to turn people into adults of a certain kind, with certain values, certain attributes and certain intellectual qualities and skills. To use Rousseau's own phrase, as we saw in Chapter 1, the child was regarded as a 'man-in-the-making' and educationists as 'always looking for the man in the child, without considering what he is before he becomes a man'. The essence of our process approach to education is that it is primarily concerned with what children are rather than with what they are to be turned into; it regards education not as a process of moulding but as one of guided growth and development, of a kind whose precise end cannot, and, indeed, should not, be predetermined. It is thus incompatible with any kind of instrumental approach to educational planning.

The 'aims and objectives' model

It is for this reason that it is especially at odds with that school of thought (or, in some cases, lack of thought) which would have us plan our curricula by first stating our aims and objectives. This, as we have suggested already, is a cry one hears quite often nowadays; and it is a theme which is especially evident in that official documentation on curriculum to which we have also made frequent reference. Not the least disturbing feature of this current fashion is that it reflects thinking which, as we indicated just now, was prevalent in the USA in the first part of this century. This is also thinking which has been almost totally discredited in much curriculum theory since that time; certainly it has been superseded by thinking about curriculum of a much more sophisticated kind. Yet there is no evidence that the elaborate and detailed debate which has subsequently occurred has penetrated the consciousness of those who purport to be leading developments in education and the school curriculum. For the evidence of the documentation is that their thinking remains at the stage of Bloom's *Taxonomy of Educational Objectives* which was published in 1956. In the thirty years since then, men have landed on the moon, colour television has arrived in almost everyone's front room, the microcomputer has become a familiar piece of equipment, jet travel has become commonplace, the steam engine has become an item of interest only to the antiquarian, and there has been comparable progress, at least in some quarters, in thinking about education and especially about the curriculum. One wonders how long it will take the leaders of our profession to emerge from the steam age and enter the second half of the twentieth century.

However, because most of those in influential positions continue to advocate, and in some cases to attempt to demand, statements of aims and objectives (we have ourselves been asked this very week by one of Her Majesty's Inspectors for a statement of the aims and objectives of our teacher education courses – a request we responded to with a polite negative), we must devote some time here to examining this phenomenon, and especially to demonstrating the ways in which it is incompatible with our view of education or curriculum as process.

The growth of the objectives movement   The move towards requiring teachers to produce statements of their aims and objectives can be seen to have started in the USA in the early part of this century when attempts were made to encourage a 'job analysis' approach to teaching in an attempt to achieve the kind of efficiency in schools that production-line methods were bringing to industry (Davies 1976). *Plus ça change . . .*

Further impetus came from the spread of interest in the testing of pupil performance. For the link between the prespecification of objectives and the testing of performance has long been a close one and that it continues to be so is apparent from the effects on curriculum planning of current demands for a closer monitoring of standards in schools. This link was made quite explicit in the work of the first major exponent of the objectives approach, Ralph Tyler. For Tyler's original aim was to design scientific tests of educational attainment and his solution to this problem was to suggest that this could be done most readily and easily if a clear statement had been made of the kind of attainment that was being aimed at. If course objectives had been formulated and those objectives defined in terms of intended student behaviour, that behaviour could then be evaluated in the light of those intentions (Tyler 1932; Davies 1976).

This provided the foundation upon which Tyler was later to base what has come to be regarded as the classic statement of the objectives approach to curriculum design. In a book which he tells us is intended as 'one way of viewing an instructional programme as a functional instrument of education' (1949, p.1) and in which he expresses alarm at the level of generality he claims to have detected in teachers' responses to questions about their work, he sets out the four questions which he says must be faced and answered by curriculum planners. Those four questions are concerned with the purpose, the content, the organization and the evaluation of the curriculum. They have thus been interpreted as offering a linear model of curriculum planning which takes us from specifying objectives to selecting the content or the educational experiences most likely to help us to attain those objectives to planning the methods best suited to the effective organization of those experiences and finally to an evaluation of whether our purposes have been achieved.

The next milestone was reached in 1956 with the publication by Benjamin Bloom and his associates of their *Taxonomy of Educational Objectives Handbook I: Cognitive Domain*. For this introduced a new dimension into this form of curriculum planning with its division of objectives into three categories or 'domains' – the cognitive, the affective and the psycho-motor – and at the same time it offered the most detailed ambitious classification of objectives in the cognitive domain that had yet been attempted. This was matched by the publication in 1964, under the editorship of D.R. Kratwohl, of a second handbook that offered a similar classification within the affective domain.

It was some time before the work of either Tyler or Bloom began to have any real impact but by the mid-1960s their influence was beginning to be felt not only in the United States but in the United Kingdom too, and, in an article published in 1969, Paul Hirst made the same kind of claim that we should begin our curriculum planning with a statement of our objectives, arguing that not to do so is to transgress a basic principle of rationality, since an essential feature of any rational activity is that it be goal-directed.

At the level of educational practice, initially little interest was shown in this style of planning. Some response to the early promptings can be seen in the planning of vocational courses but that was as far as things went. One reason for this may well have been the wordy and jargon-ridden nature of most of what was written about it. But at least two other reasons have been posited (Hirst 1969). One of these is the fact that at Secondary level the obsession with subject-content, reinforced by the demands of largely monolithic examination syllabuses, rendered it unnecessary for teachers ever to think about what their purposes or objectives might be. The second of these is central to the case we are propounding in this book, since it is the suggestion that at Primary level the 'romantic' or 'progressive' movement, in particular because of its emphasis on 'child-centredness', also had the effect of deflecting attention from a clear formulation of objectives. Paul Hirst explains this as an obsession with methods or procedures but it is our claim here that it is the result of a concern with education as a process and that this has very different implications. At all events, although teacher-trainers demanded from their students and inspectors from their probationer teachers and even some headteachers from all of their staff, lesson notes that began with a clear statement of the aims and objectives of their lessons, few responded to such requests with any degree of clarity or effectiveness and the practice was not taken seriously by any who were engaged in the realities of teaching.

The statement of clear course objectives, however, was a major feature of most of the curriculum projects that emerged during that period of widespread innovation that followed the establishment of the Schools Council in the United Kingdom in 1964, and this was a key factor in the growth of interest in this approach to curriculum planning that came in the 1960s. The allocation of public money to curriculum development on this scale brought with it the requirement that a proper account be given of how that money was being spent. For this reason, as well as because of considerations of a purely educational kind, evaluation was a central concern of most new projects from the outset and a proper evaluation was interpreted as requiring a clear statement of goals, aims, purposes, objectives.

The main characteristics of the objectives model of curriculum planning
The first thing to be clear about is that the term 'objectives' has come to be used quite specifically to denote short-term educational goals and a distinction is usually drawn between goals of this kind and those that are described as 'broad aims' (Taba 1962). This reflects the distinction that was made from the beginning by Bobbitt's division (1918, 1924) of objectives into 'ultimate' and 'progress' objectives and in the definition by Charters (1924) of curriculum planning as the identification of those 'working units' that will lead us step by step to the achievement of our 'ideals'.

Others have offered further refinements to this general scheme. Thus Kratwohl speaks of three kinds of educational goal – goals for the planning of the whole curriculum, behavioural objectives derived from these for the planning of courses and objectives for the planning of specific lessons (1965). And Wheeler (1967) calls these 'ultimate', 'mediate' and 'proximate' goals.

It must further be noted that the relationship between these different kinds of goal is hierarchical, the goals at each level being in some way derived from those at the level above, so that they are seen as welded into a structure or taxonomy of goals and, as a result, as was suggested by Charters, can even be set out in the form of a chart or graph.

The more sophisticated taxonomies, like that of Bloom (1956) for instance, are further refined in that there is a hierarchical structure within each category as well as between them, or, to express it differently, the relationship between objectives is seen as one of progressive refinement. For, in addition to creating that horizontal categorization of objectives delineated by the three domains, Bloom's taxonomy also offers us a hierarchical model of the relationships between the objectives within these domains. Thus, within the cognitive domain, it is claimed that there exists or should exist a graded sequence of objectives from 'knowledge of specifics' to 'classification' to 'comprehension' to 'application' to 'analysis' to 'synthesis' and so to 'the making of evaluative judgments'; and within the affective domain from 'receiving' to 'responding', 'valuing', 'organisation and characterisation by value' and 'value complex'. In a similar way, the Schools Council's Aims of Primary Education project divides its aims into those related to intellectual, physical, spiritual/religious, emotional/personal and social/moral development and then divides these different kinds of aim on a second axis into those 'to do with knowledge, skills and qualities' (Ashton, Kneen and Davies 1975, p.13)

Thus the interrelationships of objectives are seen as essentially hierarchical and all learning is viewed as a linear activity.

There are many examples of this kind of approach to be found among the schemes for the teaching of reading that teachers have been offered in recent times and, in particular, among the more sophisticated 'reading workshops' or 'reading laboratories' designed for use with pupils in Junior schools and Middle schools, or in the lower classes of Secondary schools. The Kent Mathematics Project, which we will examine in some detail in Chapter 6, is also an example of the use of this model in the teaching of mathematics.

A further important characteristic of this view of curriculum planning is that the objectives it requires us to prespecify are clearly and unequivocally behavioural. Tyler, for example, tells us that 'the most useful form for stating objectives is to express them in terms which identify both the kind of behaviour to be developed in the students and the context or area of life in which this 'behaviour is to operate' (1949, pp.46–47). Bloom calls them 'intended learning outcomes' and says that they are to be defined in terms of the behaviour the pupil is intended to display through his thoughts, actions or feelings. Mager (1962, p.13) says, 'A statement of an objective is useful to the extent that it specifies what the learner must be able to *do* or *perform* when he is demonstrating his mastery of the objective.' And Popham (1969, p.35) tells us that 'a satisfactory instructional objective must describe an observable *behaviour* of the learner or a *product* which is a consequence of learner behaviour', giving as examples of the former 'skill in making impromptu speeches or performing gymnastic feats' and of the latter 'an omelet from the home economics class'. The Schools Council's Aims of Primary Education project offers the same kind of definition, declaring that 'if the teacher's aims are to help guide his practice, then they should be expressed in behavioural terms. That is to say that they should state what the child will actually be able to do when the aim is achieved' (Ashton, Kneen and Davies 1975, p.15).

This concern with observable changes of behaviour is most apparent in some of the forms of record-keeping that have recently been urged upon Primary teachers and which we also examine in Chapter 6. At this point it is sufficient to note that the focus of this approach to educational planning is on the modification of pupil behaviour and the success of such a curriculum is to be evaluated by an appropriate assessment of the behaviour changes that the curriculum appears to have brought about in comparison with those that it was its stated intention to bring about.

A final feature of the behavioural approach to curriculum planning that we must note is that, like all scientific approaches to the study and planning of human activity, it endeavours to be value-neutral. This is not entirely true of the work of the early exponents of this view. Werrett Charters, for example, speaks, somewhat confusingly, of 'ideals' and 'activities' and it seems that, in doing so, he was attempting to make some allowance for the value dimension of educational activities. Subsequent writers within the behavioural tradition, however, have avoided such confusion by refusing to acknowledge this dimension and denying that questions of value are their concern. Bloom's taxonomy, for example, has been criticized on these grounds, since it is not based on any clearly worked out concept of education (Gribble 1970), but this is not a criticism that he or any of the others would accept as valid, since they are concerned only to present teachers and curriculum planners with a scheme or a blueprint for them to use as they think fit; it is not their concern to tell them how to use it. They regard education as a matter of changing behaviour but they do not accept responsibility for questions about what kinds of behaviour education should be concerned to promote or what kinds of behavioural change it should be attempting to bring out. They maintain their scientific stance, therefore, and leave it to the persons using their scheme to make the decision about how it should be used. Thus this approach deliberately sidesteps the most difficult and intractable problem that faces curriculum planners – that of deciding what kinds of activity shall be deemed to be educational.

Arguments for the use of objectives   These, then, are the major features of this approach to curriculum planning. We must now consider briefly the main reasons why some people have been and still are concerned to urge it upon curriculum planners. There would seem to be four of these which we might call the logical, the scientific, the politico-economic and the educational arguments for the use of objectives.

The logical argument we have already referred to in considering the case put by Paul Hirst. Briefly, it claims that part of what it means for an activity to be rational is that it should be directed towards some clear goal or purpose. If education is to be regarded as a rational activity, therefore, it must state its goals or purposes. If it does not, then, as both Tyler and Hirst have argued, it becomes literally aimless. Another way of putting this is to accept the analysis made by Israel Scheffler (1960), Richard Peters (1967) and others of teaching as an intentional activity and to claim that we should, therefore, acknowledge and state the intentions of our teaching. How can one teach, it is asked, if one doesn't know what one is doing it for. The power of this argument is difficult to deny, although it is not regarded even by its proponents as leading necessarily to the use of objectives of a strictly behavioural kind. On the other hand, as we have just suggested, it leads to some comparable difficulties when these intentions are seen as end-states.

The scientific argument we have also touched upon briefly. This represents an attempt to bring into the practice of education some of the precision, accuracy and technological efficiency that is admired as the key to advances elsewhere and thus to render it more 'respectable'. This was clearly the major motivation of the early exponents of this view and the application of scientific method to the study of human peformance and achievement in industry by men such as Frederick Taylor obviously aroused the interest and enthusiasm of certain educationists of his day (Davies 1976). This argument also gained force from the predominance of largely behaviourist forms of psychology within educational theory in the 1920s and 1930s. For the main impact of behaviourist psychology on education theory, as we saw in Chapter 1, if its effects are not modified and tempered by the application or acceptance of other disciplines, is to reduce it to scientific analysis of an essentially means–end kind and to advocate this sort of approach to educational planning.

The politico-economic case is made at a rather more mundane level but it is one that is becoming increasingly influential, so that both its existence and its effects must be clearly recognized. Fundamentally, what it claims is that most educational provision is made at the expense of the tax-payer and that most curriculum development is financed in the same way, so that the tax-payer is entitled to a clear statement of what his/her money is being spent on and thus of what it is intended should be achieved by it. More significantly, perhaps, it is argued that there must be a careful evaluation of the effectiveness of measures that are taken in schools or at other levels of curriculum planning in order to ensure that public money is not being wasted and that the country is not being deprived of the talents and skills its economic welfare requires of its citizens. Such evaluation, it is felt, can only be made properly if it is based on a clear statement of intentions, and such intentions have been seen in terms of end-states. Thus the effect of current attempts to monitor standards, particularly in Primary schools, in the United Kingdom and to raise the level of teacher-accountability is to push teachers towards the prespecification of their objectives, just as the need for evaluation to demonstrate that the tax-payer was receiving value for money pushed most of the early Schools Council projects towards the same curriculum model.

Lastly, some reasons that might be described as educational have been advanced in support of the prespecification of curriculum objectives. Again, however, they make the assumption that evaluation requires such prespecification. Thus it has been argued by Hilda Taba (1962) that objectives must be prespecified because this is crucial for evaluation and that evaluation in turn is crucial for effective teaching and for curriculum development itself. 'It is well known', she tells us (op. cit., p.199), 'that those things that are most clearly evaluated are also most effectively taught.'

She also claims that evaluation is essential for the continued development of the curriculum since we can only change it effectively if we obtain appropriate data concerning its effects. 'Evaluation thus serves not only to check the hypothesis on which curriculum is based but also to uncover the broader effects of a program which may serve its central purpose well, but may, at the same time, produce undesirable by-products' (op. cit., p.315).

This emphasis on evaluation and the assumption that it can only take place if objectives are clearly prestated is typical, of course, of an approach to education whose base is essentially psychological. It is important to note, however, that more recent studies of curriculum evaluation (Macdonald 1973; Hamilton 1976) have demonstrated that it is possible to evaluate a curriculum whose objectives have not been clearly stated in advance. Indeed, it might be argued that those very educational advances that Taba is concerned with are better promoted by the use of more sophisticated forms both of evaluation and of planning.

The case for the prespecification of curriculum objectives, then, is a powerful one. Many of the objections to it, however, are equally cogent. It is to a consideration of these that we now turn.

Some problems presented by the objectives model   The most fundamental criticism that has been levelled at this approach to curriculum planning is that its attempt to reduce education to a scientific activity, analogous to the processes of industry, commits it to a view of 'man' and of human nature that many people find unacceptable and even unpalatable. For to adopt this kind of industrial model for education is to assume that it is legitimate to mould human beings, to modify their behaviour, according to certain clear-cut intentions without making any allowance for their own individual wishes, desires or interests. Like the materials upon which the industrial worker operates, children's minds are to be fashioned by teachers according to some preconceived blueprint.

This kind of view also requires us to accept that human behaviour can be explored, analysed and explained in the same way as the behaviour of inanimate objects, that it can be studied scientifically by the same methods as are used by the physical scientists or even the biologist and that it can be explained in terms of causes rather than purposes, by reference to external forces acting on the individual rather than internal drives and choices of a personal kind.

Fundamental to the view, therefore, is a psychological theory of a behaviourist kind and it is with behaviourist psychology that the movement has been associated from the start. In fact, most of its theoretical proponents have been psychologists rather than educationists or teachers. This passive model of 'man' is endemic to the theory and it is thus not acceptable to those who take the view that 'man' is to be regarded as a free and active agent, responsible for his/her own destiny and who, as a direct consequence of this, believe it to be morally wrong to deny him/her that responsibility and freedom by attempting to mould his/her behaviour to suit the ends of someone else. Such a process, they argue, is indoctrination rather than education and thus to be deplored.

It is for this reason that it has also been attacked as being based not only on an inadequate and unacceptable model of 'man' but also on an equally unsatisfactory concept of education, or perhaps on no concept of education at all. For as we have seen, those who have attempted to disentangle the concept of education from other related concepts such as training, instruction or indoctrination have done so by drawing attention to certain features of education that are not necessary parts of these other processes and, indeed, are sometimes explicitly excluded from them (Peters 1965, 1966). Pre-eminent among these features is that of individual autonomy without a concern for which, it is argued, no process of teaching can be called education. Such a view of education clearly entails the kind of active model of 'man' we have just been discussing and precludes an approach to educational planning that begins from a clear idea of the kinds of behaviour modification that teachers are to try to bring about in their pupils.

A second major kind of criticism has been directed at the views of knowledge and of learning which underpin this approach to educational planning (Pring 1971). There are several aspects of this.

In the first place, the hierarchical form of the relationships between objectives that is characteristic of taxonomies such as that of Bloom (1956) does not reflect the realities of the learning process. The linear model that it assumes, which attempts to break down all learning into a step-by-step procedure, is not suitable for most of the learning that goes on in schools. We do not acquire knowledge and then, at some later stage, attain understanding;

the two must go hand in hand. Any view of knowledge that does not recognize this must be regarded as too simplistic to serve as a basis for any but the most unsophisticated of teaching activities.

Secondly, the division of objectives into domains that is a major feature of Bloom's taxonomy or into the categories or spheres offered by the Aims of Primary Education project (Ashton, Kneen and Davies 1975) is an attempt to create distinctions that are unrealistic in practice and untenable in theory. For it is not possible to envisage an activity that concerns itself only with certain cognitive or intellectual goals without simultaneously involving affective or emotional considerations and probably the development of psycho-motor skills too. Indeed, we have been arguing that it is of the essence of an educational activity that it should be concerned not only to develop cognitive abilities but at the same time to promote a recognition of the intrinsic value of the activity and a feeling for those standards of truth and beauty which are an essential component of what it means to have knowledge and to be educated (Pring 1971). For how could one attempt to ensure that 'the child should be able to read with understanding material appropriate to his age group and interests' (Ashton, Kneen and Davies 1975, p.17) without, at the same time, endeavouring to see to it that 'the child should be developing a personal appreciation of beauty in some of its forms, both natural and artistic' (op. cit., p.19) and that 'the child should find enjoyment in a variety of aspects of school work and gain satisfaction from his achievements' (op. cit., p.21), not to mention that 'the child should be happy, cheerful and well balanced' (ibid.)? Conversely, how can one hope ever to achieve these affective goals if one has largely to ignore them when setting out to attain the former 'aims related to intellectual development' (op. cit., p.17).

A further serious criticism is that made by Charity James (1968) when she argues that this approach restricts the freedom of both teacher and pupil. For both will be inclined to see the objectives as fixed or given, just as Secondary teachers tend to see examination syllabuses as immutable, so that not only will they concentrate on what must be rather simple instructional goals, they will also lose the opportunity to play an active role in the educational process, a process which, it is claimed, is only fully educational if both teachers and pupils are active within it. The curriculum on this view has to be seen as the dynamic interaction of teacher and pupil and this cannot be promoted by a scientific, 'industrial' model requiring careful preplanning of outcomes. Every act of education takes place in its own individual context (Sockett 1976) and thus cannot be predetermined. Education is an art as well as a science and far too complex and sophisticated an activity to be elucidated in terms of this kind of simple model.

This view of education as an on-going, open-ended process, subject to constant reassessment and modification as a result of pupil–teacher interaction is supported by the practical experience of many teachers. We noted earlier that teachers and student-teachers, even in the face of concerted pressures upon them to prespecify the objectives of their lessons, have in practice rejected this approach and we suggested that this might be seen as evidence of its impracticability. We can perhaps see now that it is precisely those teachers who are concerned to offer something that goes beyond mere training or instruction who have found this model impossible to use. The realities of the teacher's task are too complex to be met by an approach like that of the industrial planner.

This has been reinforced by the experience of many of those curriculum projects that have attempted to use this kind of model, such as the Schools Council's project, History, Geography, and Social Science 8–13 (Blyth 1974) and the Nuffield 'A' level Biology project (Kelly 1973). For even when sets of objectives are presented to them in clear terms, teachers do find it impossible not to modify them continually in the light of the experiences that they and their pupils have from the moment the work begins. It is thus not bloody-mindedness on their part that causes them to cannibalize what they are offered; it is a realization that, if they do not make this kind of constant adjustment, then the goals of their teaching will remain at a simple level and that which is truly educational will be at risk. It is here that the practitioners may fairly claim to have been ahead of the theoreticians. It is here too that the most serious threats are posed by the growing pressures on teachers from outside the school.

The criticisms of the objectives model, then, are as strong as, if not stronger than, the case for its use. That strength derives largely from the claims that for proper educational planning a concept of education is necessary and that the only satisfactory concept we can attain is one that refuses to see 'man' as a passive creature and to regard the process of education and the acquisition of knowledge as purely instrumental processes. On the other hand, it is desirable that the process of education should be a rational process, even if it is not to be scientific in a narrow sense, that it should not appear to be aimless and that teachers and others should have a reasonably clear idea of what they are about.

It is because this has been seen as a dilemma that some people have wished to argue for what we might call compromise solutions to the difficulty. Our solution, as we have made clear throughout is to reject this kind of approach, this curriculum planning model, along with the content-based approach we examined earlier, in favour of a process-based approach which we believe can be shown to satisfy all these demands. That we will discuss in greater detail in Chapter 4.

We must first, however, consider some of these attempts at compromise, not least because it has been our contention throughout that the process approach is not compatible with either of the other two approaches we have considered, so that it has to be our view that no compromise solution is possible.

Attempts at compromise

One attempt at such compromise has taken the form of suggesting that we should examine each area of the curriculum separately on the assumption that different subject areas or curriculum activities will require different approaches to their planning.

This argument has taken two main forms. The first of these has distinguished the teaching of science and mathematics from teaching in other areas of the curriculum and has proposed that, while the prespecification of objectives would appear to be inappropriate in the latter context, the teaching of 'factual' material in 'linear' subjects like mathematics, where a clear progression of step-by-step learning may be discerned, does lend itself to clear initial statements of intended outcomes. Certainly, it is the case that most of the examples used by those who have wished to argue the unsuitability of the objectives model have been derived from Humanities subjects. The most cogent and often quoted example is that used by Laurence Stenhouse (1970) in the attack he mounts on the objectives model, the example of the teaching of *Hamlet*. To introduce any work of literature to pupils of any age with clear intended learning outcomes in mind is at best to reduce that work to a purely instrumental role, a means to something else rather than an end in itself, and, at worst, to use it as a device for imposing one's own moral and aesthetic values on one's pupils. The teaching of literature must involve an attempt to elicit a personal response from each individual pupil and the form that this will take cannot be stated in advance.

This argument would appear to be irrefutable and it is not difficult to appreciate its force in relation to all those subjects that comprise the Humanities. However, is it possible to approach the teaching of mathematics and the sciences differently? Some have certainly felt that it is and in practice a good deal of the teaching of these subjects can be seen to reflect an acceptance of the validity of this model. This is particularly true of some of the schemes for the teaching of mathematics in the Primary school, such as Fletcher Mathematics and the Kent Mathematics Project, to which we referred earlier and which we shall consider in greater detail in Chapter 6. We must also note the degree of preoccupation with curriculum objectives shown by the team associated with the project Science 5–13.

It has been argued, however, that this distinction between the Humanities and the sciences is difficult to maintain. In particular, it has been suggested that nothing could be more unlike true scientific method or enquiry than to begin an experiment with a clear statement of what one intends to prove by it (Sockett 1976), that the old-style 'required-to-prove' approach to the teaching of science indicates a misunderstanding of the nature of scientific exploration and is unlikely to promote an appreciation of what science truly is. For this reason, although, as we have said, the prespecification of objectives played a major part in the evolution of the Science 5–13 project, those objectives on examination prove to be rather more loosely framed than at first sight they appear to be and in practice they have been used to support an approach to the teaching of science in the Primary school that is enquiry-based. This is even more apparent in the work of the follow-up project, Learning through Science.

It becomes increasingly clear, then, that in all areas of the curriculum, if our concern is with education and we wish to distinguish this from instruction, training and other teaching activities, one of the things we must do is to eschew the prespecification of objectives.

It is this that has led some to propose a different kind of division of curriculum activities, a separation of those whose justification is clearly eductional from those which are equally clearly instrumental, forms of training for which statements of intent are not only acceptable but even necessary. Some support for this view comes from the fact we have already noted that the most widespread practical use of systems of objectives has occurred in the area of vocational preparation and training. Certainly, in such contexts the content, of what is taught is clearly chosen on instrumental grounds, so that most or all of the objections that have been raised would seem not to be applicable. In teaching someone to drive a car, for example, it would be foolish not to have a clear idea of one's goals, expressed in quite explicit behavioural terms – 'she shall be able to bring the car to an immediate halt when confronted by an obstruction, human or material' and so on.

However, while this is undoubtedly a proper and acceptable approach to the teaching of basic skills, it is not as easy to identify and single out these skills in the context of education as many theorists appear to believe, and serious dangers lurk in those attempts to make this kind of distinction within the school curriculum. Not much of what goes on in schools has this kind of single-minded vocational goal. The impossibility of making this kind of division between the development of skills and other elements of learning in an educational context is a major feature of the argument we are deploying in this book.

For it is central to the case that we are trying to present that the teaching of basic skills, even those of a psycho-motor kind, cannot be separated out from other kinds of goal without the loss of that essential ingredient of education that we are concerned to draw attention to. It is possible to teach basic skills in an intructional manner – the basic skills of reading, for example, of using a saw or a wood-chisel, of drawing straight lines or circles and many others – and it is in this area that the use of the behavioural model in Primary schools has appeared to be successful. The wide adoption and evident commercial success of those 'reading workshops' and 'reading laboratories' we mentioned earlier provide ample evidence of this. However, if we do not at the same time have clearly in mind the educational dimensions of the activities we are engaged in, then, while our efforts might well result in highly skilled performance at the behavioural level, they are likely to result in our achieving little beyond that and may even be counter-productive to any further attainment and, indeed, to education itself. For, as the Bullock Report (DES 1975) pointed out, it is possible to help pupils to a high level of reading performance and at the same time to kill or to inhibit any love or appreciation they may have developed for the written word. Indeed, as the Report also pointed out, even that high level of skilled performance itself will be short-lived. There are more 'non-readers' about than those who merely cannot decipher the symbols of the written word. This is a major danger of attempts to measure standards of attainment in schools in terms simply of performance or behaviour. It is thus a danger not only of the objectives model of curriculum planning but also of those popular, public and political demands for improved standards in the 'basic skills' which have this kind of simplistic model of education at their tap-root. This issue we will discuss in greater detail in Chapter 5.

A second kind of compromise solution has emerged from the practical experience of a number of curriculum projects that we have aleady briefly referred to. A number of project teams have discovered that no matter how carefully their objectives have been framed they quickly come to be modified by teachers in the light of the experience and feedback they begin to receive as soon as they begin to implement the project. They have thus come to realize that the objectives they framed would have to be regarded as tentative and open to constant modification and adjustment. Those, for example, who were associated with the Schools Council's project, History, Geography and Social Science 8–13, came to recognize that they must regard their objectives only as 'provisional' (Blyth 1974) and those concerned with the Nuffield 'A' level Biology project came to describe their objectives as 'mutable' (Kelly 1973). This view not only reflects more nearly the practical realities of the classroom and of teacher behaviour and experience, it is also closer to what we really mean by scientific exploration which, as we pointed out earlier, is characterized not by possessing a clear idea of where it is going but rather by being hypothetical, open-ended and subject to constant modification. This development is reflected in the growing practice of some local authorities of offering curriculum 'guidelines' to their Primary teachers rather than statements of objectives, although it is sometimes the case that these guidelines are so tightly framed that their point is lost and their impact on the curriculum continues to be restrictive, as we shall see when we examine some examples of them in Chapter 6.

Such an approach is also supportive of the development of the curriculum, since it allows for the kind of continuous change and adjustment that the notion of development entails. It thus recognizes that in education 'objectives are developmental, representing roads to travel rather than terminal points' (Taba 1962, p.203). It also acknowledges the force of one of the criticisms levelled by Paul Hirst at the behavioural objectives model of educational planning, namely that it assumes that curricula can be planned in a Utopian, *carte blanche* manner rather than recognizing that the curriculum development must take place in a specific context and must be seen as essentially a piecemeal activity (Hirst 1975).

A recognition of the developmental nature of educational goals leads also to a willingness to accept unintended learning outcomes (Hogben 1972) and to state our goals not in highly behavioural terms but as broad long-term aims. It is thus closely linked to a third kind of attempt that has been made to resolve the problem of curriculum objectives, the search for a form of objective that might be free of the difficulties of the behavioural model.

For, as we noted earlier, some commentators have wanted to claim not that educational goals cannot be prespecified but that they are too complex to be expressed in the simple form of behavioural objectives. Thus Paul Hirst has argued (1975) that the behavioural model is inadequate because it loses sight of the fact that educational objectives must be concerned with much more complex forms of personal and mental development than that model allows. The behavioural model leads to a view of education as a form of engineering and we must find a model that will allow us to approach education with the kind of intentionality that rationality demands but without losing those essential ingredients of education that we have seen are put at risk when we begin with limited objectives of a behavioural kind. Neither the 'engineering' model nor the 'horticultural' or 'growth' model is satisfactory. A new model must be found for educational planning and this will be based on a different and new conception of what an educational objective is.

Eliot Eisner's suggestion that we distinguish between 'instrumental' and 'expressive' objectives can be seen as an attempt to meet this challenge. It is also, however, an attempt to divide the curriculum into instructional and non-instructional areas in the way we have just discussed. The distinction he is attempting to make also suggests a resurrection of that made by Charters between 'ideal' and 'activity' objectives that we referred to earlier. For Eisner, an 'instructional' objective is a behavioural objective of the kind we have been discussing. An 'expressive' objective, however, 'describes an educational encounter. It identifies a situation in which children are to work, a problem with which they are to cope, a task in which they are to engage; but it does not specify what from that encounter, situation, problem or task they are to learn. . . . An expressive objective is evocative rather than prescriptive' (Eisner 1969, pp.15–16). Among the examples he gives of such objectives are 'to interpret the meaning of *Paradise Lost*', 'to examine and appraise the significance of *The Old Man and the Sea*' and 'to visit the zoo and discuss what was of interest there' (op. cit., p.16).

It is this kind of thinking that lies behind those statements of objectives offered by several Schools Council projects which we noted earlier were not strictly behavioural in form but appeared to be seeking a more satisfactory educational basis. It is also another way of attempting to express as objectives those complex forms of development of which Paul Hirst speaks. This in turn reflects the thinking of many teachers who, while acknowledging the difficulties created by attempts to specify the goals of their teaching in narrow behavioural terms, feel it quite appropriate to speak of the 'broad aims' of education, to view from this kind of perspective such things as the development of autonomy, rationality, understanding and so on, and thus to regard these as the objectives of their teaching.

This kind of thinking has also led to the emergence of what, from our perspective, we must regard as the bastardized term 'process objective' (Barnes 1982) and the idea that processes can be stated as objectives (Skilbeck 1984). It is the coining of this term and the appearance of this kind of notion which for us more than anything else symbolizes and encapsulates the problem we are attempting to address, the muddled thinking we are anxious to avoid and to help others to avoid, not least because it reveals a complete failure to understand what the term 'process' means for those who are advocating a process curriculum.

It is quite understandable that teachers should want to be given, or to establish some idea of what should be the end-products of several years of continuous effort on their part. However, what is wrong with this approach is that it assumes that these qualities can be regarded as end-states and thus as extrinsic to the processes and activities of education, when in fact, as we have suggested several times, the two cannot be separated in this way, since they are integrally linked and interwoven. Such qualities of mind are not the objectives, goals, purposes, intentions of educational activity but rather the principles which must inform all such activity and the processes of teaching from the outset. A concern with the principle of autonomy, for example, must be there from the beginning – even in the work that is done with the three-year-old – if autonomy is to be developed. To suggest that we might engage pupils in certain activities now in order that they may achieve autonomy later is to misunderstand totally the educational process or at least to offer a gross caricature of it. For, if we take this view, what we do now will often be counter-productive to our intentions, since the temptation will always be present to permit the end to justify, rather than to permeate, the means. It is this that is at fault with all forms of educational planning that are instrumental and thus with all forms of educational objectives.

It is clear that both Eisner and Hirst are endeavouring to avoid defining an educational objective in instrumental terms because they are aware of the fundamental contradiction that that entails. However, if that contradiction is fundamental, then it cannot be resolved by seeking for a different kind of goal for educational activities; it can only be resolved by replacing the notion of an educational goal with something entirely different. This, in effect, is what Eisner's notion of an expressive objective actually does. For, as the examples given clearly show, it does not provide us with a goal so much as offer us a statement of procedures or principles. It is, however, misleading to use the term 'objective' with its connotations of extrinsic purposes to denote a notion whose central concern seems to be with processes (Kelly 1977).

Similarly, it is not helpful to suggest that we should plan in terms of objectives but treat these as 'provisional' (Blyth 1974) or 'mutable' (Kelly 1973). For such a proposal points us, or should point us, immediately to the question of the criteria by which we are to make subsequent adaptations and changes (as well as those by which we are to select our objectives in the first instance). It thus should alert us to the fact that there is a stage of planning which is logically prior to the stating of such objectives – that of delineating the criteria of choice, the underlying planning principles.

This leads us naturally to a consideration of the final solution that has been proposed for the problem of educational planning. For it has been suggested that, for all the reasons we have attempted to set out in this chapter, it is not appropriate to attempt to plan activities that are intended to be educational by the prespecification of objectives of any kind (Stenhouse 1970, 1975). It is proposed rather that we begin by setting out the procedural principles that are to underpin our teaching and form the basis of all the decisions we make or by defining the 'value positions embodied in the curriculum specification or specifications' (Stenhouse 1970, p.82). In short, the suggestion is that we reject the objectives model for the planning of an educational curriculum and adopt a process model instead.

It is our contention that a recognition of the validity of this claim has long been implicit in the developing tradition of the Primary school and that the essence of that approach to education that we have claimed can be traced to the so-called 'progressive' movement which began with Rousseau, is that it is founded on a curriculum model of this kind. In the context of this book, therefore, and of our general case, this curriculum model deserves a full discussion. This we hope to give it in the next chapter.

Summary and conclusions

We have in this chapter attempted to look at the two major models of curriculum planning which are alternative to, and, in our view, incompatible with, the process-based approach we are advocating. In particular, we have been concerned to highlight our reasons for insisting on their incompatibility.

We considered first the content-based approach, that which begins the planning of the curriculum from statements of the knowledge-content it is concerned to transmit. We acknowledged that there cannot be education without knowledge-content, but attempted to make clear that our criticism is directed at the view that makes this the first and most important consideration. For we suggested that it is this approach that has led to the rejection of education by many pupils, so that it has often proved to be counterproductive to education. We also drew attention to the fact that, when it is not openly instrumental and utilitarian, it is based on a rationalist epistemology of precisely the kind we are concerned to challenge, and it is for this reason that it is incompatible with the process-based approach which we have argued begins from a different epistemological position. We also suggested that those who have advocated knowledge based planning on educational grounds have done so because of certain assumptions they have made about the kinds of development the content they have advocated would promote, so that at root their concern is the same as our own, the development of the pupil. It is our contention that, if this is our central concern, then it must be the starting-point for curriculum planning, and considerations of the appropriate knowledge-content must be subordinated to this. We also suggested that this will mean that there cannot be any specification of what is an appropriate common content for all pupils, since, pupils being human (a factor not always appreciated), they are likely to require different kinds of educational diet, just as they require different kinds of food and different sizes of shoes.

Our conclusion, therefore, was that, while knowledge is important, it cannot be regarded as the most important factor nor as the first concern in educational planning, and that we cannot even reach any kind of compromise model which would give it claims equal to those of the development of the individual.

We then turned to the second major approach to curriculum planning which can be discerned in current practice and especially in the policies of our political masters – that of planning education in terms of what it is *for*, from instrumental or utilitarian considerations. In particular, we considered in some detail the 'aims and objectives' school of curriculum planning.

We began by tracing its history and suggesting that it can be seen as the result of a desire to make the practice of education more 'scientific' and thus as an effect of the influence of psychology, especially that of the behaviourist school, on education theory.

We then tried to pick out the essential characteristics of this view, and, in doing so, we laid particular stress on the fact that those systems of objectives that have been proposed are behavioural, hierarchically structured and value-neutral. We next suggested that support for this approach to curriculum planning came not only from those who wished to make education more scientific but also from those who felt that in order for it to qualify as a rational activity it needs to have clear goals of some kind, from others who have felt that they could see advantages of an educational kind in it and, most recently, from politicians and others who have seen this as the only way of evaluating what schools and teachers are doing and testing their effectiveness and efficiency.

Having thus outlined the case for this model of curriculum planning, we then considered some of the criticisms that have been levelled at it. Most of these seemed to focus on the claim that, both in theory and in practice, to approach education in a manner that regards it as an instrumental activity is to lose one essential ingredient that makes education what it is, namely a process whose justification must lie within itself. Thus we saw that the critics of the objectives model base their attack mainly on the fact that it treats education and knowledge as instrumental and, as a corollary of doing so, often adopts a passive model of 'man', that model of 'man' that is at the root of behavioural psychology. We saw too that in practice this leads to teaching that is better described as instruction or training or even indoctrination than education and that it places constraints on both teachers and pupils that inhibit that freedom of interaction that some have claimed to be central to the educative process.

Inevitably, therefore, when we came to consider some of the solutions that have been proposed to this problem, some alternative approaches to curriculum planning, we found faults in those that fall into this same trap of regarding education as an instrumental process that is to be planned as a means to ends beyond itself. The solutions that appeared to offer something of value were those that in one form or another rejected that means–end stance and attempted to allow for unintended learning outcomes and for constant modification in the light of the continuing experiences of teacher and taught.

This led us finally to the view that the notion of an educational objective might be a contradiction in terms and that an educational curriculum might have to be planned by the use of or on the basis of a totally different model. Such a model would have to recognize that if education is not to be viewed in instrumental terms its planning must begin not with a statement of goals but with the specification of procedures, principles or processes. Such a model, we suggested, exists in that view of education and curriculum that is described as 'progressive', in that view which we are describing as process-based and in the approach which we are arguing is fundamental to the philosophy of the Primary school. Its implications must be examined in some detail, therefore, and it is to this that we now turn.

Suggested further reading

Alexander, R.J. (1984) *Primary Teaching*. Eastbourne: Holt, Rinehart & Winston.
Davies, I.K. (1976) *Objectives in Curriculum Design*. Maidenhead: McGraw-Hill.
Stenhouse, L. (1975) *An Introduction to Curriculum Research and Development*. London: Heinemann.

CHAPTER 4

CURRICULUM PLANNING IN THE PRIMARY SCHOOL 2 – PLANNING FOR EDUCATION AS PROCESS

The previous chapter set out to elucidate those features of the two major alternative approaches to curriculum planning which we see as being incompatible with a process-based approach. It will also have revealed why it is that so many teachers slip so readily into content-based or objectives-based planning. For clearly, these approaches are not very complex, they have the appearance at least of being concrete and practical, they can more readily satisfy the demands of those outside the school or the classroom for some clear statements of what it is teachers are doing and they seem to offer more scope, or at least to provide relatively easy means, for the assessment of the pupils, the appraisal of the teachers and the evaluation of the curriculum.

There is a second, more important reason, however, why teachers slip so readily into these forms of planning. And that is the fact that they are unsure how to set about planning any other way. They often lack a full understanding of what process based planning entails and of how it can, or should, be undertaken. Nor is this surprising, since, as we have already noted on several occasions, the same lack of clarity is apparent elsewhere, so that for most teachers their initial education and the expectations and advice to which they continue to be exposed from senior members of the profession, and especially the Inspectorate, have not only failed to open their minds to the possibilities and the practicalities of this form of planning, they have usually pointed them very firmly in those other directions.

It is the aim of this chapter to explicate the main elements of the process-based approach, and to explain how teachers may set about the task of translating its basic principles into the realities of their classroom practice. In doing this, we hope to show clearly that a decision to reject the other two approaches does not leave the teacher without a plan – or 'rudderless' as one commentator suggested in reviewing the first edition of this book. For it is equally possible, and quite valid, to state the intentions of one's teaching in terms of principles and processes as it is to express them in terms of end-states, products or 'aims and objectives'. Indeed, it is our claim that this approach provides a better plan for education, not least because it places the rudder – or, to be precise, the tiller – firmly in the hands of teacher and child. That, of course, is the source of great concern to some people.

We will set about these tasks by exploring some of the major features of a process model of education, in particular by picking up some of the points that were made in Chapters 1 and 2 and subjecting them to a more careful examination.

Once we have done this, we will proceed to a consideration of the present-day practice of education in the Primary school, not only to show what the adoption of such a model implies for classroom practice but also to demonstrate that the major features of this view are implicit in the current practice of many Primary school teachers even if they are not always explicitly recognized or acknowledged by them.

We thus hope to offer two complementary viewpoints which together should provide a clearer picture of the essential nature of this approach to education.

Some negative points

First, however, it is worth briefly reminding ourselves of some of the negative points which emerged from our examination of the other models in Chapter 3, to establish clearly first of all what a process approach is *not*.

Before we do that, however, there is another negative point that we must make, and that is that, although the term 'process' is being used with increasing frequency in discussions of education, it is not always given the connotations that we wish to give it in our analysis of curriculum. Like all terms which denote complex concepts, it can be seen to be used with a variety of meanings, so that we must be sure that when we use it, and especially when we come across it being used by others, we are clear about the precise meaning that is being given to it.

In particular, we must distinguish those uses of it which go no further than methodological considerations and our use of it which treats it as a central concept in a new philosophy of education. The word 'process' has now entered the vocabulary (some might say the jargon) of the educational debate. And there are many, such as the Inspectorate, who are quick to pick up new terminology but slow to understand the conceptual changes which that new terminology reflects. Thus, in many of its current uses, such as in the recent HMI/DES literature and in some recent discussions of science education, the term denotes no more than the procedures or methods by which children are to learn and acquire that knowledge which someone has predetermined they should learn or acquire. This is also the source of what we regard as the fundamental misunderstanding which, as we saw in Chapter 3, has led Malcolm Skilbeck (1984) to claim that educational processes can be expressed as objectives. The concern is with the processes of learning rather than the processes of education, the procedures by which children acquire knowledge rather than those by which their development is forwarded. One thing, then, which a process model of curriculum is *not* is a new form of methodology for the transmission of knowledge.

We are not attempting to establish a 'patent' on the word nor to claim any kind of proprietary rights to it. It is important, however, that we point out, and that the reader should be very clear, that some of those who have appropriated it since it came into fashion have, whether wilfully or through ignorance and misunderstanding, given it a very different, even incompatible, meaning.

Let us now turn to a brief resume of those other negative points which emerged from our discussion of the alternative models in Chapter 3.

There are three major things which we would claim a process model is *not*, three views of education and approaches to curriculum planning it is opposed to and is incompatible with.

First, it must reject the notion that education is centrally concerned with the transmission of knowledge-content for its own sake; in this model content is merely the vehicle by which the child is conveyed towards further levels of development. Our point is that, as we noted in Chapter 1 the Hadow Report (Board of Education 1931) asserted, by this approach, 'knowledge will be acquired in the process, not, indeed, without effort, but by an effort whose value will be enhanced by the fact that its purpose and significance can be appreciated, at least in part, by the children themselves' (op. cit., Introduction).

Second, it follows from this that it cannot accommodate the idea that this will be, or can be, a uniform process for all children; its approach to education is a personal one; its concern is with the development of each child as a person, so that it recognizes that, since every child is a unique individual, his/her education must be an individual and personal matter. To say that is not, as we shall show later, to be committed to what some, notably the behavioural psychologists, have meant by an individualized approach to education; it is, however, to recognize, indeed to insist, that educational development must be attended to and promoted at the personal level.

This is one important way in which this view goes beyond that of Hadow, and, indeed, that of Plowden, and of the view which is generally understood by the term 'progressivism'. In our view, it represents little more than a clarification of what seems to be entailed by the underpinning philosophy of that view, but it is certainly not appreciated in most statements of so-called 'progressivism'. For we continue to see reflected in these statements those rationalist assumptions about the superior status of certain kinds of knowledge, to which we referred in Chapter 3, and the corresponding assumptions that children will somehow develop if exposed to them. Even major figures associated with the 'progressive' movement have continued to hanker after some statements of desirable knowledge-content, believing, like Herbart for example, that exposure to the great achievements of Western European culture would automatically lead to the kind of development they have wished to promote. Such a view reflects what is at root little more than a change of methodology; in our opinion, a process approach is far more revolutionary than that, and represents a genuine and fundamental change of philosophy. This is one of the main reasons why we are at pains to argue the incompatibility of these approaches. It is also a view which is difficult to maintain in a multicultural society (Kelly 1986), or in face of that work in developmental psychology to which we are constantly making reference, but that does not prevent people from wishing to advocate a common content for the Primary curriculum.

The third thing we would wish to claim here that a process approach is *not* is that it is not compatible with, indeed it is positively opposed to, the view that education can be planned in instrumental terms, by reference to what it is *for*; education, on this view, is not any form of training; there is an important distinction between these two concepts, or aspects, of schooling and this is a distinction the process model sets out to stress.

All of these are negative points which have emerged from our discussions in the earlier chapters of this book of the origins of this view, the criticisms which have been offered of it and, especially, our examination of the alternative models in Chapter 3.

It is now time to pick up the positive features, some of which have also been identified earlier, and to consider these in greater detail. Those features are the empiricist view of the knowledge which is the very base of this approach, its concern with education as a process of development, its emphasis on the centrality of experience to this process. Its recognition that such a process must be seen as completely personal, and, most importantly, the interaction of these features, their unification in a coherent theory of education and a consistent curriculum policy.

All of these features we must now consider in turn.

The essential elements of the process view

Before looking in detail at these major elements in the theoretical basis of the process-view, it may be worth attempting a brief, and perhaps oversimplified, statement of the value position from which its advocates start. The basic principle is the conviction that education is the provision of opportunities for the development of potential. There are powers, abilities, capacities – any or all of these terms will do – which, given the right kind of assistance and support, everyone can develop; and education is the process of providing that assistance and support. Another way of looking at this is to see education as offering scope for the development of awareness, the extending of horizons of all kinds, the enrichment of life here and now and, especially, for the future. The years of compulsory schooling create the opportunity to do this for everyone; but we must not lose sight of the fact that continuing education, 'second chance' education as it is sometimes called, can and should be planned on the same principles, its main function being to provide these opportunities for those whose compulsory schooling has not done this for them, or to extend the process for those for whom it has.

If we look at it for a moment from the opposite end, as it were, this view of education derives also from the conviction, or rather the awareness, that a large number of people, too many, a majority perhaps, even in so-called 'advanced' societies, continue to be educationally stunted – not only intellectually but emotionally too – and thus enjoy reduced opportunities for obtaining value from their lives. To assert that is not necessarily to be claiming that it is a great loss to them not to be able to appreciate Shakespeare or Shostakovich, although this may be part of it. The main concern, however, is that they are not equipped to gain full satisfaction from those things they do appreciate, whether these be cricket, football or even television soap operas. Whatever their interests, their levels of awareness remain too often very low, and there is much scope for the enrichment of their lives in the extension or the raising of these. Too many, for example, remain until old-age at the level of 'concrete operations', and their powers of abstract thinking – about *anything* – are never developed.

Further, this view does not believe, like Plato and many latter day 'Platonists', that this is because they are endowed with inadequate mental or intellectual equipment, with a small allowance of what they would call 'intelligence'; they are not doomed forever by their intellectual inheritance to be 'men of bronze', 'C' stream, 'half our future'. The reason for their obvious limitations is to be sought, and found, in the kind of educational provision that has been made for them, a form of provision whose emphasis has been on utility or on knowledge-content, and which has taken insufficient account of what they needed as individuals to maximize the capacities they have.

The form of curriculum we are advocating is concerned primarily to correct this by starting from the desire to assist in the development of those capacities. We have called this a 'process' curriculum. We also sometimes refer to it as a 'developmental' curriculum. It is not very different from what Alan Blyth (1984), following Sheila Browne, has dubbed the 'enabling' curriculum, although we feel our concept goes a little way beyond what seems to be encapsulated in that.

The detailed, and perhaps complex, theoretical arguments in support of this which we now offer – and those which emerge in the general debate over this view as people subject it to conceptual analysis or whatever is the current intellectual fad – must not be allowed to blind us to the essential simplicities of this basic stance. The concern is to provide everyone with the opportunity for enhanced capacities, understanding and awareness, in order to enrich existence and increase the potential it might offer.

Let us now look in some detail at the main theoretical elements in this view.

Knowledge

The role of knowledge in education is far more complex than most commentators have appeared to recognize. We have already suggested that most of the advocates of a knowledge-based approach to curriculum have made the, unwarranted, assumption that exposure to certain kinds of knowledge would bring about certain forms of cognitive development. We have also drawn attention to the fact that this seldom occurs as they envisage it. It is also worth noting that many educationists have wished to stress that it is not *what* children learn, what knowledge they acquire, but *how* they learn or acquire it that is crucial in education. This was what A.N. Whitehead (1932) wished to alert us to when he spoke of the dangers of 'inert' knowledge, knowledge acquired without meaning or significance, knowledge 'plastered on' but not properly integrated into the individual's understanding, knowledge imbibed but not digested, not assimilated in such a way as to become a real part of a person's cognitive functioning. And it is certainly what the Hadow Report meant by its assertion of activity and experience as the central concerns of the curriculum rather than 'knowledge to be acquired and facts to be stored' (Board of Education 1931, p.93).

We have noted too, however, that this kind of claim, important as it is, has seldom been accompanied by a full understanding of what such a view of education implies for knowledge itself. For it must imply, as we have suggested on several occasions, that the value of knowledge is to be sought in the response of the individual to it and not in some assumed properties of the knowledge itself. And this in turn must require that we view knowledge not as having some status and existence of its own, independent of human beings, not as 'out there', not as God-given, not as reified, not as 'bigger than the both of us', but as a human construct, as tentative, as hypothetical, as subject to change and evolution, even as something which in the last resort, whether we go as far down this road as the phenomenologists or not, is very largely personal. In short, this view of education is based on an empiricist/pragmatist epistemology and expressly rejects that rationalist epistemology which under-pins all knowledge-based approaches to education (other than the overtly economic and instrumental).

It cannot be overstressed that the process view of education and curriculum starts from this completely different theory of what knowledge is, of what gives it its validity and, indeed, what form of validity it is susceptible to. Knowledge is our understanding of the world, and it is that understanding which gives it whatever, temporary and tentative, validity it has. Not only does this view not see knowledge as divided into seven or eight timeless forms of rationality (Hirst 1965, 1974) – an issue we will take up in Chapter 5 – it also rejects the idea that it is timeless in any way, that it is in any sense a fixed quantum. It sees all knowledge as tentative and subject to constant modification and change.

It cannot, therefore, envisage how a curriculum can be defined or planned in terms of this kind of shifting knowledge-content. It can only argue from this basic position that education must be concerned to help children to develop an understanding of this shifting nature of knowledge, to adapt to it and to contribute to the constant development of this kind of evolutionary under-standing. If knowledge is constantly evolving, as, for example, Dewey claimed it is, then to treat it within education as if it were a fixed, static entity is, first, to hinder children from appreciating that crucial aspect of knowledge, and, secondly, to contribute to a process by which knowledge must become ossified, and the very process of its evolution retarded, since to deny the next generation that kind of understanding is to inhibit it from contributing to the continuing development of human knowledge.

The process view, further, acknowledges that, if knowledge is a human creation, and especially if it is 'socially constructed' (Young 1971), a creation of particular groups within society, then we must recognize the values inherent in that knowledge and especially in the selection of that knowledge-content which is to be included in the school curriculum, the values implicit in those subject hierarchies we have already noted as characteristic of any rationalist approach to education. It is only if we accept the rationalist view of knowledge as timeless, eternal, God-given, 'out there', bigger than all of us, that we can view it as being value-free. Once we reject that notion, as we have seen an empiricist/pragmatist epistemology does, and as our process model consequently does, we have to recognize that any view of what knowledge is important, any notion of a hierarchy of subjects, must be predicated on the values of the person or persons advocating such a notion, and, since values on this theory of knowledge can be no more shown to have eternal, timeless status than any other kind of 'knowledge', such notions must be recognized as being totally subjective.

It is this that has led to the rejection of much of what has been offered under the guise of education by many pupils whose value systems are different from those of the planners, pupils from different cultural backgrounds, whether social or ethnic. And it is this, therefore, that has led to those attacks on the education system which have seen it as a device for social control, a use of the distribution of knowledge to disseminate and transmit that knowledge, and thus those values, which the dominant ideology in society wishes to have disseminated or transmitted (Young 1971).

Some of those who have mounted this kind of attack have gone on to argue that the curriculum should be developed from the 'commonsense knowledge' of the pupils rather than the 'educational knowledge' of the teachers or curriculum planners (Keddie 1971). That is a view we would not wish to dissociate ourselves from. For essentially our case is that the first consideration should be the development of the pupil and that knowledge-content should be selected in the light of what seems most likely to promote that, so that this would seem to imply that we go for that which has meaning within the existing experience of the pupil rather than that which is regarded as enjoying some kind of intrinsic status in the eyes of the planner. Criticisms have been offered of this view on the grounds that it limits pupils to the horizons set by their own cultural and social backgrounds (White 1968, 1973), but such criticisms only carry weight if one adopts that rationalist view of worthwhile knowledge to which all should have access which we have tried to make it clear we have rejected. Horizons defined in terms of human capacities and awareness can be extended from any kind of cultural or experiential base.

This point clearly leads us on to questions about the role of experience in education and what we mean by experience, so that we must now turn to that as the second major element in our process model.

Experience

The importance of the role of experience in this form of education is summed up in the often quoted words of John Dewey, 'no such thing as imposition of truth from without is possible'. If knowledge is as we have just described it, then it cannot be imparted or transmitted to children; they must be helped to see and to appreciate its significance, its meaning, its 'truth' for themselves. This is what is implied by that notion of 'active learning' which we discussed in Chapter 2. Essentially, this is an internal process, and that internal process is what this theory means by 'experience'. It is the process by which children's understanding, awareness and general capacities develop through genuine and meaningful interactions with their environment.

On this view, education is, to use Dewey's phrase, 'the continuing reconstruction of experience'. 'The programme of the school should be so organised that it will provide opportunity for the young to engage in activities in actual life situations whose consequences will expand, revise and test whatever ideas they develop' (Childs 1956, p.143). And it is perhaps worth remembering here that it is a process which does not cease when we leave school or formal education. It is in part because Dewey sees education in this light that he wishes also to claim that it is a 'continuing and lifelong process'. His point is that if children learn to adapt and modify their understandings constantly in the light of their continuing experience, they will go on adapting in this way throughout life. It is worth noting here, however, that this also constitutes an argument for planning the continuing education of adults along similar lines.

Two further points need to be made about the notion of education as experience. The first of these is a response to the criticism that is made that experience is subjective, and even idiosyncratic. There are three things to say about this.

The first is to note briefly that the idea that any other form of education enjoys some kind of objective status is, as we suggested just now, entirely spurious. The claim to, or the appearance of, objectivity only serves to conceal from us the fact that such views encapsulate the highly subjective values of those proffering them.

The second comment is that, if we take Dewey's view, although such experience itself may be subjective or idiosyncratic, it is not necessary to assume that it leads to a subjective view of knowledge (Kelly 1986). Certainly, there are those who would claim that all knowledge is subjective, simply because it is derived from idiosyncratic perception and experience. But Dewey's view, which is not by any means difficult to go along with, certainly in the 'scientific' sphere, is that a certain degree of objectivity is attainable – not the timeless objectivity of the rationalist but a form of objectivity based on the current, temporal and, perhaps, temporary acceptance and agreement of those who here and now are together considering the evidence, and, indeed, sharing the experience. As C.S. Peirce, in deploying his pragmatist theory of truth, said, 'The opinion which is fated to be ultimately agreed to by all who investigate is what we mean by the truth, and the object represented by this opinion is the real'.

A third comment needs to be made, however, in response to the charge of subjectivity. For sometimes it is clearly directed not at this view of knowledge but at this view of education; and the concern that is expressed is that this approach to education will lead to different experiences and a different content to the education of different pupils. Our response to this is to agree and to reassert that that is precisely the point. We have said on several occasions that this view must lead to an acceptance that education is a personal matter, that, if there is to be genuine development, it must begin from where the pupil is currently at, and we recently noted the claim that education should start from the 'commonsense knowledge' of the pupil (Keddie 1971). All of this requires us to recognize and accept that the experiences which will lead to this kind of development, and the content which will promote it, will differ from pupil to pupil. It is only if we continue to hanker after that rationalist view of knowledge that all must be exposed to, that all must acquire, that we find this unacceptable.

The same point has to be made in response to those who claim that, because experience is unpredictable and because much of it is gained outside the school, it cannot provide an adequate base for educational planning. Alan Blyth (1984, p.24), for example, tells us, 'If it is unpredictable, then the most assiduous follower of Herbart or Dewey will not be able to go more than a certain distance towards planning what experience an individual is to have. Neither of them really allows for an attack of measles, or the death of a pet, or the movement or termination of a father's (*sic*) job by a firm. Neither of them really allows for crazes or bullying or family holidays. Yet all of these are parts of experience'.

To this we again reply that that is exactly the point. If one can cease to hanker after experience which can be used – in the methodological sense only – as a device for developing the knowledge which the teacher or the curriculum planner has decided ought to be transmitted, then it is exactly the kinds of experience instanced there that constitute the 'commonsense knowledge' of the pupil and thus the base from which the process approach would have us develop further experiences. The good teacher will be looking, as many do, especially in Infant schools, for precisely the kinds of experience listed there as a basis for developing his/her pupils' work. Neither Herbart nor Dewey may have gone that far; the process model we are advocating certainly does. And it does so because one of the ways in which it has outstripped 'progressivism' is that it has a clearer view of its epistemological base and can thus escape from the demands of supposedly God-given knowledge.

This leads us, however, to the second major problem we need to address. If the knowledge to be acquired or transmitted is not the criterion by which we select from among the many experiences children have or might be offered, what criterion do we appeal to? How do we decide what kinds of experience to offer, to encourage, to promote? This is a question which is also raised by some of the criticisms we noted in Chapter 2 have been offered of the notions of 'needs', 'interests' and 'growth' as bases for educational planning.

The answer again has to be sought in the kinds of development we feel we should be forwarding. We must first of all be looking to the kinds of experience which will extend the individual's existing experience and develop his/her understanding, capabilities, awareness and those other powers we listed earlier. The question of the direction in which these experiences should be extended must be answered in similar terms; they must be extended in such a way as to promote those kinds of development which are our concern; their direction must be determined by reference to the need to support continuing experience, what Dewey called the 'experiental continuum'; we must discourage experiences or activities which are likely to lead to developmental 'dead-ends and encourage those which will forward the whole process of active learning and experience-based development. 'The central problem of an education based on experience is to select the kind of present experiences that live fruitfully and creatively in subsequent experience' (Dewey 1938, pp. 27–8).

Thus the major criterion to which the teacher will refer in making his/her decisions is not that of 'directional aims' (Dearden 1976) derived from a rationalist view of knowledge as created in several distinct 'forms' but rather that of continuous growth and development, the 'experiental continuum', and s/he will promote and encourage those experiences that are likely to lead to continuing development of this kind. His/her focus will thus be on the processes by which children acquire and develop knowledge and discover truth rather than on the particular bodies of knowledge or truths that s/he has decided they should assimilate.

The view of education that derives from this particular epistemological standpoint, therefore, as we have suggested before, reinforces the general thrust of developmental psychology, and suggests that we should concern ourselves with the processes by which the cognitive development of each child proceeds, adding to that, however, a further important argument, that it is only in this way that education will also be able to promote the process by which human knowledge itself develops.

We saw in Chapter 2 that curriculum planning can be undertaken by reference to the needs of the child, the needs of society or the requirements of knowledge. This view of curriculum places the emphasis on the first of these. For, in its simplest form, this view is asserting that the prime criterion by which the teacher is to select and advance the experiences of each pupil is his/her judgement as to what will promote the development of that pupil's powers of understanding.

The demands of the particular society in which the child must live and work cannot, of course, be completely ignored, not least because they will introduce certain constraints, especially of a moral kind, into teachers' decisions. The experience of planning a bank robbery might contribute much to intellectual development but would rightly be discouraged on these grounds. Such considerations, then, may have the negative role of debarring certain kinds of experience, and reflections on the nature of society may even provide an important basis for the selection of experiences and activities, so that, for example, in an advanced industrial society that selection might well reflect the importance of such things as scientific and mathematical understanding. But to grant such considerations the central role in making our curriculum decisions is to slide into that instrumental and utilitarian approach we discussed earlier. The development of the child remains the focus and the demands of society must be recognized as offering criteria of a secondary kind in curriculum planning.

Similarly, the demands of knowledge must be seen as a second-order consideration. For, as we saw earlier, the answer to our problem of selection is not to turn to academic studies, on the grounds that these are non-utilitarian, and to plan our curriculum by reference only to them. That was the error of the traditional 'Grammar school' curriculum, whose main feature came to be its lack of relevance. Nor is the solution to adopt 'directional aims' that are derived from what are claimed to be the present structures of human knowledge. For this too is likely to result in the ossification of those structures as well as placing limitations on the development of the pupils. Again, therefore, we must recognize that these structures have their place and that we cannot simply forget them in our educational planning, but we must also note that there are strong arguments for not allowing them to dominate it.

If we are to plan children's experiences, then, primarily by reference to the kinds of development education is concerned to promote, we must attempt to gain a clearer view of the notion of education as development. It is to this that we now turn as the third major element in our process model of of curriculum.

Education as development

It is perhaps worth noting at the outset that education cannot be planned without some reference to development, that 'formal education cannot take place without the adoption of some stance towards development' (Blyth 1984, p.7). We have noted on several occasions that even knowledge-based approaches to education have some notion of development at their base. One strength we are claiming for our approach is that it accepts this as the starting-point for educational planning.

The second point to be noted is that one can adopt a number of different views of development. One can, for example, have some notion of the ideal or perfect human being, such as that which can be seen in Plato's theories, and, less obviously but no less significantly, in modern-day versions of rationalism, and conceive of development as the process of leading people towards this. This is clearly the view of development which lies behind the knowledge-based approach to education. And it is worth noting that, on this view, childhood is seen as an inferior state, from the inadequacies of which children have to be extracted. The most extreme form of this view is the Christian doctrine of 'original sin'. And it is worthy of note also that a central tenet of our process view, as of the 'progressive' view from which it is derived, has, from the time of Rousseau, been a rejection of that stance as literally meaningless, an acceptance of the child as a child, and the adoption of a positive view of childhood.

A second view of development is that which sees it as natural growth. Such a view is not far from the work of Rousseau, and has been the source of much criticism of so-called 'child-centred' approaches to education. For it has been claimed, quite rightly and fairly, as we saw in Chapter 2, that the policy of non-interference is the very opposite of what we mean, or could mean, by 'education', and that, when it has been accepted by teachers, it has led to the worst kinds of *laissez-faire* and unstructured forms of learning.

We argued in Chapter 2, that this is not a view adopted by the process model. Mention of it, however, leads us to the first major point we wish to make about the concept of development adopted by the process model. For it is an essential feature of that model that, within the context of *education*, development is to be seen as *guided* development. It is characteristic of physical development that it happens whether it is in any way deliberately directed or not. So long as a child has food, drink, warmth etc., physical development will take place step by step. In physical terms, childhood will give way to adolescence, adolescence to adulthood and adulthood to old-age. This is largely a matter of maturation. It is a basic tenet of the process view of education that there is no such maturation, no such automatic progression in the development of the individual on any other dimension – intellectual, emotional or moral. Development along these dimensions requires guidance – or perhaps we are merely saying that it requires the right kinds of food and sustenance generally. We noted earlier how many people have reached physical adulthood, and even old-age without revealing much progression on other fronts. Hence, in a very real sense, development, other than physical development, is dependent on education. Without education it will not occur. And, in our view, education is the process of ensuring that it does occur and that it is maximized.

The second major point we wish to make about the view of development which is encapsulated in our process model is that it is not limited to intellectual or cognitive development. Such a limitation is endemic to the knowledge-based view of the rationalist which cannot, as the work of Plato and, perhaps more so, that of Kant reveal, cope with the affective or emotional dimension of human life – except by reducing it to some form of cognition (Kelly 1986). The process view attempts to correct this and, because of its rejection of the rationalist stance, it is in a better position to do so. Like the empiricist epistemology upon which it is built, it endeavours to see human beings as *human* beings and not merely as rational beings, as being essentially endowed, even gifted, with feelings as well as powers of reasoning, and thus needing to have those feelings educated along with their powers of reasoning, rather than devalued or suppressed. Thus this view interprets development as implying personal, social, moral, aesthetic and emotional development as well as intellectual development. It is difficult to find a single adjective which will describe this holistic view of development – and that in itself may be a significant comment on the Western European cultural tradition – but the concern is to help children, and indeed adults, to develop and to continue to develop as human beings, in all the fullness that that term encapsulates.

For both of these reasons, if we are really concerned to promote education in this form, it is necessary to understand more fully how children develop along these many dimensions and, in particular, how teachers can assist with these processes of development. It is for this reason that, as we have indicated on several occasions, this view of education is especially dependent on the work of developmental psychology. And it is to a consideration of some relevant aspects of that work that we again turn for the final ingredients in our theoretical recipe for the view of education as process.

The contribution of developmental psychology

It was noted in Chapter 1 that the main emphasis of Piaget's work has been to describe as invariant the sequence of stages through which every child passes.

The child's view of the world and his/her approach to the solution of problems – especially that of the young child – will be qualitatively different from that of his/her teacher. In addition, Piaget's theoretical framework is founded on the view that the origins of development lie in action – the human interaction with the physical environment.

Using these two fundamental insights as starting-points to be elaborated on, and indeed, challenged, developmental psychologists have engaged in extensive work during the past two decades. Donaldson, Grieve and Pratt (1983) offer a lucid summary of this work, identifying three major themes which have been pursued.

The first derives from the notion of 'the competent newborn' and has shifted interest, even in studies of very young babies, to what childen can do rather than concentrating on what they are incapable of. It is not concerned of course to argue that there are no limits to the child's understanding, but it has led to a more positive emphasis on using what the child understands and is able to do as the main reference points for supporting the development of competence and understanding.

The second theme has taken the researchers beyond a study of the individual to the social context of learning, in order to understand more fully how individual development occurs. For it is argued that thought develops in an interpersonal context and that even the youngest children are sociocentric rather than egocentric. Interaction in a social environment, therefore, becomes as important to the individual's cognitive development as interaction with the physical environment – if not more so. An active concern to make sense of their social interactions becomes a major preoccupation of humans from the earliest stages of learning. This has led Hughes and Grieve (1983, p.114) to argue that 'psychologists and linguists – and all others who rely on questioning young children – can no longer treat the child as merely a passive recipient of questions and instructions, but must instead start to view the child as someone who is actively trying to make sense of the situation he is in – however bizarre it may seem'.

The third theme directs attention to the relative importance of goals and means in childen's learning. It is argued that, 'while spontaneous behaviour of an everyday kind will often focus on goals, disembedded tasks require more deliberate control and monitoring of the process involved in attaining goals' (Donaldson, Grieve and Pratt 1983, p.5). Formal or disembedded tasks – that is those activites which are not dependent on and do not arise from everyday human interaction – are central to the kind of learning that is undertaken and promoted in schools. For this reason, it is considered to be more important to pay attention to and support children's developing consciousness of what they themselves do in the process of achieving goals rather than merely assessing their achievements, as 'the growth of a greater consciousness of the means of achieving goals is a precondition for the development of greater deliberate control and reflectiveness, which in turn is necessary for many of the activities demanded in school' (ibid.).

The implications of this recent work will be discussed more fully later. At this point however, it must be noted that three points emerge in support of a process model if this explanation of the nature of intellectual development is accepted.

The first is that teachers must develop a thorough understanding of child development, both in general terms – that is, with reference to the most recent findings in this field – and in terms of their resultant knowledge of the individual children in their care. As was shown in Chapter 1, the child study movement has a long history of influence in Primary education, and Primary teachers have also placed stress on a personal approach to the planning of work with childen. As our understanding of the child and his/her development has increased, however, the demands on teachers have become more specific and more complex. For, if each individual child's development is to be catered for in the sense described in Chapter 1, that is if notions of cognitive conflict are to be planned for realistically and appropriate modes of representation used, then teachers must be able to engage in what can be seen more as a diagnostic approach to the planning of experiences for children. This must be an approach which attempts to match the activities provided for children to both their interests and their levels of understanding. These activities must also be designed to promote the process of intellectual development. Teachers are expected therefore to engage children in work which is interesting not only in the sense that it will be eagerly participated in but also in that it will challenge the child's existing understandings and lead – through what Piaget terms 'disequilibrium' and Bruner terms 'cognitive conflict' – to an urge on the part of the learner to resolve the problems presented. The activities engaged in, therefore, will provide a kind of intrinsic motivation which will lead to true intellectual development. This diagnostic approach to planning, which draws heavily on an understanding of the child and his/her development, not only emphasizes personal learning, but also places stress on the need for teachers to be developing and refining their own understanding and abilities to diagnose and make suitable provision. In other words the teacher should not only be a good learner in the sense that Sadler (1974) gives to the term when he speaks of the teacher's ability himself or herself to acquire knowledge, s/he needs also to be good at developing such understanding as relates directly to his/her professional competence. A major part of the expertise of all teachers, therefore, whatever the age of their pupils, is an understanding of the fundamental processes of child development.

Before we move to the second point it is worth noting that this developmental style of learning theory, by stressing the limitations of the child's own reasoning powers and thus giving adults the responsibility for guiding the child's development through increasingly complex stages of thought, can be seen as permitting adults to assume total responsibility for the directions of learning. As we saw in Chapter 2, therefore, it can become a more palatable way of justifying the teacher's absolute authority (Darling 1978), a view that will be considered more closely later.

We now turn to the second feature of this developmental view of intelligence which supports the process model that we have been describing.

We have noted several times when describing Piaget's theory of intellectual development that he views action as a central requirement of such development. It is this feature of his view that supports the methodology of 'progressive' education – 'discovery' or 'enquiry' methods. Piaget criticizes teaching methods that 'feed' lessons to students while ignoring their intellectual and emotional needs and advocates the kind of approach discussed in Jerome Bruner's short book, *The Process of Education* (1960), which stresses the importance of action on the part of students who are trying to 'learn' science. The view of knowledge taken here, again as we saw in Chapter 2, is not of something that comes to us from outside, 'ready-made', nor of an inborn capacity, but of a reality that we construct slowly over many years through action (Piaget 1969).

Early interpretations of the importance of action for intellectual development led to an unwillingness on the part of teachers to 'meddle' in the child's physical activity. Action in this sense, however, does not imply only physical activity. For we also explained in Chapter 2 that the activity of the mind too is a part of what is meant here by action. Nor does it imply only action upon the physical environment or interaction with other children. Many writers have drawn attention to the fact that we have learned from earlier attempts that stimulating children to action simply by providing rich environments is not adequate. Lilian Katz, for example, argues that many children suffer 'from insufficient adult help in making sense out of their rich environments. In this sense many children can be said to "starve in the midst of plenty" and to appear to be understimulated' (Katz 1977, p.87). Developing a similar point, about allowing the actions of children to occur unaided, Margaret Donaldson draws our attention to the important role of the teacher in raising to the child's consciousness the implications of his/her intellectual development. She argues that it is the teacher's role to help children 'to learn to be conscious of the powers of their own minds' and to help them 'decide to what ends they will use them' (Donaldson 1978, p.122). She argues further that, unless children are helped in this way, intellectual development will be a long, slow business and few would make much headway. This is the dimension that Bruner's prescriptive theory of instruction has added to Piaget's descriptive theory of cognitive development. Because of the important role of action in learning, the teacher must be a guide and interpreter rather than an instructor.

The third point to be made is that the cognitive emphasis in this approach is significant. Despite comments that nowadays a consideration of the child's intellectual development is always left until last in Primary schools (Dearden 1976), there is much evidence to support the view that in Primary education the main emphasis in the last decade has been on cognitive development and there has been increasing attention given to cognition in education. Martin Woodhead, in a discussion of intervention programmes designed for young children, comments that 'in all cases promoting aspects of cognitive learning has been emphasized more than any other aspect of development. The other aspects have been neglected not because they were considered unimportant but because the research teams believed that the nursery was already catering adequately for physical, social and emotional development' (Woodhead 1976, p.38). As was shown earlier, the creation of a context within which education can occur has long been a commonplace matter in the best of our Primary schools, so that educationists in this sector have been left free to devote much attention to how to promote intellectual development, which is seen as the key to educational progress.

Two further points need to be made and the first necessitates stressing a significant distinction between academic and intellectual development (Katz 1977). For it must not be assumed that the case that is being argued is for purely academic activities – for tasks in which children acquire 'prespecified vocabulary, conventional concepts and some rudimentary pupil role behaviours and skills which are typically sampled in standardized tests of academic achievement' (Katz 1977, p.19). If intellectual development is viewed purely in this academic way as the pursuit of useless knowledge for its own sake, we come close to the sort of concept that seemed to lie behind traditional views of a 'liberal' education as one that involves the study of subjects such as the ancient languages whose utilitarian value was difficult to see and therefore probably non-existent. To argue that sort of case is to argue for a definition of education framed only in terms of certain kinds of subject content, albeit content of a non-instrumental kind, and certain social skills associated with the academic life, and such a view does not go far enough and certainly not as far as either the 'progressives' or the advocates of a process model want to see. For the acquisition of certain kinds of academic knowledge and skills, even if undertaken for their own sake, will not necessarily lead to the development of those intellectual capacities that it is claimed are a better basis for a definition of education.

A second point must be added to this, however. As was noted above, intellectual development progresses as the child's capacity for disembedded thinking is increased, and disembedded or formal thinking depends on his/her increasing ability to reflect upon and control thought processes in any given situation. For, as Margaret Donaldson argues, 'if a child is going to control and direct his own thinking . . . he must become conscious of it' (1978, p.94), and, further, 'we are conscious of what we do to the extent that we are conscious also of what we do *not* do – of what we might have done. The notion of choice is thus central' (ibid.). It is reflective self-consciousness, control of thought process and choice that are the key features of the development of cognition, and it is providing experiences and opportunities for advancing these that is the major responsibility of education.

The process view claims, therefore, that education is concerned with the intellectual development of the individual and is therefore to be defined not in terms of certain kinds of academic subject content but in terms of the kinds of intellectual development that it is concerned to promote. In contrast to academic activities, intellectual activities involve 'exploration, experimentation and the engagement of the mind in thinking, analysing, recording and, in a variety of ways, extending, deepening, refining and improving children's understandings of their own environments and experiences' (Katz 1977, p.19).

The developmental view of intelligence, therefore, has supported firstly the individual development of both child and teacher, secondly active learning and ideas about how this can be supported by teachers and thirdly, a stress on cognition and examination of the manner in which this relates to educational progress. In short, it has led to an emphasis on the processes of education and has thus reinforced those more theoretical considerations whose thrust, as we saw earlier, has been in a coincident direction.

We began this chapter by asserting, as a general principle, that it was the development of powers, abilities, capacities, capabilities, and the extension of awareness that our process model was essentially concerned with. In the first part of the chapter, we have endeavoured to elaborate on that by identifying the central principles which derive from that basic position, those principles upon which all our planning must be based, if we adopt such a view. Pre-eminent among these principles are a rejection of any view that would give knowledge some kind of timeless and unquestioned status; a consequent theory of knowledge as the developing understanding and awareness of the individual child; a conviction that, on that definition, knowledge can only be promoted through the provision of genuine experiences; a recognition, as a consequence, that we can only select such experiences by reference to the continuing development of the child; the adoption of a view of development as all-embracing, as inclusive of all dimensions of human development and not restricted to the intellectual; the acknowledgement that development of this kind requires the deliberate intervention of the teacher; and, as a refinement of this view of development, the assertion that, as recent work in developmental psychology has suggested, such intervention should be concerned centrally with the growth of reflective self-consciousness to provide understanding and control of thought processes and opportunities for the making of choices.

The acceptance of these principles calls for an immediate rejection of the simple linear approach to curriculum planning which is appropriate to the other models of curriculum which we discussed in Chapter 3. For we can no longer settle with certainty all the decisions that need to be made about the experiences which will promote the child's development and understanding before the practical activity of teaching is embarked upon, nor can we leave evaluation to the end of practical activity. This is not to say that no planning can take place before teaching begins or, worse, that no planning can take place at all. It is to say, however, that a different style of planning is required and a different structure must be adopted.

It is to the practical implications of this that we must now turn.

The implications of the process model for curriculum planning

Teachers who begin from this kind of theoretical standpoint will approach their planning of the curriculum in a way that is quite different from that of other teachers. To begin with, they will approach it with a broader, more comprehensive notion of what curriculum planning involves. At Secondary level, for example, curriculum planning is usually of the 'à la carte' kind, as the recent survey completed by HM Inspectorate (DES 1979) has made clear, occurring within particular subject areas and thus becoming rather a form of syllabus planning. Primary teachers, on the other hand, rather than approaching their planning from the point of view of a specific interest – an area of content or a particular skill – and thus creating a syllabus or a timetable, are more likely to approach curriculum planning as a totality. As a result, they do not always recognize that what they are engaged in is in fact a form of curriculum planning; indeed, they are often somewhat reticent about using the term 'curriculum' because it is usually regarded as bringing with it connotations of this kind of fragmented approach.

They will also be giving consideration not only to what they should teach and how they should set about teaching it but also to what children can learn and how they can best learn it. In short, they will be aware of the interaction between the child and what s/he is to be presented with.

It is, therefore, of the very essence of this planning style that it will display a unity which takes account of the interrelatedness of all of the child's experiences and that it will be concerned to promote the development of the child's abilities to conceptualize and to perform in a skilled manner. In other words, the planning will be for education as a process.

This general position leads to the adoption by teachers of a different basis for the planning of pupils' learning. They concern themselves with the creation of a structure for the learning processes that they are endeavouring to encourage, rather than concentrating their attention exclusively on particular aims or areas of subject content. Once this structure has been created, aspects of it may be focused on and considered in detail – the development of writing, for example, or how learning might be promoted through scientific experiences – but such special attention is given only in relation to the contribution that these aspects make to the total experiences that are offered. They are integral parts of the planning structure and can only be considered as such.

This structure can best be planned, and, indeed, best discussed and examined, by reference to or in terms of three different levels or points of consideration – first, the educational context and environment, second, planned experiences and areas of exploration or enquiry, and, thirdly, the development of competencies and reflection.

The educational context and environment

Everything that we have said so far emphasizes the importance of the context or setting within which education is to take place. The first consideration in the planning of this kind of education, therefore, must be with the creation of an environment within which the child will be stimulated to learn. Our first task here, then, is to attempt to describe such a context and to identify those elements in it that are crucial for the advancement of education of the kind we have described.

The underlying principle of such a context will be that it will enable the child to be active – developing both the capacity to act upon the materials presented in a purposive way and, at the same time, the ability to enquire and to be independent in the choices s/he makes. The teacher is unable to attain these fundamental goals if his/her planning it too tight and if s/he imposes too many of his/her own structures on the available materials. The overall conception of the classroom, therefore, is informal both in arrangement and in atmosphere. The teacher plans for a classroom organization which stresses openness – opening choices for both the teacher and the children. The classroom thus functions as a workshop rather than a lecture theatre (Grugeon 1973).

This starting-point – this informality in both atmosphere and arrangement – has misled many teachers into a *laissez-faire* attitude to planning. Each aspect, therefore, requires closer consideration, for within these informalities come important but subtle structures or planning strategies which are difficult to define and therefore often missed by teachers.

The first kind is to do with selection, organization and presentation of materials. In Dewey's words, 'it becomes the office of the educator to select those things within the range of existing experience that have the promise and potentiality of presenting new problems which by stimulating new ways of observation and judgment will expand the area of further experience' (Dewey 1938, p.75). The selection and arrangement of materials, then, is by no means random. These materials might include a selection from natural materials (sand, water, clay etc.), construction materials (bricks, boxes etc.), materials for expression and craft (pencils, paints etc.), materials for drama (socio-dramatic play areas, miniature world play etc.), living things (plants, animals), reference materials (displays, book areas etc.) – all the stuff of our good Primary schools and, when organized and presented appropriately by the skilled teacher, the physical context for education.

Even at this earliest stage of planning it should be noted that, although we can be confident that certain resources will both absorb children and enable certain kinds of development to occur, teachers should always be open to considering other basic provisions which might hold the potential for new educational experiences. Who could have envisaged twenty years ago, for example, that having a computer with a LOGO program as part of the basic classroom provision would support children's development in the way described by Seymour Papert (1980)?

One of the teacher's tasks is to select and arrange these basic materials so that they are at all times available to the children and can be used without interfering with other on-going activities. Another task is to ensure that they are presented in such a way that they challenge the particular group of children that is using them. Immediately, therefore, the teacher is required to make skilled judgements in shaping the physical environment, including within it basic resources presented in such a way as to challenge the curiosity of the children.

This is why it is so important that teachers should have a deep understanding of the theoretical principles underpinning this approach to education, since it is only by reference to those principles that they can make appropriately the on-the-spot decisions and judgements that are essential to its effective practice and to planning in all its aspects.

The second kind of consideration is perhaps even more elusive but nonetheless important in this first stage of planning. It is to do with the atmosphere or climate of the classroom and the human relationships that are fostered there. The approach that we are endeavouring to describe requires that the teacher will seek to establish the kinds of relationship with every child in the class that encourage individuals to have both the freedom to use these materials and the confidence and inclination to sustain and consolidate enquiries. The children will be encouraged, in other words, not only to use the materials, but also to create, experiment, explore and above all to talk with each other and with their teacher about their experiences. This is the implication of the notion of a personal approach which recurs throughout the literature and it is an approach which is complex for and demanding of the teacher. In order to establish working relationships of this kind with the children, s/he needs to reduce the rigidity imposed by prescribed timetabling and grouping of children to a minimum.

It does not follow, however, that having adopted a looser approach to planning and working, the right kind of atmosphere and relationships will automatically ensue. Three more subtle requirements will also influence teachers' planning.

First, teachers need to know their children so that they are able to assess levels of understanding and plan experiences in accordance with this assessment, a point that has been stressed throughout our discussion. They need to ensure, therefore, that adequate time is spent with each child in a variety of situations and that they have devised an economic means of recording their resultant observations and knowledge of each child. An example of this aspect of planning is given by Maggie Bierley (1983) in her account of how the staff of one Primary school set about developing a system of record-keeping that would be supportive of their process approach to education. Important though this aspect of planning is, however, it may suggest a purely cognitive emphasis in planning, and it has become increasingly clear in recent years (Barnes 1976; Shields 1978) that children's learning from their manipulation of physical materials is not readily separable from their social interactions, and also that teachers' social responses to them are a key influence in their developing self-esteem and application to learning.

Secondly, therefore, teachers need to be accepting and supportive of each child. They need to accept and understand each child's background and experience as valid starting-points for development. Indeed, the responsibility should go further than this, as Tizard and Hughes (1984) have shown. For teachers should mediate between the child's experiences at home and at school and, where possible, work in co-operation with parents, recognizing the crucial and positive role that they too play in the child's education. The relationship, therefore, is of essence friendly and warm, and the teacher starts from 'where the child is', respecting as valuable his/her home background.

Third, they must add to this warmth an intensity of relationship. This third point, which has recently been deduced from research into the nature of mother–infant attachment, is discussed by Lilian Katz. Her concern is that the provision of a stimulating school environment with a warm, accepting teacher is clearly insufficient 'to engage the learner's mind and to help that mind as it attempts to improve and develop understandings of its experience' (Katz 1977, p.20). She argues that each child needs to feel or sense that what s/he does – or does not do – really matters to the teacher and this she sees as requiring more than warmth in the relationship. Katz's thesis is that optimum intensity of relationships between children and their teacher (that is, relationships which are both warm and intense) cause young children to develop their capacities for intentional behaviour and that this is 'related to the growing child's ability to organise his own behaviour, to set, pursue, realise and achieve his own purposes' (op. cit., p.23).

Clearly all three points overlap and all are partly dependent on the teacher's sensitivity towards children, a quality which cannot be planned for in the deliberate way suggested above. It is equally clear, however, that the teacher's manner and personality can only partly explain the successful use of this approach. In addition, both aspects of context – the physical environment and the social climate of the classroom – do depend on careful planning of time, materials, grouping and recording. Before moving to the second set of considerations, therefore, it is worth stressing that at this first level the teacher's planning is crucial.

It is also as well to note that informality that has been ill-thought out and lacking in the kind of structure described above has led some teachers – even sensitive and kindly teachers – to be uncertain of their role. The result has been that they either opt out completely and merely 'stage-manage' a happy environment or they prescribe programmes of tasks to be completed (usually practice in the skills of reading, writing and numeracy) before the children are allowed to choose their activities (the 'play-after-work' syndrome).

As far as organization of the context is concerned, therefore, the whole classroom – and indeed the accessible environment outside of the classroom – is set up in such a way as to encourage action, interest, talk and listening of different kinds, using everyday experiences as starting-points for development.

Setting the context, then, is a complex planning activity for the teacher which goes far beyond the mere organization of the physical provision of the classroom and embraces all aspects of the creation of a truly educational environment.

Planned experiences and areas of exploration and enquiry

The provisions made within the environment will, if carefully planned and presented, create many opportunities for learning and many starting-points for developing children's understanding of their world and themselves. These are only starting-points, however, so that the ways in which this development can be supported and the consequent planning that this entails must be considered as part of the second level of planning. Before doing this, it is important to note that, also at this second level, planned experiences are selected and introduced by the teacher in a more deliberate and direct manner.

Planned activities of this kind might include a range of experiences – those offered by music, for example, or related to social or environmental studies. Their selection is based on a decision about whether or not they have the potential for provoking and extending reflective thought and understanding. This is, of course, a difficult judgement to make and, as we noted in Chapter 1, many experiences and the modes of expression they lead to are neglected because our understanding of their potential in promoting cognition is incomplete (Eisner 1982). The extent of our understanding, however, does allow some planned experiences to be included with a certainty of their worth.

It has long been known, for example, that the narrative form holds important potential for supporting human learning in addition to being absorbing to children and adults alike. As Kieran Egan argues (1985, p.399), 'stories have this crucial feature, which life and history lack, that they have beginnings and ends and so can fix the meaning of events'. For this reason, experiences presented in this form – whether factual of fictional – are important, and, when appropriate, experiences should be planned and presented to children in this manner. Egan goes further than this, however, showing that in its fictional form – stories and children's literature, for example – narrative provides two other important supports to thinking. First, it presents events in a fantasy form – a form commonly used by children to reflect more clearly on real experiences through powerful imaginary ones. Second, it makes use of what Egan calls binary opposites, such as good/bad, alive/dead, love/hate, and these provide structural devices and reference points between which meaning can be established. These devices are very engaging to children and are also important in supporting aspects of their learning, for the more subtle shades of opinion and judgement can only develop and be made in a sensitive and authoritative manner if the binary opposites are fully understood (Egan 1979). For these reasons, a programme of stories and literature is an important part of the planned experiences.

Another example of experiences that can be planned in this more deliberate manner is taken from those experiences that provoke curiosity and productive enquiry in school. There is a wealth of evidence to show that children from every kind of socio-economic background are curious and questioning in their approach to learning at home (Wells 1981; Clark 1976; Tizard et al. 1981; Southgate et al. 1981). There is also evidence, however, that they are unlikely to adopt this style automatically in school. Indeed, Willes (1983) argues that, partly because of the way that the pupil role is perceived by children – a perception which is based on what they have learned from parents, peers and often from teachers themselves – their spontaneous behaviour in school is more likely to be passive and responsive largely to teacher direction, behaviour which makes productive enquiry difficult, if not impossible. Mindful of this problem, the members of the team responsible for the Schools Council's Learning Through Science Project devised open-ended workcards to supplement basic classroom provisions and promote productive enquiries. In planning these cards, the team was attempting to pose problems which would help children to show initiative, challenge ideas and, in general, develop an enquiring mind and scientific approach to problems. The resultant design is flexible and 'allows children scope to bring forward their own ideas . . . and leaves scope for children at different stages of development to take things as far as they can' (Richards 1983, p.112).

Another approach to resolving the same problem is taken by Lilian Katz (1977) when she shows how teachers of even the youngest children in school can teach their pupils to signal effectively when they do not understand what is expected of them or when they are confused by the activity that they are engaged in. Here the teachers intervene to teach the children strategies which will overcome their stereotyped view of the pupil's role.

The examples offered above show how deliberate intervention by the teacher can provide children with experiences which are designed to support and forward their development in quite specific ways. Most of the planning at this second level, however, is directed at the experiences that are derived by the children themselves from their activity in the planned environment of the classroom. For choices need to be made not only about the kinds of experience that are provided, but also about how these should develop. This leads us to considerations related to the resultant areas of study.

The first point to be made is that the start of any study will be the child's activity, interest or enquiry. In line with the general approach, children will be engaged for part of their time at school in 'activities'. The first decision to be made by the teacher, therefore, will be whether or not it is appropriate to intervene. As soon as the adult does intervene, the nature of the child's activity changes and takes on a different meaning and purpose and it might be helpful here to make a distinction between 'play' and 'engaging in an enquiry'. Note should also be made of the importance, on occasions, of a teacher's non-intervention in a child's play.

As was shown in Chapter 3, teachers have been, especially in the late 1970s, under pressure to establish efficient institutionalized learning and are now understandably worried if time is spent in school on activities that are not clearly planned and overtly productive. It is timely, therefore, to be reminded of the importance of human playfulness and note that its value for the child can be undermined by an excessive eagerness on the part of the adult to intervene. In Tinbergen's words, 'what many adults seem to be unaware of is that too much joining in, too much encouragement, too much taking the lead, too frequent switching of the child's attention – what I like to call the 'grand-parent syndrome' – has deleterious effects. Like a superabundance of toys, so an overdose of social intervention either interrupts the child's play or forces it to too fast a pace, and this leads to restlessness, to short attention spans, and to an inability to amuse itself' (Tinbergen 1976, p.8). The child's play is one activity to be encouraged and respected, not least because of its importance in the educational process. It is also important, as Douglas Barnes (1976) points out, for children of all ages to be allowed to 'play with words', to produce written work of a kind that is not intended for the eyes of the teacher.

The support and development of enquiries from the initial interests of the children as they use the materials in their environment does depend, however, on the adoption of some more structured planning strategies by the teacher. The usual approach that results is a form of interdisciplinary enquiry about the nature of experiences which has been variously called the development of 'an interest', 'a theme' or 'a topic'. Again the approach can be individual or can involve small groups of children or the whole class. The range of development of the interest would depend partly on the age and level of development of the child and partly on the teacher's ability to sustain and guide understanding. The essence of it, however, is that the starting-point should be as a result of either an experience which has been of interest to the child or a question that s/he himself/herself has asked.

This approach to developing and widening the skills and understandings of children through developing their interests has led to the most serious kinds of confusion in practice. For some teachers, in their anxiety either to demonstrate that their children have interests, or to make the work interesting to their own satisfaction and not necessarily their children's, have engaged pupils in topics which begin with the teacher's interest, develop along lines that the teacher has planned out carefully and come to a conclusion when the teacher has exhausted his/her own resources.

The first misunderstanding hinges on the fact that the teacher may see the theme itself in a form similar to a content or subject area, and therefore be led to ensure its development by planning it out carefully, deciding in detail what should be studied and which aspects should be developed. The net result of this would be to say that each term a new 'project' would be embarked upon and care would be taken to involve children in as many different 'projects' as possible during their time in school, taking care where possible that the same 'topics' don't recur.

This 'pre-packaged' view of centres of interest has led to one distortion of what is implied by areas of study. For there is a difference between, on the one hand, deciding to develop a project on, shall we say, ships, and planning the provisions for this and the directions it should take, and, on the other hand, noting that one child began to make a model boat with boxes and so may need to know more about the skills of construction or about modes of transport or about an infinite number of other things which may, in turn, interest other children or, indeed, the whole class. The teacher needs to be sure of what it is that is of initial interest to the children, for this will also influence the selection of possible developments. It may also result in developments in directions which were not initially foreseen, if these are routes which interest the children. Thus the child's initial interest in making a boat can be sustained to develop skills, knowledge and understanding of a more general kind. The teacher's role is partly to indicate to him/her possible extensions of the interest (through added provision, discussion etc.) and partly to indicate the need to learn skills and develop understanding if his/her enquiries are to be sustained.

A second kind of confusion occurs when the teacher decides to intervene only in relation to the promotion of a particular content area through the child's interest. The distinction to be drawn here is between, on the one hand, using the child's interest in boats in order to promote mathematics and, on the other hand, showing him/her how, by developing mathematical understanding, she/he is able to enhance his/her ability to construct a more efficient boat, to classify the many types of boats more effectively or whatever. The crucial distinction is between intervening to promote processes of a more general kind and focusing on an end-product or a particular kind of content.

In addition to the provision of a suitable context for learning, then, the need to assist the development of pupil's enquiries introduces a second set of planning considerations. For the teacher must be mindful that the starting-point of a theme should be rooted in a real interest of the child and, although she/he must plan and provide fully for the likely directions that that interest can take – not least by opening up possibilities for the child – each development (even unexpected ones) must reflect what is the child's own concern.

In addition to this, the teacher plans not only to develop a 'topic' but also to help the children to make sense of their enquiries and interpret or represent their findings through appropriate modes of expression. Many examples of this happening can be found in Michael Armstrong's long-term study of a class of eight- and nine-year-olds at work in a richly resourced classroom. Armstrong argues that the children's intellectual concerns fall within the various traditions of human thought as they strive to understand and express their own experiences. In other words, their modes of expression become literary, mathematical, scientific or whatever, according to what is appropriate. Armstrong, argues, however, that 'such acts of appropriation are not to be interpreted as mere spontaneity . . . They emerge, rather, out of children's absorption in subject matter, and that depends, as far as school life is concerned, upon the quality of environment which a teacher prepares and sustains within the classroom' (1980, p.129).

Stephen Rowland, the class teacher of Armstrong's observed children, expands upon this point, arguing that 'there appear to be certain principles which underlie the learning of adult and child alike, and certain concerns that each express as they strive to make sense of their world' (1984, p.149), and that these principles lead the child, as they do the adult, to appropriate conventions of expression and understandings that have been established within their culture. Rowland stresses that it is the learner's control over this process of appropriation which is of greatest significance for development and argues that 'this idea that learning is controlled by the learner presupposes that knowledge is not transmitted directly from teacher to learner' (ibid.) and that 'where new activity is initiated by the teacher, control over it must be handed back to the children at some point, by encouraging them to make their own reinterpretations of its purposes in order that the ideas can be related to their existing knowledge and concerns' (ibid.).

The teacher's responsibility is twofold – to sustain interest through presenting problems and extensions within an interest, and to give attention to the child's performance, how s/he tackles problems, as well as to the products of his/her thoughts. The approach is, therefore, diagnostic of various processes rather than prescriptive of end-results.

The planning that is necesssary at this second level, therefore, relates to experience and is concerned with the kind of knowledge – whether expressed in its more traditional way, as was the case with children's literature, or in relation to the child's own interest – which will support and promote development and understanding. It is concerned, in short, with the subject matter of education and with the role that this planned experience plays in promoting the child's development.

It is clear from the above discussion that a concern for the child's control over his/her development and learning is an issue of great importance to the process curriculum. And it is this fundamental principle which must guide our planning at the third level – that of the planning required for the teaching of skills.

The development of competencies and reflection

The third set of considerations in this approach to planning comes much closer to what has traditionally been regarded as curriculum planning, for, at its simplest level, it relates to planning for the specific learning of skills in response to the requirement that schools should ensure that each individual should become literate and numerate in order to function adequately in society. One of the most important tasks of the Primary teacher is seen as teaching the 'basic skills'.

Before considering how the learning of skills and facts is approached and attended to within the process model that we have been describing, two points need to be established. The first is that the teaching of 'basic skills' is not exclusively the responsibility of the teacher of young children. In the past, skills have tended to be viewed in this way, as young children, performing at the rudimentary stages, make their needs more obvious. As soon as some expertise is acquired on the part of the child, however, the teaching of that skill has tended to be neglected.

This attitude is changing (notably through the work of the Schools Council projects in the area of language skills and through the influence on teachers of such writers as Frank Smith and Margaret Donaldson), but there is still a tendency to believe that, once 'basic skills' have been mastered, skills-learning warrants no more attention, unless the child has failed and is in need of remedial help. It must be stressed, however, that although in the context of this discussion early skills-learning is the main concern, the learning of skills is a concern of teachers at every stage of the system.

The second point is that, although in a school context the term 'skill' conjures up performance in reading, writing and arithmetic or in games activities (the traditional 'basic skills'), in fact the learning of skills is a feature of most aspects of school-learning (indeed of learning in general) and it is, therefore, a complex and wide-ranging concept, which is perhaps better termed the growth of competence. We will return to these points in Chapter 5.

At this point, however, we must note that, if the process model of planning is employed, the teacher will find it difficult to adopt a purely utilitarian approach to the teaching of specific knowledge, skills and facts. For to do so would be to abandon all of those educational principles we identified earlier upon which this general approach to education is based. As part of the process, therefore, of planning for pupils' enquiries and understanding, the teacher must plan for the acquisition of relevant skills, must ensure opportunities for reflective thinking and must have available appropriate factual knowledge, all of which are integral to such planning.

The planning of the factual knowledge that will be relevant is, in a sense, the easiest aspect to resolve, assuming that it is remembered, as we saw in Chapter 1 when we discussed the distinction made by Piaget between learning and development, that facts may be learned without this having any impact on the child's understanding. Careful research will inform the teacher of a range of facts that might bcome relevant to the child who is absorbed in a particular experience. If a conversational relationship is established with the child, it is often clear that s/he needs factual information either to add new perspectives to a problem or in answer to a question. In these instances, the child needs to be told – on condition, of course, that the information is accurate. (On one occasion recently, when visiting a sanctuary for birds, we listened in horror as a father answered his child's question with total confidence, telling him that a huge and very sick gannet was a herring gull.) The teacher, therefore, needs to be well-informed, but cannot be an oracle, and so, perhaps more importantly, needs to be prepared to admit when s/he does not know and to be able to indicate to the child that s/he knows how to find out. It must be noted too that being given factual information when it is relevant in no way undermines a conviction that planning should enable the child to pursue his/her own enquiries. It is for this reason that the emphasis on the acquisition of subject knowledge in the preparation of teachers is based on a serious and fundamental misunderstanding of the role of the teacher in the education of the child. It is not the possession of knowledge by the teacher so much as his/her ability to deploy this to support the development of the child which is crucial.

If the planning of appropriate factual knowledge is relatively straightforward, requiring a certain amount of research on the part of the teacher, a recognition by him/her of what is relevant to the child and the availability of reference sources, the other two aspects to be planned at this level are, by comparison, much more demanding and complex. For it is the child's growth of competence through deploying complex skills, such as literacy, for example, and his/her increasing ability to be reflective and to be in control of thought processes that are the crucial factors which support his/her cognitive development. Planning to support these processes, therefore, becomes of vital concern in this approach to education.

Space restricts us from offering a detailed outline of such planning. This we have explored elsewhere and we have considered the kinds of practical planning strategies which teachers have employed to support these aspects both in relation to the individual class teacher (Blenkin 1983) and in relation to the policies of a whole school staff (Whitehead 1983; Richards 1983). In the context of this discussion, therefore, it will serve to give consideration to one example of how reflective skills learning can be approached and note the resultant planning implications. This example relates to both competence and reflection, as it is our contention that the two are connected and interdependent – a point to be expanded upon in Chapter 5 – and in particular to considerations that are necessary when planning to teach the reflective skill of reading.

Preliminary considerations that need to be made in relation to reading are set out clearly in Frank Smith's analysis of this skill (Smith 1971). He argues that a child coming to reading instruction has had a considerable experience with all the cognitive skills required in learning to read. In other words, the child knows how but not where to look. Smith also draws our attention to semantic as well as acoustic and visual categories in learning this particular skill, to say nothing of the emotional response to the reading situation, and the value judgements made in the selection of reading material by both child and adult (Smith 1971, p.224).

In short, the kind of learning involved is complex and, as we suggested in Chapter 3, it is difficult to treat the motor skills of reading in the discrete way that the utilitarian approach seems to suggest. To separate the cognitive aspects from the psycho-motor aspects of learning to read (comprehension from skilled deciphering of words, for example) is difficult, if not impossible. Also, the affective response of both child and adult to the reading situation is an essential ingredient at every stage. The skill of reading can certainly be set out in a hierarchical manner, with sub-skills interlinking in stages which lead to a complex skilled performance. To use this hierarchy, however, as a blueprint for the learning of the skill is to adopt a reductionist view of the enterprise. This is useful only as a diagnostic instrument to the teacher, and can be applied only in the assessing of the child's overall progress. Skills of this level of complexity cannot be learned in isolation from other kinds of learning.

If we consider learning to read from another perspective – that offered by Margaret Donaldson, for example – different, but equally important, dimensions become apparent. For reading can be seen not only as a skill that gives children access to the world of books and writing, but also as a tool for 'thinking about thinking' (a phrase coined by Seymour Papert (1980) in relation to a different form of language, the language of the computer). The written word, Donaldson argues, is a device which places language in a setting that is context-free and this enables the reader to think in this kind of setting. She goes on to point out that reading also enables the child 'to begin to consider possibilities in relation to at least one important act of thought: the apprehension of meaning' (1978, p.95), and to argue that 'the critical things are that the written word is enduring, and that it can be free of non-linguistic context' (ibid.). This means that learning to read is a process which gives to the child – probably for the first time – a chance to experience a high degree of self-consciousness, and an opportunity to stop and think, both of which encourage the development of control and reflectiveness in learning which, as we saw earlier in this chapter, are crucial to an ability to think rationally. She concludes by arguing that the intellectual demands which can be made of the child in the process of reading have 'incalculable consequences for the development of the kinds of thinking which are characteristic of logic, mathematics and the sciences' (ibid.).

Both of these sets of considerations, gleaned from two very different perspectives on learning to read, provide insights of a profound kind on how the teaching should be planned. For, as we will see in Chapter 5, it does not automatically follow that the experience of reading will have this impact on every child. Much depends on how the teaching of the skill is approached. For, if the child is to grow in competence, as described above, s/he needs to be able to see the skill of reading as part of him/herself. The experience, therefore, must be personal and invested with meaning. The teacher will need to be aware that the tasks that s/he invites the children to participate in must be such that they encourage active learning and give each child the opportunity to see him/herself in control. Most important of all, attention is drawn to the fact that reflective skills and the thought processes that they engender are of central importance to cognitive development. They are not a preliminary to education, therefore, but an integral part of it at all stages, and the teaching of them must be approached as such.

The fundamental consideration at this third level of planning, therefore, must be that in the learning of facts and specific skills and in the development of reflective thinking, as in all other kinds of learning, the child must be helped to see the meaning and worth of the process. The child must develop skilled performance, with the teacher's help, in the same meaningful way in which his/her overall development is fostered.

Summary and conclusions

We have attempted in this chapter to pick out the major features and implications of the adoption of a view of education as process, first, by identifying the basic principles of such a view and, second, by considering their practical implementation.

This exploration revealed several important underlying principles. First, we noted two negative points, that this approach to education does not take as the first consideration in planning the curriculum either its content or its intended products, so that the planning does not start with the writing of syllabuses or lists of 'aims and objectives'. Secondly, we drew attention to the fact that this developmental view of education must be seen as a highly personal matter, not individualized in the customary sense, but requiring planning by reference to the developmental needs of each child. Thirdly, we identified what we see to be the three major features of this view, which, together and in interaction with each other, provide the basic principles from which planning must start – a view of knowledge as 'man'-made rather than God-given, and thus subject to evolution and change rather than enjoying some kind of timeless status; an acceptance that such knowledge can only be acquired through genuine and meaningful experience on the part of the learner; and, as a consequence of this, a recognition that such experience must be selected, controlled and guided by the teacher by reference to the development of the child. We also noted that this view sees development in an all-embracing sense, as including all dimensions of human development and not merely the cognitive. And we stressed that, unlike some of the 'progressive' views which have been advocated, and, indeed, sometimes practised, this view recognizes that this kind of development can only be fostered if the teacher takes a very active role in the process, the degree and timing of teacher intervention being the most crucial issues teachers have to face in implementing such an approach. Finally, to round off our discussion of the theoretical bases of this view, we suggested that teachers might look to the contribution of recent work in developmental psychology for a better understanding of the aspects of development which are important and how they might respond to these.

This led us naturally into the second task we set ourselves in this chapter, a consideration of the implications of this view for planning and for practice. In pursuing this, we explored several major areas or dimensions of planning. The first of these was the context which, if it is to be truly educational, must offer the child freedom to explore and to experience, although there must also be appropriate and skilful intervention from the teacher if his/her experiences and explorations are to forward his/her development. We note too the importance of both the warmth and the intensity of the relationships s/he is able to develop with the teacher for his/her educational advancement.

Secondly, we discussed the planning of experiences and it was shown that some of these experiences might be planned quite deliberately by the teacher, although such planning would always have the developmental needs of the child in mind. In short, content of all kinds might be selected and provided by the teacher but for the child's rather than the content's sake.

It was noted too that the areas of interest a child explores must also be genuine areas of experience and must not be selected or pursued in order merely to satisfy the teacher's demands. Rather the teacher must help the child to develop appropriate devices for dealing with the elements of his/her own enquiries and promote his/her intellectual growth in that way. Again the concern is with the process of education rather than with its content or with its possible or potential products.

This in turn raised the question of how we can through this kind of approach foster the development and learning of those 'basic skills' and areas of knowledge and understanding that society, quite reasonably, expects its schools to impart to children. In response to this, we drew attention to the close connection between the learning of skills and the development of reflective thinking, and we suggested that it is thus not an issue only for the teacher of young children but for all teachers. This also alerts us, however, to the fact that there is a potential conflict with those principles we have discussed above if we attempt to separate the teaching of these skills from our concern for the wider aspects of children's development.

This issue, and indeed the general problem of a unified approach to knowledge of which it is a part, is central to the question of the efficiency and the practicality of adopting a view of education as process and requires much fuller discussion than it has had so far. It is, therefore, to a more detailed examination of this issue that we now turn.

Suggested further reading

Egan, K. (1979) *Educational Development*. New York: Oxford University Press.
Blyth, W.A.L. (1984) *Development, Experience and Curriculum in Primary Education*. London and Sydney: Croom Helm; New York: St Martin's.

Donaldson, M., Grieve, R. and Pratt, C. (eds.) (1983) *Early Childhood Development and Education*. Oxford: Blackwell.

Armstrong, M. (1980) *Closely Observed Children: The Diary of a Primary Classroom*. London: Writers & Readers Publishing Co-operative, in association with the Chameleon Editorial Group.

Blenkin, G.M. and Kelly, A.V. (eds.) (1983) *The Primary Curriculum in Action*. London: Harper & Row.

CHAPTER 5

A UNIFIED CURRICULUM

We noted in Chapter 3, when discussing the knowledge-based approach to curriculum, that there are two main strands to the argument of those who would recommend, on educational grounds, that we begin our curriculum planning from a consideration of its knowledge-content. The first of these is the view that some knowledge is intrinsically worthwhile, or at least more worthwhile than other kinds, that there is a hierarchy of knowledge. And we noted there that this view is firmly and essentially based on that rationalist theory of knowledge which we have made it quite clear our view rejects.

The second strand to this argument is the claim that rationality has several discrete forms, that, consequently, its embodiment in human knowledge must reflect these same forms and that the curriculum must therefore include a range of content of a kind which will provide access to these several forms. This is the case deployed by Paul Hirst (1965, 1974) and taken up, or even taken as read, by many who have followed in that tradition, perhaps most notably, from our point of view, by Robert Dearden (1967, 1968, 1976), who, as we noted in Chapter 2, has mounted a number of criticisms of the 'progressive' or 'child-centred' approach to the Primary curriculum, all of them predicated on the view that education is concerned primarily to provide access to the seven or eight forms of rationality that Paul Hirst has claimed to have identified.

It is our case here that this view too is similarly based on a rationalist epistemology, so that, when we reject that epistemological base, the notion of seven or eight forms of knowledge derived from seven or eight timeless forms of rationality must also go. Just as we claimed earlier that intrinsic value is 'in the eye of the beholder', so, in our view, rationality is in the mind of the knower, or at least the divisions of knowledge and understanding are. If knowledge is divided into separate pieces or subjects, these divisions, like knowledge itself, do not reflect timeless and God-given forms of rationality, but rather ways in which mankind has found it most convenient to organize knowledge. They are human, even social, constructs. Furthermore, these divisions, and the boundaries between subjects and bodies of knowledge, again like knowledge itself, must change and evolve. Current divisions are very different from those in vogue even a matter of decades ago. And so again we must not adopt an approach to education that will lead to an ossification of these boundaries, any more than we should encourage the ossification of knowledge itself. Again, therefore, our main concern should be to assist children to organize their own knowledge and understandings in ways which have meaning for them.

When we speak of a unified curriculum, then, we are not exploring ways in which we might put discrete bodies of knowledge together, as has been the case with many discussions of 'curriculum integration'. We are concerned much more, and consistently with our basic stance, with how we can develop a unity of understanding in the mind of the individual pupil.

There are, in fact, two aspects of this, two major and related issues that we are now in a position to face and, indeed, must now face as the next step in the development of our exploration of that view of the curriculum that we are discussing here. First there are the general questions raised by the adoption of a unified approach to the acquisition of knowledge and the unwillingness to accept the sanctity of traditional subject divisions. Secondly, there is the narrower issue, whose topicality may afford it greater current importance, of distinguishing the teaching of those 'basic skills' that society, in the particular form of parents, industrialists and politicians, is demanding of schools with an apparently increasing urgency from those wider aspects of education which are also recognized as of importance.

It is to a consideration of these associated questions that we now turn and we will begin by exploring the narrower issue of the teaching and learning of skills.

The teaching and learning of skills

So far, although our references to skills-learning have been brief, several important points have emerged, important both for the content of the work of the Primary school and their impact on the model of planning we are arguing is appropriate to the work of the Primary teacher. It is worth reminding ourselves of these points.

The first point we have noted is that, contrary to popular mythology, for much of his/her time in school, the young child will be engaged in learning skills – mostly the basic skills of literacy and numeracy. This has been the finding of all major surveys of Primary schools. Indeed, in the report of the survey by Her Majesty's Inspectors, *Primary Education in England* (DES 1978), it was argued that so much time was devoted to the 3 Rs that sometimes it worked to the detriment of other aspects of learning. Because the learning of skills is allotted so much time during the school day and because so much importance is rightly attached to the teaching of skills, not just by parents and employers but also by the Primary teachers themselves, the approach to the teaching of skills becomes a major consideration, and so the planning style adopted in this sphere will have a major impact on overall planning.

The second point emerged from our discussion of the objectives model of curriculum planning. We noted there that it was often argued that, as schools were responsible for various kinds of activity in addition to promoting the educational process, teachers should adopt different planning styles for different kinds of pupil activity. This division of activities, we saw, could be viewed in various ways, but the one that is apposite at this point is that which seeks to separate those activities whose justification is clearly educational from those which seem to be clearly instrumental. For the teaching of 'basic skills' is often justified in instrumental or utilitarian terms.

Many curriculum theorists seem to find this kind of separation acceptable. Even some writers who attack instrumental planning styles as anti-educational are prepared to concede that such styles are eminently suitable for the teaching of skills. 'Like all universal panaceas in education, the objectives approach (one might fairly say the objectives ideology) has some valid limited applicability. If we want to train pupils in certain narrowly defined practical and physical skills, or if we want to check up on their capacity to make correct verbal responses, then the approach has much to be said for it' (Dearden 1976, p.26). And again, 'The objectives model appears more suitable in curricular areas which emphasize information and skills' (Stenhouse 1975, p.97). If we pursue this argument, then, it seems to be perfectly acceptable to treat the learning of skills differently and separately from other aspects of learning.

One is left by such arguments, however, with a feeling of unease, as it is usually unclear whether or not the intention is that the full range of skills-learning or even all aspects of one complex skill are to be treated in this way. The examples of skills that are usually given by writers promoting this view are those of a narrow, easily defined kind – making a canoe, speaking a foreign language, baking a cake, learning to swim are among the examples given by the two writers quoted above. The point at which we should cease to treat the teaching of a skill as an instrumental training exercise is never developed or clarified. The tendency is to treat all skills-learning somewhat fleetingly and as a package and one is left feeling that something of importance has been glossed over, for few of the skills taught in school are easy either to define or to teach. It is our contention that the lack of clarity on this particular issue is an important source of confusion both in curriculum theory and in classroom practice.

This brings us to the third point that we have already raised which is that the difficulty is compounded by the common and uncritical use of the term 'basic skills'. Admittedly, by implication the learning of skills of numeracy and literacy are seen to be fundamental to all school-learning. However, when listening to parents, employers, Secondary school colleagues and the public in general bemoaning as fact, despite well-documented research evidence to the contrary (NFER 1955, 1960, 1970; DES 1978), that the standards of attainment in the 3 Rs of our young people have dropped and that this is largely the fault of teachers in the Primary schools who should get back to teaching the basics, one cannot help but deduce that 'basic' is understood to imply that the skills of this kind are not only fundamental but also that they are easy to acquire through simple practice. The implications are that 'basic skills' are less complex than other kinds of human activity and can, therefore, be planned for and learned in a more simplistic and mechanical way and usually in the first few years at school. This indeed is the popular view of what Primary schools – and Infant schools in particular – are for, and if we are in doubt about this we can consult reception class teachers who know that most five-year-olds come to school with definite preconceptions gleaned from parents and others. School for most of them is the place where children learn to read, write and do sums – 'the real work' – and the young child commonly expects that these abilities will be acquired almost magically within weeks or even days of entering the school's portals.

It can be claimed further that it is not just external pressure that leads many teachers in Primary schools to become anxious about their children's performance in 'basic skills' and to devote a large proportion of time to teaching the mechanics of the 3 Rs in a somewhat simplistic way. As the majority of these teachers are people who have enjoyed a reasonable success themselves in the school system, it is not unreasonable to assume that most of them acquired these skills – certainly the skills of reading and writing – with ease. When most of the children in their care seem to be faced with a more difficult struggle and sometimes consequent disappointment, many teachers resort to planning daily exercises for the children, often at the expense of any other activities, on the assumption that repetition of the mechanics of reading, writing and computation is the only solution. Practice, in other words, makes perfect.

What we are arguing is that, because the 'basic skills' are popularly viewed in this simplistic, mechanical way, teachers in the Primary schools are often

pressured into thinking that children who do not acquire them with ease –
assuming, of course, that these children are physically normal – must be very
slow, very disturbed or very obstinate and in any case need to be made to spend
a disproportionate amount of time repeating the mechanics of the skill until
they succeed. Conversely, the teacher who has succeeded in promoting the
mechanics of the 3 Rs – even if this has been achieved at the expense of
everything else – is afforded status by parents, employers and, one suspects, by
him/herself and his/her colleagues.

Another dimension of this same point has been developed more thoroughly
elsewhere (Blenkin 1980) and that is that teachers of young children are not
viewed and, indeed, do not view themselves as specialists in the academic sense,
largely because their major reponsibility is regarded as being for the teaching of
the 'basic skills'. In other words, since it is their task to teach skills which most
normal adults have readily mastered, the assumptions are made, even sometimes by the teachers themselves, that, unlike the specialist teaching of, say,
French, this does not confer any particular status, that it does not require any
great expertise and that their planning for the child's acquisition of these 'basic
skills' is a simple matter. Ronald King, for example, noted that the Infant
teachers he observed did not regard themselves as specialists of any kind. He
writes that they were 'experts in arranging for children to learn', but that
'writing and reading and basic number work were regarded as skills that most
adults possessed in some degree' (King 1978, p.32). On the other hand, as the
reverse is true of most adults' understanding of mathematics, they approach
this aspect of their work with much more caution. As King goes on to record,
'mathematics was not defined in this way. It was regarded as being slightly
esoteric' (ibid.). He notes the ready confidence, therefore, with which the
teachers tackled the teaching of the mechanics of the 3 Rs, including basic
number work, and the contrasting unease with which they approached the
teaching of mathematics.

This point, therefore, explains at least in part, why teachers commonly
adopt a different stance when discussing the planning styles that are appropriate, on the one hand, for encouraging skills-learning and, on the other, for
the advancement of processes of a more strictly educational kind.

What must be asked, however, is how many of those adults who seem to
have grasped these mechanics so readily have developed a level of competence
in numeracy and literacy which would support an active use of these skills, and
this brings us to the fourth point that has been raised which is that, on closer
examination, it is not as easy to identify and single out these skills for separate
treatment as many appear to believe. And we have also noted that, when they
are learned in isolation, they can even serve to undermine the child's educa-

tional advancement. He may learn the mechanics of reading and writing but, in doing so, may be put off books and writing for ever. She may learn to compute efficiently, but in doing so may develop an abiding fear of mathematics. We have noted repeatedly how serious this dilemma is.

The fifth point is one that we raised in Chapter 4 and this is that, while, on the one hand, the style of planning that we described there offers a unity of approach which gives it its educational strength, on the other hand, many see this very unity of approach as undermining the standards of achievement in the basic skills. It has become increasingly apparent in much of what has been said above that a major problem for the Primary teacher is how to make what seems to be a compromise between the teaching of skills and the teaching of the more generally acknowledged educational activities. How, in other words, can the teacher ensure not only that the learning of basic skills does not put the child's education in jeopardy, but also, conversely, that, when time and attention is given to the child's educational advancement, his/her standard of competence in skills-learning is not undermined.

It is to a close examination of this tension that we must now address our attention for we have seen that it is only when an appropriate style of planning for skills-learning is found that a truly unified approach to education in the Primary school will be a practical possibility. We will do this first by discussing what is meant by a skill, second by exploring more closely how it is that skills – and especially the basic skills of literacy and numeracy – can effectively be taught and learned, and thirdly by examining, in the light of this, the connections between skills-learning and the overall process of becoming educated.

What is a skill?

One problem in any discussion of skills-learning in school is that the meaning of skill is rarely questioned and it is taken for granted that there is clarity and agreement in this sphere. The assumption is often made, therefore, that skills are readily identified, learned through training rather than education and therefore best dealt with separately and as early as possible in the child's school career. We argued in Chapter 4, however, that, firstly, there is an element of skills-learning in most aspects of the learning that takes place in school and that, secondly, an individual will be developing his/her performance – certainly in the skills of literary and numeracy, for example – throughout his/her school career. These two points are important, therefore, for all teachers and not just those working in Primary schools.

They are also points which follow naturally from the view of knowledge which we have adopted and which we have attempted to make clear in our earlier chapters. For we have persistently stressed our conviction that knowledge must be viewed from the point of view of the knower or the learner, so that the learning of skills must be seen as part of that process of developing such knowledge and understanding which we have made plain is our view of what education is.

Another way of expressing this (and one which offers additional support for this view) is to explain these points about skills-learning as stemming from a recognition that skills are a central feature of the learner's ability to 'know how' rather than to 'know that', and, further, from the view expressed by Gilbert Ryle (1967, p.27) that 'in the special business of teaching, we are much more concerned with people's competence than with their cognitive repertoires . . . we are interested less in the stocks of truths that they acquire than in their capacities to find out truths for themselves and their ability to organise and exploit them, when discovered'. Ryle's main thesis is that there has been a mistaken tendency to view 'knowing about something' (understanding its meaning) as a quite distinct and somehow superior activity from 'knowing how to do something' (efficient performance) and he objects strongly to this tendency, calling it an 'intellectual legend'. Others also have pointed to the intimate link between the child's developing intellect and the growth of his/her conscious mastery of his/her world (Bruner 1971; Sadler 1974; Donaldson 1978).

If we are right to assert that skills-learning is an essential component in a wide range of kinds of learning, then we must establish more clearly which areas involve or are supported by skills. We must begin, therefore, by identifying first where skills are part of what is to be learned. A broad framework for categorizing skills is a useful starting point for this. When do we use the term 'skill' to describe the learning that is occurring?

The categories which emerge include, for example, the simple motor skills which are acquired in infancy with little apparent guidance. In addition, four types of skills-learning can be identified as occurring partly, if not largely, in school and can be termed as essential to the learning that occurs there. First there are the basic skills of numeracy and literacy; second, specialist skills taught as a part of other curriculum activities (e.g., drawing, using hand tools, performing athletic feats); third are the social skills (e.g., how to co-operate with others, to judge the moods of others etc.); and fourth, critical thinking (e.g., the application of knowledge to new problems, cognitive skills, etc.) (Downey and Kelly 1979).

It becomes immediately apparent, then, that, when attempts are made to identify skills-learning through examining the usage of the term, the currency is wide and embraces what appear to be, in some cases, very different kinds of human activity and, in others, overlapping activities.

The next question to ask, therefore, is why the term 'skill' is used in all these contexts, for it is obvious that a clearer definition of the term needs to be sought. Psychologists have long been concerned with this question and their initial descriptions map out certain features common to a skilled performance as opposed to a habit. Reed (1968), for example, argues that, in order to acquire skills (apart from the simple motor skills), the learner must have some instruction and guidance, must have knowledge of results or feedback, so that mistakes can be rectified and performance improved, and lastly must have practice. The implication seems at first to be that skills can be identified as particular sequences of behaviour which form into a hierarchy of competences requiring more and more efficiency and skilfulness from the learner. Elliott and Connolly develop this description.

> To an extent skill is synonymous with efficiency. It refers to the organisation of actions into a purposeful plan which is executed with economy. Even in the case of such relatively imprecise concepts as 'social skills', the essence of the skill lies in the ability to achieve a goal. Unlike efficiency, however, skill carries connotations of task difficulty. A broad description of skill therefore is 'an ability to achieve defined goals with an efficiency beyond that of an inexperienced person' (Elliott and Connolly 1974, p.135).

Further than this, skills can be seen to form a sequence – a series of subroutines which can be ordered into levels of difficulty – and simple subroutines can be shown to be essential precursors of more complex aspects of the skill.

It would seem, therefore, that it is a relatively simple task to identify the skills to be learned and then to prespecify the objectives to be achieved in their learning, using the sequence of subroutines as a basis for sequencing the material into units or goals. Indeed, this is how skills teaching is often planned as we shall see in Chapter 6.

As Reed goes on to explain, however, it is not as simple as that. He draws our attention to the fact that much work is still to be done in the area of skills-learning and how this takes place. He argues that 'there has been a conventional tendency for studies of skill to be more concerned with what has been learned than with learning itself' (Reed 1968, p.139). This has meant that instruction in skills has begun with sequences based on the units that form the parts of an observable skilled performance, feedback has tended to be based on knowledge of results at the end of each unit and practice has focused on repetition of each element until it is perfected. In other words the assumption is often too readily made that the description of the sequences of skilled performance translates readily into a blueprint for learning the skill, a point that we have noted several times, and this may explain why the objectives approach to skills-teaching is advocated as the most appropriate planning model.

This point is developed by Elliott and Connolly in their analysis of skill. They show, however, that a surface description of skill ignores on the one hand the important underlying link between the skilfulness of the performer in one element of the skill and his/her overall skill, ability or competence, and on the other hand the link between the skill itself and its application or use. These elements they see as separable in analysis, but not in function. They argue that

> A sub-routine is an act, the performance of which is a necessary but not sufficient condition for the execution of some more complex, hierarchically organised sequence of sub-routines of which it is a member. A correctly organised sequence of actions constitutes what is generally considered as a skill, such as walking, tool-using or singing. The sub-routine thus gains its significance as an act from the context in which it occurs. Thus if skill is modular, the distinction between problem-solving and skilled performance might be the distinction between the organisation and the execution of sub-routines (Elliott and Connolly 1974, p.136).

The problem then, is that, although the learning of a skill can be described as structural or modular, other elements of the description, such as the relations between acts, the context in which the acts take place etc. are equally important in the learning of the skill. If all aspects are not incorporated into the description of skill, they argue, skills will be viewed in a distorted way and success in the performance of sub-skills will be stressed on the assumption that these will automatically build into a whole. If this happens, attention is diverted from other equally important aspects such as 'an understanding of the relations between them (the performances) and their significance to the organism' (Elliott and Connolly 1974, p.167).

It is clear, then, that, although our understanding of the nature of skill is still rudimentary, we can no longer assume that skills can be taught or learned in isolated units. Nor can we assume that skills are learned independently of the context in which they are used. This takes us to the second part of our discussion which is to focus on the learning and teaching of skills.

How can skills be learned?

We have stressed throughout our discussion that teachers have been encouraged to view the teaching of skills – even the complex skills of literacy and numeracy – in isolation from other forms of teaching. In addition to this, sequential descriptions of skilled performances have led to the encouragement of the view that skills are best learned in a linear fashion, with each step an essential precursor to the ensuing one. Indeed, Reed's elements discussed earlier:

instruction/guidance → performance → feedback → practice

form a linear planning model which matches admirably the behavioural approach to planning which was discussed in Chapter 3.

If we take note also of the points discussed above, however, several factors begin to complicate matters. If the skill to be learned is driving a car, then as we saw in Chapter 3, these factors are reduced to a minimum and the learner can be engaged in what is purely a training exercise. The learner is presumably committed to acquiring the skill by his/her own choice, a factor that cannot be assumed about learners in school. The skill of driving a car is also not an integral part of a related activity that is intended to be educational (i.e., non-instrumental), as many skills learned in schools are. And the units that form the total skill – for safety reasons at least – must be learned in a prescribed sequence.

In itself, a skill, such as decoding printed words, can be seen in a similar way, and, if it is so viewed, it does not raise the obvious problems in relation to the effects of instrumental approaches on education outlined in Chapter 3, because the decoding sub-skills of reading are not in themselves educative. Such skills are, however, normally justified as, amongst other things, part of a broader skill (literacy) which in turn is a part of education itself. In other words, one would teach the subskills of reading for several reasons, but these will include the aim that the learner should become literate in the widest sense, and thus have independent access to the widest culture through literature, scientific writing and so on.

It is unlikely, therefore, that prespecifying the objectives of, shall we say, the learning of phonics will advance the learner towards this broad educational aim. Indeed, the writers of some reading schemes have attempted to do this and the result is generally accepted to be counter-productive to the achievement of the broad aim, as the reading material becomes distorted by the focus on one aspect of this complex skill and learning to read becomes associated only with completing books as quickly as possible. The learner certainly can be observed to change his/her behaviour in the sense that s/he can apply phonics to his/her word attack. S/he is not being encouraged to use visual cues, however, and s/he is likely also to find the activity tedious, and one that s/he will wish to drop as soon as possible. For the impoverished material that s/he is asked to handle in order to acquire this particular subskill may be damaging other aspects of his/her reading skills. This approach also debars him/her from taking an active role in his/her own language development, removes the relevance and meaning from his/her reading and, in Halliday's terms (1965), denies him/her that intention to 'mean' which is a powerful force in acquiring all types of language skill.

In short, if a skill such as reading is to be viewed as supportive of an educational activity, if not as an educational activity in itself, an approach to the teaching of it by way of prespecified behavioural objectives and a concentration on skills of a simple kind is not only inappropriate, it is also often counter-productive, as we saw in Chapter 3 the Bullock Report (DES 1975) claimed.

Parallels can be drawn in the skills of numeracy, for not only may children be encouraged to 'bark at print' or become non-readers who can decipher print, but also – and perhaps more commonly – they can learn to recite computations without being aware of either the rules or the concepts that govern the activity.

The skills of numeracy are perhaps even more interesting in this respect as they are intimately and more obviously linked with the development of logical and abstract thought, so that the approach we adopt to the teaching of them can either promote or inhibit the kind of development our process model is concerned with.

The skilled operations of numeracy are themselves based on abstract concepts from the start. As Matthews explains,

> Mathematics is an abstract subject and the very word 'abstract' suggests there should be a variety of concrete experiences from which a particular idea can be abstracted. For example, numbers themselves are abstract. No one has ever seen a three . . . children can see three birds, three beasts, three crayons, three brushes, a miscellaneous collection consisting of one ship, one shoe and one stick of sealing wax (three things altogether) . . . and eventually they distil what all these sets have in common, namely the number three (Matthews 1978, p.168).

He goes on to argue that, although mathematics can be considered as a set of skills and concepts, meaning must underlie the learning of both. Indeed, it is even more difficult to conceive of someone who is numerate without having some conceptual understanding than it is one who is literate without understanding the meaning of the text. There is undoubtedly an intimate relationship between skill and understanding throughout such learning.

A further difficulty which emerges when a linear and discrete approach is adopted in teaching a skill was mentioned, again in relation to learning to read, in Chapter 4. This is the assumption that intellectual activity is at a minimum when learning a skill, and that the learner is passive. Frank Smith, for example, asserts that the child acquires language 'by making assumptions about what are the relevant elements and relations of his language, looking for significant differences in the physical representation of speech, establishing his own grammatical categories and rules, and testing his hypotheses on a trial and error basis' (Smith 1971, p.56).

He also asserts that this active learning is the best approach to adopt when learning written language. The teacher's role is also seen to be active and supportive. It is argued, therefore, that 'given the opportunity and active assistance from a teacher who can accept him as a constructive, active learner, a teacher who understands the reading process, and who knows how to appraise the status of the child's present understanding of reading, the child can be helped to induce a set of rules' (McKenzie 1975, p.25). In other words, even the mechanical, decoding aspects of this skill are most meaningfully learned if the child is encouraged to be active. For, if the teaching is approached in this way, the learner, in learning even these apparently mechanical decoding sub-skills, can be helped to induce rules and generalizations.

Further than this, the notion of feedback, which we saw was an important element in the successful learning of skills, has also been examined closely and shown to be operating in a variety of ways throughout the time when a unit or sub-skill is being learned and not just after the attempt or performance has been completed. Again, Elliott and Connolly discuss the various kinds of feedback that have been postulated. They break the notion down into, for example, intrinsic and extrinsic knowledge of results 'to distinguish between knowledge of performance inevitably available to the subject as a result of his movements, and terminal knowledge of results giving information about the consequences of action' (Elliott and Connolly 1974, p.138). They also examine action feedback and learning feedback, or feedback and feedforward, all of which, they argue, support a modular rather than a linear theory of skills-learning. If this modular theory is accepted, it again draws attention to the facts that planning must focus on the individual and that it must be recognized as being far more complex than the advocates of the linear approach appreciate.

Finally it is important to note the similar arguments that have been made in relation to the development of social skills. Maureen Shields (1978), for example, shows how intellectually demanding the development of skills of communication are for the young child in the nursery. In doing so, she also questions our assumptions about what constitutes a cognitive, affective or psycho-motor activity. If we continue to associate cognitive development almost exclusively with knowledge of the inanimate world, then we are led to overlook the strong cognitive component in other areas of experience. She says, for example, of the skill of communication,

This skill displays his ability to make hypotheses about the communicative competence of persons, hypotheses about their perceptions, their concepts, their intentions, inclinations, moods and states, their memories and systems of rules . . . This is by far the most elaborate and by far the most compelling of our human intellectual systems (Shields 1978, p.556).

Again, therefore, this recent work highlights the problems of categorizing kinds of learning, and the development that might be missed if we too readily assume that the learner engaged in learning skills is passive and that such skills are relatively simple so that they can be prespecified and learned in strict sequence.

This is not an argument for avoiding clarification of the hierarchical nature of skills to be learned. It is an argument, however, for suggesting that many of the skills that need to be acquired in school are not as separable from the educational activities that they relate to as writing about skills often suggests. The usefulness of spelling out the levels of a skill lies in its advantages to the teacher's performance in teaching rather than to the means by which the child will acquire that skill. In other words, an understanding of the interrelationship of sub-skills is likely to improve the teacher's 'diagnostic' abilities and thus assist him/her to function more efficiently in helping pupils. For it can be seen that the most effective teaching of skills, that teaching which encourages learners to relate their learning to broader principles of an educational nature and supports them in their development, requires a teacher who is constantly developing his/her own expertise and understanding of the process.

It also requires a learner who is positively encouraged to be active whilst s/he is learning, to invent and discover as well as practise, and judge his/her own performance, using the teacher's instruction as a starting-point. For, in Donaldson's words, 'This way of proceeding would not only appear to offer the best hope of mastering word decoding skills. It must have the further general advantage . . . of encouraging reflective thought and awareness of the processes of the mind' (Donaldson 1978, p.106).

In summary, it has been shown that it is often a mistake to prespecify the objectives of learning a skill in order to produce a blueprint for practice. If the arguments above are accepted, and it is seen that the child must be active in learning to use the sub-skills in his/her search for meaning, such an approach is not effective; nor, if it is counter-productive to the broader aims of education, is it desirable.

We have seen too that skills-learning is linked to activities that help individuals to become more competent. We have also shown that, although the complex skills taught in schools can be described in sections which are linear or hierarchical in form, this structural description does not necessarily provide us with a suitable programme for teaching, as description does not necessarily translate easily into function. Learners are faced with a demanding intellectual task when learning a skill, and the best way of encouraging children to acquire skills that are meaningful is both to provide them with points of reference as starting points and to encourage active rather than passive learning. The structure of the skill, then, becomes a diagnostic instrument for the teacher who can then help each child individually towards competence.

Skills and process

The discussion so far has shown that recent research into the learning of skills is moving away from an exclusive concern with the mechanical – or even psycho-motor – elements of learning to a much closer concern with the links between skill acquisition and intellectual development. Also, resulting from this, we have seen a much closer link between the development of skills and the development of other abilities more conventionally recognized as educational. In other words, skills are being viewed increasingly as processes which are closely linked to and supportive of intellectual development, and the teaching of skills in this manner is coming to be acknowledged as the teacher's most appropriate way of contributing to that intellectual development and to the advancement of the processes of education.

If the skills to be learned in school are to be seen as the means by which the child is helped to make conscious sense of his/her world, in the way envisaged by Donaldson, then the skills themselves must be seen as processes which have as much meaning within education as those processes which have hitherto been regarded as central to it. It is no longer possible, therefore, to define education in terms only of those intellectual processes the philosophers have identified which it is concerned to promote, and in doing so to ignore the integral role within it of skills-learning. Indeed, as Bruner (1978) argues, work in the area of language acquisition has not only sparked a revolt against traditional 'cause-effect' psychology by showing positivist theories to be inadequate, but has also brought psychologists and philosophers closer together in outlook if not in method. It was after all Dewey who argued at the end of the last century that

> No one can estimate the benumbing and hardening effect of continued drill in reading as mere form. It should be obvious that what I have in mind is not a Philistine attack upon books and reading. The question is not how to get rid of them, but how to get their value – how to use them to their capacity as servants of the intellectual and moral life. To answer this question, we must consider what is the effect of growth in a special direction upon the attitudes and habits which alone open up avenues for development in other lines (Dewey 1898, p.29).

When we look at the problem almost a century later, in the setting of the increased understanding of human development that has been gained as a result of the work in child development, we can see even more clearly that skill and process must be interlinked.

As a consequence of this, if skills both relate to the individual's increasing competence and are central to most aspects of school learning, then it becomes of paramount importance that all teachers are helped to develop a clear understanding of the most effective ways of making this link. Furthermore, it is in this area that success and support can most readily be offered, for it is in this area that most is known about structure in teaching and its effects on the learner. It is worth noting, in this respect, Susan Carey's argument:

> Whatever the cognitive differences are among people they can best be seen in terms of differences in their arsenal of modularised skills. There is not a small number of such skills, rather the number is staggeringly large – each piece of knowledge can be thought of in this way. Because each new skill depends upon the last, the effect of unmodularised skills is to detract from building new ones. This becomes cumulatively more disastrous in school, where a pace is set for mastering new material (Carey, 1974, p.190).

She goes on to argue that this is where our efforts should be concentrated because we already know enough in this sphere to be able to design structured and supportive environments in which children can steadily increase their competence and conscious mastery of their world.

If this view of skills is adopted, we are no longer able to treat skills in a coincidental way, in a peripheral way or in a way separate from other forms of learning. For skills become the principal means by which the child learns to represent, organize and shape his/her world and his/her experience within it. They are, therefore, integral to his/her development, since they are his/her principal means of becoming independent and shaping his/her own development.

Clearly the way that the teacher resolves or interprets structure in this sphere is important and a theme that we must return to in Chapter 6. At this point we must conclude that skills and competencies are increasingly seen as an integral part of the child's developing abilities to control his/her world. The more competent s/he becomes, the more independent s/he is in setting and achieving his/her own goals. Hence competence is important to individual development, for as the child increases his/her skill – his/her 'know-how' – s/he also increases his/her view of him/herself as a competent human being who has some control over his/her own destiny. It is one important way in which his/her reflective self-consciousness can be developed in order to increase control of thought processes and to extend the range of choice, as we suggested in Chapter 4 education should be centrally concerned to do.

The integration of knowledge

The case for seeing the learning of skills as an integral part of the total process of education is, as we said at the beginning of this chapter, one aspect of a wider argument for regarding all learning and hence all knowledge as a unity. It thus leads us naturally to a discussion of the question of the integration of subject-matter or, to look at it from the other end, an approach to learning that does not accept or base itself on any notion of the sanctity of traditional subject divisions.

Discussions of curriculum integration have been a feature of education theory in recent years but they have for the most part taken place within the context of Secondary education, being prompted by the advent of projects such as the Keele Integrated Studies Project (KISP) and the Goldsmiths' College scheme for Interdisciplinary Enquiry (IDE). They have thus begun from the opposite standpoint to that we must start from here, since they have sprung from attempts to bring about integration in a curriculum that is already subject based and divided into clear-cut categories. In short, they have been concerned with whether one can, and whether, how or why one should break down barriers that are already there rather than with the question of whether such barriers should be erected in the first place.

Such discussions have also and inevitably been largely philosophical in flavour, or, more accurately, epistemological. They have been centrally concerned with questions about the organization of bodies of public and propositional knowledge into subjects and disciplines. Questions of an administrative kind have also often been to the fore and it has been argued (Kelly 1977) that the constraints both on this debate and on the realities of the practice of schools and other institutions have more often been administrative than epistemological. However, it remains the case that all such discussions have begun from the standpoint of the teacher, the school, even society and the public organization of knowledge, and little attempt has been made to look at the issue from the viewpoint of the individual child and the organization of his/her experience, knowledge and understanding of his/her own world. In this connection, it is interesting to note that the result of this approach to curriculum planning has been the generation of a system which, as the recent survey of Secondary education in England by HM Inspectorate (DES 1979) has shown, has led to an unbalanced curriculum for many individual pupils, so that concern is now being shown with the problem of how we can plan Secondary education in terms of its total curriculum. Our point here is that this has never been a cause for concern at the level of the Primary school precisely because it has for a long time viewed the curriculum as a totality.

It is for that reason that we have reached this particular point of the curriculum debate from the opposite end. For we have come to it as the next step in the development of our examination of what it means to develop a curriculum from the needs of the individual child, what it means to plan education in terms of developmental processes. In exploring this, we have come to the point where we can now see that a basic tenet of this approach is the concern to guide and assist the child in the development and organization of his/her own knowledge and experience. We noted in Chapter 1, when we were looking for the fundamental principles of this view of education, that one of these principles, as Dewey pointed out, is that the child should be able to organize his/her own knowledge rather than have that organization predetermined for him/her by the imposition of the categories used by his/her teachers or even by society itself. S/he must be permitted and, indeed, helped to develop his/her own categories and to create his/her own subdivisions and boundaries within his/her own developing experience. This is the only route, Dewey argued, not only to a proper education for the individual but also to the continued evolution and development of human knowledge itself. We are now in a position to consider the implications of this.

In doing so, we must also note that the major flavour of this discussion will be psychological rather than philosophical or, more accurately, that to approach the issue of curriculum integration from this angle will lead to our considering it from a psychological as well as from a philosophical standpoint. For, as we suggested at the beginning of this chapter, our concern is with the unity of knowledge and understanding in the mind of the individual child, so that we must pay as much attention to the question of what it means for an individual to possess knowledge as to that of what knowledge is. In short, it will lead us to recognize the validity of what Jean Piaget and, as we saw earlier, more recently, Jerome Bruner have been asserting, namely that the gap between philosophy and psychology in discussions of education is not as wide nor as clearly recognizable as some seem to believe, a point which may in itself tell us something about the integration of knowledge. It is a point too which follows naturally from that rapprochement of the work of philosophers and developmental psychologists which we saw in Chapter 1 has created the foundations for this approach to education.

This is a point that needs to be stressed as much in the context of this present issue as it was in our earlier discussion of the teaching and learning of skills. For it involves the same kind of tension, even conflict, between the demands of education when seen as the promotion of the development of the capacities or competencies of the individual and the pressures of external demands and standards. Furthermore, it creates the same kind of problem for teachers in their attempts to respond both to what they see as the educational needs of their pupils and to the demands of important agencies outside the school.

It is a problem which some teachers resolve by developing policies for the teaching of history or geography or science and accepting with too great a feeling of humility and self-abasement the criticisms of those who accuse them of lacking the necessary knowledge of subject-matter to teach these subjects adequately. These accusations sometimes come even from those who ought themselves to reveal a better understanding of education, such as certain professors of the subject and those members of HM Inspectorate who were responsible for the recently published survey of Primary schools (DES 1978).

For that survey, although supportive of the work of Primary teachers in many ways, has added to these particular pressures on them by suggesting that there might be an increase of specialist teaching of particular subjects in Primary schools on the grounds that many teachers will be unable to deal adequately with all of the important aspects of the curriculum. It suggests that in some cases 'advice and guidance from a specialist, probably another member of the staff, may be enough' (DES 1978, p.118), but it goes on to say, 'In other cases, more often with older than with younger children, and much more often in junior than in infant schools, it may be necessary for the specialist to teach either the whole class or a group of children for particular topics' (ibid.). Its ambivalence towards this issue is shown by its parallel discussions of the advantages of the 'one class to one teacher system' (op. cit., p.117) and the dangers of fragmentation and lack of co-ordination that too much specialist teaching may lead to. In this it reveals within itself those tensions faced by Primary teachers which we are discussing here.

These tensions are now being resolved very firmly in favour of the subject-based approach. For, recent years have seen a significant increase in the number and the status of specialist posts with subject responsibility in Primary schools (Campbell 1985). We now find fewer such posts being allocated for general responsibilities, even for such major areas as the school's Infant Department or for Curriculum Development of a cross-curricular kind, and more being linked to specific subject areas.

Clearly, there are political forces at work here. For it is not so much that teachers and headteachers are of themselves coming to view the curriculum in this way; it is much more the case that these are the only kinds of post which, in the current political climate, are, in many places, likely to obtain the approval of governing bodies and, more importantly, of County Hall. This political process is also reflected in the newly established criteria for the approval of courses of initial teacher education. For the body which has been set up to give, or to withhold, such approval, the Council for the Accreditation of Teacher Education (CATE), has been given quite strict criteria to apply; and one of those criteria, as we saw in Chapter 3, is the requirement that at least two full years of a four-year (B.Ed.) course must be devoted to the study of a subject – even for intending Infant and Nursery teachers.

The political message, then, is clear. And we must be equally clear about its implications for the curriculum of the Primary school. For this requirement of concurrent courses of teacher education entails a consequential reduction in the emphasis which can be placed on other aspects of the preparation of teachers – such things as the study of Child Development and, indeed, of curriculum. And the imposition of this ideology on all teacher education represents the imposition of a particular ideology of curriculum on our Primary schools, a subject/content/knowledge-based view of the kind we have been arguing is, especially in this stark form, inimical to our view of education as process.

For, as we have noted so often, this view regards subjects as bodies of knowledge that somehow have to be transferred to the consciousness of the learner rather than as media for the development of his/her intellectual or cognitive capacities. If we view these subjects in this latter way, we realize that the interaction between teacher and pupil becomes more dynamic and the focus shifts from the knowledge to the learner. The role of the subject becomes adjectival or adverbial rather than substantive, descriptive of the learning process rather than reified as a separate entity. Again, therefore, this is a logical extension of the view of education as concerned with processes rather than with products. It is also one aspect of the notion of development as the aim of education (Kohlberg and Mayer 1972).

It is the appreciation of this that is one of the strengths of the Schools Council's most recent work in the area of Primary school science (Richards 1979). For the emphasis there, as we noted earlier the project title makes clear, is on learning *through* science rather than the learning *of* science. In other words the project has begun from an awareness that the central concern is with the development of certain cognitive capacities rather than the acquisition of certain kinds of factual knowledge, so that the practical questions to be faced become those about what kinds of knowledge contribute to that kind of development rather than how one can promote the acquisition of knowledge in particular areas or fields. A similar point is made by Eliot Eisner (1979) in his discussions of the contribution that painting can make to the cognitive development of children. Both of these examples we will examine more fully in Chapter 6.

The second aspect of this current political trend, and the one which is of

more direct significance in the context of this chapter, is that it not only places an emphasis on subject-content as the prime concern in curriculum planning, it also encourages the idea that that content can be divided up into neat subject parcels and presented to pupils in this way. It is worth considering this briefly, therefore, in the context of the debate which has raged over the last two decades or so over the question of curriculum integration.

That debate began in the context of Secondary education in the UK in the 1960s and was prompted for the most part by the dissatisfaction expressed first of all by pupils and then by their teachers with the traditional curricular diet that was being offered by most schools. Questions began to be asked about the relevance of that diet to the needs of pupils, especially those of lower ability, and the problem was accentuated when the school-leaving age was raised to sixteen and those pupils who were clearly gaining least from the curriculum that was offered were to be required by law to experience, or to endure, a further year of it. It was claimed, as we noted in Chapter 3, that the curriculum lacked relevance and meaning for such pupils and it was felt that this was in the main due to the traditional subject divisions that formed its vital framework, a point that illustrates very well in itself what we are saying here about the unified approach of the Primary school. This point was later taken up and developed, as we also saw, by the 'new sociologists' who argued not only that this kind of curriculum was irrelevant and meaningless but that it represented an attempt by the dominant culture of society to impose itself and its control on its less articulate elements (Young 1971). This is a point which seems to us to have far more significance and weight in the context of current political initiatives in education than it had in 1971 when it was first clearly articulated.

Attempts by teachers to act on these feelings of dissatisfaction, however, led to the introduction of many botched-up schemes of integrated studies, to the cobbling together of subjects and bodies of knowledge with little concern for the coherence of what resulted, to integration from without rather than from within.

Furthermore, these schemes were no more satisfactory when they were based on nationally sponsored curriculum projects than when they were the result of the initiative of individual schools or groups of teachers. For neither the Keele Integrated Studies Project nor the Goldsmith's College Inter-disciplinary Enquiry scheme attempted to be 'teacher-proof', both accepting the desirability of local variation and interpretation, and, indeed, the viability of different methodological approaches, but the result of this was a very large credibility gap between the thinking of those at the centre of these developments and the practice of the teachers at their periphery.

One of the major reasons for the unsatisfactory nature of these early attempts at curriculum integration was that, as we suggested earlier, they were attempts to approach the problem from the wong end. The validity, even the sanctity, of traditional subject divisions was accepted. The issue was seen as essentially epistemological, and philosophers, such as Philip Phenix (1964) and Paul Hirst (1965) responded to these developments by attempting to shore up the traditional 'disintegrated' view of curriculum, arguing, as we saw earlier, for several discrete forms of knowledge or understanding or awareness or meaning, deriving from the several discrete forms of rationality which they claimed to have identified. And their case was accepted and interpreted as providing a justification for at least some of these subject divisions, so that, as a result, curriculum integration was seen by many as an attempt to do the impossible, to reconcile the irreconcilable, to integrate totally discrete elements of knowledge, to mix oil and water. Thus some opposed the idea violently, claiming it to be insane and impossible, and others attempted to bring it about against great opposition and often with a lack of personal conviction about its viability. There were even some who suggested that we adopt a typical British compromise and establish a curriculum which consists of all the major disciplines and an interdisciplinary component (Lawton 1975), a suggested solution whose logic has always escaped us – but not apparently those who would advocate a similar approach to current curriculum planning in the Primary school.

The same problem, and, indeed, the same muddle, has in the Primary sector emerged from the lengthy debate concerning what has been called the 'integrated day'. For again, both in discussions of this and in attempts to put it into practice, it is clear that both organizational and epistemological difficulties have arisen and, again, it is also clear that these have often been confused.

In many cases, the term 'integrated day' is used to describe nothing more than the absence of a formal timetable and the consequent freedom for the teacher to arrange the teaching of subjects to suit him/herself or his/her pupils, either individually or collectively. Thus, in much of the extensive debate about the 'integrated day', the assumption is made that the major issues facing the teacher are organizational issues, such as those of time, space and grouping, and, since it is these that have usually been uppermost in the minds of teachers, the complex problems of planning which they raise have understandably been the main concern of those attempts that have been made to advise them in this area (Taylor 1971).

It is important to be clear, however, that, while these organizational arrangements are a necessary condition for the implementation of an integrated curriculum and the adoption of a unified approach to knowledge, they are not a sufficient condition. Without them such an approach to learning would be impossible, but to say that is not to say that to adopt them is to have adopted such an approach. This is a distinction that it is important to be clear about and one that has not always been clearly understood. To organize a school on the basis of the 'integrated day' is not in itself to have embraced a unified curriculum.

Those who have in fact gone further than this, however, and have adopted not only the 'integrated day' but also an integrated curriculum, have found themselves faced by problems that are identical with those that, as we saw earlier, have been met by their Secondary school colleagues, and their practice has been attacked on exactly the same grounds, namely that it transgresses certain canons of logic and the requirements imposed by the structure of knowledge itself (Dearden 1971). This is a point which we saw reflected in the notion of 'directional aims' which we discussed in Chapter 2. The only difference is that these arguments may be felt to have more force in the context of the Primary school, since it is likely here that the attempt will be made to integrate the whole curriculum rather than to offer some form of 'integrated studies' alongside the continuing study of traditional subjects, as has been the practice of most Secondary schools. Indeed, it is this feature of the Primary curriculum that has attracted most criticism, particularly after it was given official support by the Plowden Report (CACE 1967).

We have noted, however, on more than one occasion, that these criticisms are based on a rationalist view of knowledge which is not the view that underpins our approach to curriculum planning. They thus have force only if we accept that view and its corollary that the central concerns of the curriculum are to transmit certain kinds of valuable knowledge and to do this in such a way as to make clear to pupils that they are divided up into certain timeless and discrete forms of rationality. They have no force at all if one does not accept that characterization of human knowledge.

We must not be interpreted as wishing to claim, however, that subjects have no place in the Primary curriculum, any more than we wished to be regarded as asserting that content, or even factual knowledge, has no place. Nor are we saying that there must not be times when children will be manifestly engaged in what is clearly history or science or mathematics, or, more precisely, in considering aspects of their environment from a historical, scientific or mathematical perspective (Alexander 1985). Our claims are that this should not be seen as the base from which the curriculum is organized; that such divisions should be natural and make sense to the child in the organization of his/her own knowledge, and not presented as derived from some notion of subjects, disciplines or 'forms'; and that the teacher's expertise should lie not in the subjects themselves, not in his/her mastery of the body of knowledge encapsulated in the traditions of the subject, but in the ability to help children, through exposure to that knowledge, to develop in the ways we have earlier attempted to define.

The other kind of confusion that has beset the practice of the Primary school in this area is that ambivalence towards specialist teaching to which we have already referred. For, as we saw, the survey of Primary schools undertaken by HM Inspectorate (DES 1978) on the one hand expresses concern about a topic-based approach to the teaching of subjects like history, geography and science and the competence of the teachers to teach these subjects as specialists while, on the other hand, criticizing those schools which have attempted to deal with this problem by employing specialist teachers and stressing the need for all teachers to be capable of developing those capacities or processes we discussed earlier.

This is an issue which, as we suggested earlier, is no longer a matter of ambivalence to our political masters nor, consequently, to HM Inspectorate. New policies in teacher education and in the appointments to posts of special responsibility in schools, as we have seen, make it quite clear that the current policy is towards increased subject-specialization. It is important, therefore, that it should also cease to be a matter of ambivalence for those teachers whose own philosophy would take them in the opposite direction.

In the present climate, it is particularly important for such teachers to be clear about what that philosophy is and what it entails. The first point they should be clear about, in our view, is that the onus is not on them to show why or how knowledge can be unified or integrated, but rather on those who would break it up or disintegrate it to justify that process. Secondly, they need to recognize that the disintegration of knowledge is a feature of that kind of rationalist epistemology which has been foisted on them, explicitly by the most influential educational theorists of the last few decades, and implicitly by the politicians and educational administrators. Thirdly, they must appreciate, and understand, that such a view of knowledge is not that which underlies the process approach to education; even more, it is a view which that approach expressly rejects. And lastly, they must remember that that approach commits them to seeking for and attempting to promote a unity of knowledge in the minds of their pupils, and that this entails concentrating their attention not on how bodies of knowledge can be integrated in some metaphysical sense, but on how they can help individual pupils to integrate their own knowledge and understanding of their world.

In an educational context, there can be only one view of, or basis for, curriculum integration and that is the promotion of the development of each individual pupil. This becomes apparent when one approaches the question from the other end, when one considers the issue from the viewpoint of the learner rather than the teacher, when one starts with the child who is to learn rather than with the subject-matter to be learnt, in short when one adds a psychological perspective to the philosophical perspective that has been permitted to dominate discussions of this issue. As those associated with the Keele Integrated Studies Project told us, 'The main thing at stake is to regard subjects as tools of enquiry and not just bodies of information' (Schools Council 1972, p.10). This is the real and only point of a unified approach to curriculum, namely that the basis of its coherence is the internal logic of the individual's organization of his/her own experience rather than merely the logic of the subject-matter itself.

We noted in Chapter 4, when discussing some of the practicalities of a process approach to curriculum, Michael Armstrong's (1980) claim that, given the right context for educational development, children's intellectual concerns will fall within the various traditions of human thought as they strive to understand and express their own experiences, that their modes of expression become literary, scientific, mathematical or whatever, according to what is appropriate. We noted too Stephen Rowland's (1984) parallel claim that they appropriate conventions of experience and understandings that have been established within their culture. This process will ensure a unity to their own knowledge and understanding of their worlds even within the divisions they will themselves make. What is crucial is that the unity is theirs, the divisions are theirs and the organization of knowledge is theirs. Furthermore, this process not only leads to what we would regard as a proper form of educational development for the individual child, it is also likely to ensure that any such divisions, even if currently accepted within the culture, are not permitted to ossify and thus to act as barriers to the subsequent development of new divisions and forms of organizing knowledge. These divisions are no more fixed or God-given than the knowledge itself. This is the essence of the empiricist view of knowledge and rationality, and it is of vital importance to an understanding of the process view of education.

It is this approach which, even when one allows for its lack of a clear theoretical base, has helped the Primary school towards the kind of view of the curriculum as a totality which has clearly eluded most Secondary schools and which, as we suggested earlier, in the light of the comments made in the survey of Secondary education undertaken by HM Inspectorate (DES 1979), is of increasing concern in that sector. It is for this reason that one must conclude this discussion of a unified curriculum by noting that the logic of attempting to make the former more like the latter, to convert the only sector of the British school system which has gone some way towards solving this problem to increased specialist teaching, is, to say the least, far from immediately self-evident. At root it can only be satisfactorily explained as a political device, prompted by economic considerations, or, worse, by motives of social control, since not only is it difficult to envisage the kinds of educational argument which might be deployed to support it, it is also a highly significant feature of the current scene that there is a notable lack of any attempt to produce such arguments on the part of the major proponents of these policies.

Summary and conclusions

We have in this chapter examined some of the attempts that have been made to break down the educational experiences that schools offer their pupils into separate packages or sections or categories.

First we considered at some length the proposal that the learning of skills should be handled as separate, or at least as separable, from other kinds of activity. In doing so, we discovered, firstly, that to define what skills are is very difficult and that it is thus quite impossible to decide on the point at which the line is to be drawn and this kind of separation made. Then we noted that this approach can be positively counter-productive to the development of other kinds of intellectual capacity and thus to the achievement of any but the most simplistic instrumental or utilitarian goals. This led us to the realization that the only proper way to view the teaching and learning of skills in an educational context is to see that both are an integral and inseparable part of the processes of education and to recognize that their prime function and purpose is to promote the kinds of intellectual development of which education itself consists.

Secondly, we looked at some of the difficulties that arise from too rigid a division of knowledge into subject categories for the purposes of teaching and learning. Again we saw that this can be counter-productive to educational development and we suggested that the only educational argument for an integrated or unified approach to the curriculum is that this also contributes to the development of the intellectual capacities of the individual and of a meaningful structure for his/her own knowledge and experience.

Our concern throughout this book has been to explicate the basic principles of a view of education which we believe most Primary teachers are at heart committed to, and to elucidate what we regard as the consequences for practice of adopting those basic principles.

We have been constantly aware, in doing this, first, that the practice of Primary teachers does not always reflect this, and, second, that this is in large measure due to other influences which have been at work on the development of the curriculum of the British Primary school, especially those which, as we saw in Chapter 1, Alan Blyth (1965) has identified as the 'elementary' and the 'preparatory' traditions. In more recent times, however, there have been new, and more readily discernible, pressures on teachers whose effect has been to deflect them from the essentials of the process approach. One of these is those overt and direct pressures which have emerged from the recent politicization of education, the recent intrusion of political forces and pressure groups into the school, the classroom and the curriculum. It is not our claim that the outside world should be excluded from the school; it is our view, however, that it should not be permitted to control and direct what goes on there in the way that is currently the case; for its form and direction too often run counter to those of the teacher, and this leads not to enhanced or more efficient practice, as is the popular current belief, but to the kind of inefficiency which must be a concomitant of confused and contradictory pressures. When contrary tides meet, they create eddies, which, as we all know, go round and round in ever-decreasing circles.

The second source of such confusing pressures is those mistaken assumptions which are made by many of the criticisms offered of the Primary curriculum, in much of the research that has been undertaken into the work of Primary teachers (Kelly 1981) and even in some of the attempts that have been made to offer positive support and guidance to teachers in this sector. For, again as we have seen, those mistaken assumptions lead to criticisms which are muddled, and often invalid, and to recommendations which are equally confused and confusing. Again, therefore, their effect is to reduce rather than to raise the general level of teaching performance and teaching quality.

Both of these sources of contrary pressures on Primary teachers have emerged as significant throughout our discussions in this book but perhaps especially in our examination of the notion of a unified curriculum in this chapter. We turn in our next chapter to a direct consideration of the more conspicuous of these.

Suggested further reading

Rowland, S. (1984) *The Enquiring Classroom*. Lewes: Falmer
Campbell, R.J. (1985) *Developing the Primary School Curriculum*. Eastbourne: Holt, Rinehart & Winston.

CHAPTER 6

THE CHANGING CONTEXT OF THE PRIMARY CURRICULUM

To give an account of particular curriculum developments in Primary schools during the past two decades is a comparatively difficult task – by comparison, that is, to that of giving a similar account of developments during the same period in the Secondary sector. There are several reasons for this and these are worth noting before we embark on this task.

This is, of course, partly a confirmation of the fact that changes that occur in Primary education do so in the setting of a separate tradition and one that we have endeavoured to show has been associated over a much longer period – in theory, if not always in practice – with a 'progressive' ideology and a consequent innovatory style. This is particularly true of the curriculum planned for the under-seven-year-olds in the Primary schools, for, as we showed earlier, in Nursery and Infant schools there has occurred, at least since the 1930s, a significant shift from the elementary school tradition with its preoccupation with the utilitarian functions of schooling to an informal, 'progressive' tradition which has sought to develop the capacities of every individual child in a more comprehensive way.

This tradition was well established at the start of the period that we are concerned with here and some of the schools for young children were, by 1960, regarded as providing an education that came closest to the democratic ideal sought for throughout the public sector of schooling. Indeed, one observer at the time argued that 'in primary education, a notable expansion of the curriculum is perhaps the century's major achievement' (Williams 1961, p.165). Up to the publication of the Plowden Report in 1967 and largely as a result of the changing of the 11+ selection procedures in many local authorities, this tradition was also having an increasing impact on the organization, if not the curriculum, of the Junior departments of Primary schools.

It is not as easy to argue, therefore, that the major advances that have occurred have done so during the last twenty years. Nor is it true to say that these changes have been characterized solely by a response to the three main phases during this period which have shaped the preoccupations of those concerned with curriculum development generally – 'the progressive movement' in the early 1960s, 'the curriculum development movement' in the mid-1960s and early 1970s and latterly 'the accountability movement' (Stenhouse 1980). This is not to say that these broad movements have been without their influence, and we hope to show in our later discussion how important they have been in influencing the curriculum of the Primary schools. It is to say, however, that to cite only these elements would be seriously to oversimplify developments in schools that have slowly evolved over a long period of time a distinctive approach to curriculum planning.

The three main movements identified by Stenhouse do not take account, for example, of a fourth influence, 'the child development movement', and we have argued throughout this book that this movement, certainly throughout the twentieth century, has been powerful in influencing any progress made in Primary education. It is important to note here that the 'curriculum development movement', whose relationship had hitherto been secondary to the 'child development movement', gradually became an integral part of that movement during the period that we are concerned to examine. It could be arued that the only developments which have occurred – if we restrict that term to mean progress that has been made – during the past decade have been a result of the merging of these movements which has led to the development of professional, or curriculum, theory. Many of the advances in curriculum planning, therefore, have been either profoundly influenced by, or the direct result of, the work of developmental psychologists, as we hope to show when we examine particular examples.

This leads us to return again to a point made in our Introduction and that is that curriculum innovation was already a well-established concept in some Primary schools (usually in the Nursery–Infant departments) when national bodies such as the Schools Council were being established to create interest in curriculum development and to generate national projects. Indeed, some of the national curriculum movements of the past two decades have tended to constrain rather than advance the development of work with young children, again a point that we will explore more closely later.

Another factor worthy of note is that most of the teachers working in Primary schools during this period had undertaken a more extensive initial professional education than many of their colleagues in other sectors and, although it is true that many have had their 'progressive' ideas 'knocked out of them by experienced colleagues who practised the formal teaching inherited from the elementary schools' (Stenhouse 1980, p.246), there has persisted throughout the past twenty years a strong nucleus of Primary teachers, headteachers and advisers, again particularly among those concerned with the education of younger children, who have continued to work within and to develop the 'progressive' tradition. In this sense, the initial professional education has had a more profound impact on teachers in Primary education than it has done elsewhere and the study of educational theory and practice has influenced and been influenced by many, if by no means all, teachers even after entry into the profession. In other words, a larger proportion of teachers in this area have shown an interest in the development of their professional expertise.

This receptivity to innovation is also partly due to the size of the institutions within which Primary teachers work. As the schools are physcially smaller than Secondary schools, they offer a setting in which it is more possible to develop a coherent policy or approach to curriculum planning. It is certainly possible for a teacher to understand and come to know in detail the views, ideas and levels of competence of all his/her colleagues and in some instances – for example, in schools whose design is open – to be aware of the day-to-day work of colleagues, even if the teachers within a school choose not actually to teach as a team. In this way, professional accountability becomes easier if not inevitable.

Being smaller in scale, it is also possible for the school community to develop a more intimate and informal relationship with the local community and with parents who are themselves at their most responsive to the school when their children are young. It is, in other words, easier to blur the boundaries between the school and its outside community and it is also possible for non-professionals to observe or even participate in the school's work, so that accountability to those served becomes a more personal matter.

We are not suggesting that innovatory activities and open styles of accountability have consequently been widespread, for the natural conservatism of many teachers together with the profound influence of the other traditions – especially the elementary school tradition – have meant that curriculum change does not inevitably occur. Indeed, the small size of the institution can be as effective a factor in halting development as it can be in advancing it and this is particularly true when staffing becomes unduly static.

It is, however, more possible for teachers in the Primary schools, in comparison to those working in other educational institutions, to be open and responsive to change and development, even in a climate of economic stringency. In reality, although the majority may limit their response to organizational rather than curricular changes (Richards 1980), the fact that non-streaming and vertical grouping has been introduced over a widespread area and into such a substantial proportion of Infant and Junior school classrooms – one of the findings of the HMI's survey (DES 1978) – is some indication that the teachers can have considerable force as agents of change, for there was no obvious external pressure on them in these instances to make these changes.

One further reason for the difficulty in pinpointing curriculum developments during the past two decades is worthy of note. Primary teachers have not been expected until very recently to respond to the same dramatic administrative and political demands that have been made of their Secondary colleagues. The comparatively rapid change to Comprehensive schools and the raising of the school-leaving age naturally placed issues related to the Secondary school curriculum in the limelight of national debate until the late 1970s. These two factors also attracted a large proportion of funding for both the Secondary schools themselves and for large-scale research projects aimed at the development of their curricula.

In retrospect, and in the light of the very recent political attention given to Primary education, it may be seen as fortunate for the Primary schools that they were, for a large part of this period, left to develop in their usual evolutionary manner. The dramatic changes made in the Secondary sector, however, did provide a stimulus for the discussions of the teachers working there and the theorists, advisers and others concerned to help them. As a result, much of the curriculum theory that was generated came from the practical problems of the Secondary schools. Primary teachers were not until recently required to face such urgent curriculum problems nor were they afforded help in articulating their view of curriculum. This, at least in part, may explain why their conception of the curriculum has remained implicit in their work for so long, has still not fully emerged and is therefore so difficult to delineate. It may also explain why they have been unduly influenced by solutions devised for Secondary schools (Blenkin 1980).

When we look at the Primary curriculum during the past twenty years, therefore, it is apparent that account must be taken of the complex and often subtle factors that are peculiar to this sector of schooling. These factors, we have attempted to show, must be considered in addition to the usual network of constraints and influences that form the more conventionally accepted context for curriculum planning.

It is the intention of this chapter, then, to describe some of the changes that have been proposed or implemented and to evaluate them both against this context and with reference to the framework offered in the preceding chapters. We have structured our discussion into three broad sections: firstly, the changes that relate to the increased political involvement in education; secondly, the influence of a perceived need for subject specialisms; and thirdly, developments designed to promote attention to process in planning. It is obvious from our remarks above that there is considerable overlap between these three areas and we will note this where possible within the discussion. We will also attempt to show, when we examine particular examples of practice within these sections, that in some instances there are developments that run counter to the process model of planning that we have argued underlies the mainstream Primary approach, whilst in others there is evidence that this approach is being supported and, in some cases, considerably advanced.

The most dominant change in context is that associated with the increasing political involvement in education, and it is to this that we must devote most of our attention.

The increased political involvement in education

There is much to be said for the assertion that, when one is not formally answerable to others for one's actions, it becomes more likely that one will neglect making any evaluation of one's work (Harlen 1979). Whether this is true of teachers or not, this was certainly the claim that came to the fore in the national debates of 1976 in what must be the bleakest year for 'progressive' education in recent history. Primary teachers were criticized, in some cases hysterically and mostly unjustly, for neglecting to plan for and achieve a reasonable standard of performance in 'basic skills' for young children and it was also claimed that, in some cases, children suffered because their teachers were unclear about their aims. There was widespread pressure that teachers should be called to account.

As a result, it is often assumed that curriculum developments that have been designed to make teachers more accountable for their work have occurred in very recent years and have been produced hurriedly and in response to the demands made by central government on the local education authorities and on schools. To view the responses from the one perspective of national pressures, however, would be to oversimplify events and would not explain the variety of interpretations and materials that have been produced.

Admittedly, most of the work undertaken has been a result of pressures that are external to the profession. These have come from both the national and local government levels. As we noted in Chapter 2, however, there has also evolved a discernible move within the profession, at least since the Plowden Report was published, both to clarify the structure of work undertaken in informal education and to define a more positive role for the teacher in this setting. The main thrust of this work was to take the insecurity out of discovery methods, to ensure, in other words, the value of work that is undertaken by children and to enable teachers to give an account of this.

The effects of demands for accountability, then, need to be examined in a variety of ways. There is the political response and its effect on the curriculum, for example, a response which is characterized at national level by the recent work of Her Majesty's Inspectors and the policy documents from the Department of Education and Science, and which finds expression at the local level in curriculum policies of various kinds. There is also the professional response, which ranges from research projects directed at helping teachers to structure, plan and evaluate their work with more clarity and understanding, to the curriculum research and development that has been undertaken at a school-based level or even by individual teachers themselves. We must note the influence that each of these has had. The most direct statements, however, have emerged from the Department of Education and Science and we will begin by briefly examining these documents and the view of the curriculum expressed within them.

Recent initiatives from central government

The pressure from government for the involvement of others apart from teachers in the curriculum has been increasing throughout the past twenty years. There is a risk of oversimplifying occurrences but several incidents are worth noting in order to clarify why teacher-accountability came suddenly to the fore and urgent action in this sphere began to occur.

Firstly, government began to heed and even sympathize with lay opinion which has always been suspicious of informal, so-called 'permissive' movements in education. When the excesses of these were open to public scrutiny (as occurred as a result of the happenings at the William Tyndale Junior School, for example) the whole issue was open to public debate and, as was stated above, it became clear that there was a strong feeling that teachers should be made to be more accountable. Secondly, the cost of education was rising, and a mood of dissatisfaction developed, as it was generally felt that such an expensive system should yield better – or at least more tangible – results. Very little of direct benefit, for example had been observed in the schools as a result of the expensive projects undertaken by the teacher-controlled Schools Council. The climate was right,therefore, for a more active intervention on the part of central government.

During this period also, two influential publications – the Bullock Report on language and literacy (DES 1975) and Neville Bennett's Lancaster research study (Bennett 1976) – were given a great deal of attention by the pr ss. The main recommendations of the Bullock Report were largely neglected by the media, but the publicity that it did receive highlighted the fact that the report advocated the monitoring of standards in literacy at Primary and Secondary levels. The members of the committee were in no doubt that 'standards should be monitored, and that this should be done on a scale which will allow confidence in the accuracy and value of the findings' (DES 1975, para. 3.26, p.44). This was the first major statement to herald the government's intention to monitor standards.

At the same time, in his research into teaching styles and pupil progress, Neville Bennett was claiming that formal teaching fulfils its aims in the academic area without detriment to the social and emotional development of pupils, whereas informal teaching only partially fulfils its aims in the latter area as well as engendering comparatively poorer outcomes in academic development (Bennett 1976). It is not insignificant that this research project, among the many that were under way at the time, should have been singled out for special attention, despite the grave reservations that were being expressed by the research community about the project's methodology, and, therefore, the validity of its 'findings' (Gray and Satterly 1981). For it seemed to offer proof to and to strengthen the case of those who maintained that 'progressive' education was ineffective and had undermined the performance of pupils in schools.

These influences and moods were not without effect on policies being made at local and national level by politicians and administrators and a series of publications began to spell out the government's intention to increase the control over the curriculum.

As a cumulative expression of these policies, the government's Green Paper, *Education in Schools* (DES 1977), marked the beginning of a concern to assess more carefully the work of the schools. Whilst rejecting rigid and uniform national tests of children's performance, it advocated that diagnostic testing should be more widely used in schools and by local authorities, to produce greater consistency of practice and greater accountability. Its main recommendations for Primary schools included that

   (i) in all schools teachers need to be quite clear about the ways in which children make and show progress in the various aspects of their learning . . .
   (ii) teachers should be able to identify with some precision the levels of achievement represented by a pupil's work (op. cit. p.8).

It was also argued that the child-centred approach had become widespread in schools (a statement that was to be refuted by the ensuing national survey.) It had 'proved to be a trap for less able or less experienced teachers and in some cases the use of the child-centred approach has deteriorated into lack of order and application' (ibid.).

In addition, therefore, it was felt that 'a core of learning' or 'a protected area of the curriculum' should be established throughout England and Wales and that literacy and numeracy should form the most important part of this core for these were skills 'for which the primary schools have a central, and indeed over-riding, responsibility' (op. cit., p.9).

To ensure that standards were maintained in this 'protected area', the Assessment of Performance Unit (APU) had been established in 1975 by the Department of Education and Science and three national research projects had been funded – one to investigate record-keeping in the Primary school, another to explore assessment techniques in the Nursery school and the third to help to provide local education authorities and schools with tests in mathematics and language so that they could test their pupils' performance against APU norms should they choose to do so (NFER 1978). In addition it was announced that the DES intended to review the curricular arrangements made by l.e.a.s as a preliminary to defining a new national framework for the curriculum. The details of this review were set out in Circular 14/77 and the aspects that were most relevant to the Primary schools were two requests – to report on aims and to examine and report on record-keeping systems.

The mood of the government's publication, the concern that it expressed for measurable standards of pupil attainment and the ensuing actions that were taken by the DES all indicated a belief 'not so much that teachers cannot be left to choose the right sorts of activity for their pupils as that they cannot be trusted to ensure that sufficiently high standards are attained unless there is some kind of outside supervision' (Kelly 1977, p.167). This, then, was the first major document to place the curriculum of the schools at the centre of the national concern.

The second was to express a somewhat different mood. *Primary Education in England: a survey by HM Inspectors of Schools* (DES 1978) appeared with much less dramatic publicity. This was the report of the work which had been undertaken nationally and in accordance with the inspectors' 'long tradition of observing children at work and forming views on the quality and appropriateness of what they do in school' (Thomas 1980, p.75).

The survey was concerned with the work of 7-, 9- and 11-year-olds in 542 schools chosen at random to be representative of Primary schools in England. Part of this work was observed at first hand, part was the result of discussion with teachers and headteachers about their planning and record-keeping and part was based on the results of tests in reading and mathematics which had been administered to a sub-sample of 9- and 11-year-olds in the case of reading, and a subsample of 11-year-olds in the case of mathematics. The survey offered no evidence to support the view that standards of attainment of pupils in schools were falling. Indeed the results of the reading tests, which it was possible to compare with three earlier NFER surveys (NFER 1955, 1960, 1970), indicated a steady improvement in this sphere. Nor did it offer evidence either that child-centred education was widespread or that the Primary curriculum was usually approached in a 'progressive' or unified way. The practice revealed in the survey was somewhat unimaginative and indicated that the majority of schools planned 'scarcely more than a revamped elementary school curriculum with the same major utilitarian emphases' (Richards 1980, p.78).

The findings of the HMI's survey largely contradicted the claims that had been made in the Green Paper about the curriculum of the schools and, as we noted in Chapter 5, the inspectors expressed concern not about the neglect of basic skills-teaching but about the fact that the teachers in the top Infant and Junior classes that were observed were, in practice, still too preoccupied with the narrow conception of curriculum inherited from the elementary tradition and were therefore predominantly emphasizing the utilitarian rather than educational functions of schooling. The idea that 'progressivism' was widespread was a widely believed myth not borne out – at least in the Junior departments of Primary schools – by the evidence of this survey (Richards 1980).

The inspectors reported that the teaching of the 'basic skills' dominated the work of many of the schools and they argued that this was often at the expense of provision for a sufficiently wide experience for some children. The consequence was claimed to be, for example, an absence of science teaching in 80 per cent of the classes and they commented on the facts that insufficient attention was afforded to the development of historical and geographical understanding and that craft was making a smaller contribution to the work than was desirable.

On the basis of their findings, they could not support the view that a narrow concentration on 'basic skills' would produce higher levels of performance. They reported that

> the basic skills are more successfully learnt when applied to other subjects and children in the classes which covered a full range of the widely taught items did better on the NFER tests at 9 and 11 years of age; also, for all three age groups the work of children in these classes was better matched to their abilities than was the work of children in other classes . . . there is no evidence in the survey to suggest

that a narrower curriculum enabled children to do better in the basic skills or led to work being more aptly chosen to suit the capacities of the children (DES 1978, p.114).

Although they expressed support for interest-based work, they criticized topic work that was self-contained and did not include sufficient opportunities for the children to make use of and develop skills and concepts. They also identified the above-average child as the one least likely to be catered for adequately in the Primary schools and suggested that Primary teachers should develop specialist abilities (notably in science) so that the able child could be challenged.

As we have noted before, the survey is an odd mixture of views and recommendations on how the Primary curriculum should develop. On the one hand it is supportive of a flexible, unified approach to planning, where children are encouraged to learn to develop skills and concepts in variety of situations and by pursuing inquiries; and its findings also support this view. On the other hand, concern is expressed that subjects such as science, history and geography are not adequately covered. They advise that teachers should develop more expertise in knowledge areas and schools should employ subject specialists to take the lead here. It is unclear, when they talk both of subject specialists and of conceptual understanding that goes beyond the content of work, whether the inspectors are promoting a process or content view of the curriculum in their report.

Its findings, as far as the realities of curriculum development are concerned, are also mixed, for, although they refute the wild claims that standards have dropped, they also show that most teachers are still content to plan for and emphasize the utilitarian aspects of schooling.

The findings of the much smaller survey of 80 First schools (DES 1982) – schools which cater for 5–8 year-olds or 5–9 year-olds – confirmed many of the findings and recommendations of the much larger Primary survey, except in two important respects. In this report, HMI note that 'in contrast to the findings of the national primary survey there is more evidence in the first schools of work intended to help children to understand the physical and natural world and which might develop the children's skills of observation and lead to early scientific understanding' (op. cit., p.58). Secondly, they recommend that 'the amount of time spent on the main area of work in a B.Ed. degree course needs to be justified by its contribution to the student's professional competence in the classroom. In some cases the main subject might evolve from an extension of the study of a professional course – involving the necessary academic rigour – for example the study of "language" ' (op. cit., p.61).

Whether the findings would have been different if the surveys had covered predominantly Nursery and Infant classes, the supposed strongholds of 'progressivism', where the teachers might be expected to have a deeper understanding of the implementation of a unified curriculum, can only be surmised. The recommendations of both reports, although contradictory and muddled in parts, are nevertheless more in line with the 'progressive' than the elementary school tradition, not least because their findings suggested that this may lead to a more rapid rise in standards of attainment.

The direction that they envisage should be taken in planning the Primary curriculum is more clearly and succinctly expressed by HM Inspectors in the next document that we must consider.

Having received and reported on the reviews of local authority arrangements for the curriculum, the DES still sought to give a lead in the process of reaching a national consensus on a desirable framework for the curriculum. As a first step towards the achievement of this, therefore, the views of the inspectors were invited and these were set out in *A View of the Curriculum* (DES 1980a), which is perhaps the most sensible and thoughtful of all these recent government publications.

In their discussion of the Primary curriculum the inspectors indicate that, in their view, there are common purposes that can be expressed at a general level and can be seen to be appropriate for every school. They are in favour, however, of schools and classes within schools interpreting these in a highly individual way and they see good reasons why this should be so. They note in particular that the children will bring to the school different experiences, teachers will vary in their interests and competencies and schools may have access to very different resources.

In general they favour the maintenance of 'a wide curriculum', that is, one that is not predominantly concerned with the 3 Rs, for they argue that children achieve a better level of performance in the basic skills if they have many opportunities to use them in a broader context.

The only two areas where weaknesses are noted are 'the provision of observational and experimental science that is seriously lacking in many primary schools' (DES 1980a, p.11) and the teaching of French which is usually attempted inappropriately. In general, however, they feel that effort should now be directed towards helping teachers to develop to a greater extent the important skills and processes that the children are already engaged in learning. They argue that 'more extensive discussion is required on the levels to which work could and should be taken, at least for some children, in the various parts of the curriculum; for example, the identification of the skills and ideas associated with history and geography that are suitable for primary school children . . . Working parties of teachers, LEA advisers, inspectors and others have already shown what useful guidelines can be produced' (ibid.).

This seems to indicate that they are concerned with processes – in their terms 'necessary skills or underlying ideas' – rather than describing the 'protected areas' in terms of content. They argue, for example, that 'as children make progress their interests diversify and what is a stimulus to one may be a barrier to another. If the necessary skill or the underlying idea can be presented as well in one way as another then it may create unnecessary difficulties to use the same way with all children' (op. cit., p.8).

In summary, two kinds of thinking were emerging from central government at the end of the 1970s and finding expression in government documents. First, there was the viewpoint of the HMI at the time, who, in their role as professional advisers, urged that ways should be found to develop the existing curriculum by helping teachers both to frame essential processes more carefully and deepen their understanding of the skills and concepts that children should be developing in schools. Although confused in parts, the substance of their views focuses on the processes of education and their view of how learning should take place is that it should be essentially unified. One means of achieving this development, they argue, is through discussions of school policy at the local or even school level: discussions which aim to deepen every teacher's understanding. Another means is to develop a clearer picture of what these processes are and how they can best be learned in a meaningful way by children in schools.

Secondly, there was the view of the curriculum that was being promoted directly from the politicians of the Department of Education and Science. Although there had been a change of government since the Green Paper of 1977, the same desires as far curriculum is concerned continued to be expressed, coloured largely by the wish for teacher-accountability, for general aggreement on a common core of subjects and skills to be taught in all schools and for greater control over education and schooling by central government.

The new decade, however, marked a turning-point. For it is in the 1980s that a consistency of approach and policy emerged from both politicians and their professional advisers. The first document to herald this approach – the consultative document, *A Framework for the School Curriculum* (DES 1980b) – is significant in that it defined the parameters of the initiatives that followed and demonstrated the values and view of curriculum that would underpin both discussions of education and policies to be adopted at a national level.

In this document, the Secretaries of State detail the form, as they see it, that the curriculum should take. This form is largely defined in terms of content and we are returned to the familiar themes of the political debates of 1976.

They see planning as dependent on a clear statement of aims which will translate into achievable objectives. They attach importance to assessment procedures combined with l.e.a. record-keeping systems designed to check the achievement of these objectives. They urge the inclusion of 'common elements' – notably English, mathematics and science – which should form a substantial part of every school's work. The emphasis is on the products of education and on clearer means of measuring achievement, particularly in certain skills and knowledge areas.

This view of the curriculum, which is a blend of the product and content models, with the content defined in terms of traditional school subjects, is assumed in all the following documents. For example, in the 1983 White Paper, *Teaching Quality* (DES 1983a), it is argued that 'all primary teachers should be equipped to take a particular responsibility for one aspect of the curriculum (such as science, mathematics or music), to act as consultants to their colleagues on that aspect and, where appropriate, to teach it to classes other than their own' (op. cit., p.10), and in a later paper, *Better Schools* (DES 1985e), the recommendations for the curriculum are introduced with the statement that 'consultations with the government's partners in the education service and with other interests have shown that there is a widespread acceptance of the need to improve the standards achieved by pupils, and of the proposition that broad agreement about the objectives and content of the school curriculum is a necessary step towards that improvement' (op. cit., p.9).

Robin Alexander (1984) gives an evaluation of the impact on the Primary sector of the teaching profession of what he characterizes as 'the subject knowledge pure and simple' approach that has been adopted by both DES politicians and the HMI. For the purposes of this discussion, however, it is worth noting the fact that, since their discussion paper of 1980, the Inspectors too have switched back from an adjectival or adverbial description of subject matter, which, as we noted in Chapter 5, gave scope for a number of interpretations of the role of knowledge in education, to a substantive interpretation in their writings about curriculum content, and the reasons for this will offer interesting points of speculation for future historians.

It is also important to examine briefly three main policy initiatives which have been introduced by central government and developed by HMI since their approaches have merged, since these have a direct impact on the curriculum of the Primary school.

The first is the policy of attempting to define the objectives of an agreed national curriculum. Although, as was shown above, this policy is outlined in the government's White Papers, the details of it are set out more clearly in a series of pamphlets under the general title of 'Curriculum Matters', which are the HMIs' 'contribution to the process of developing general agreement about curricular aims and objectives' (DES 1984). (It is worth noting incidentally that the terms 'process' and 'developing' as used there have rather different connotations from our own usage of them throughout this book.) The publication of these pamphlets began in 1984, and the topics – or, more correctly, school subjects – covered so far are English (DES 1984), Mathematics (DES 1985b), Music (DES 1985c), Home Economics (DES 1985d) and Health Education (DES 1986a), with one pamphlet devoted to the whole curriculum (DES 1985a). These have been issued in the space of little more than one year. Comments are invited and one assumes that the views of the Primary teacher, as a class teacher, are sought on all of them.

The difficulty of commenting constructively upon them if one's model of curriculum is not one that places subject and product as the first considerations in curriculum planning will be obvious. Sometimes, as in the *English from 5 to 16* document (DES 1984), the difficulties of the approach are acknowledged, but this never leads to a questioning, or even an attempted justification, of the approach itself, not even in the HMI response to the comments and criticisms that were offered of this paper (DES 1986b). The problem is perceived as technical rather than fundamentally educational.

Although the matters under discussion purport to concern the curriculum from five years to sixteen years, which could imply that education is seen as an on-going process, at least until age sixteen, these matters are defined in terms of the subjects being studied currently at the end of this period. It is noted that teachers may refer to these subjects by different names at different stages – 'English' may be called 'language development' at the Primary stage, for example – but it is claimed that these different names have an identical meaning.

Each of these papers outlines aims, objectives and principles for the subjects, and objectives are defined, in some cases, for 7-year-olds and in all cases for 11- and 16-year-olds. These objectives are offered in a variety of taxonomies. In *Home Economics from 5 to 16* (DES 1985d), for example, objectives are grouped in relation to their contribution to 'values and attitudes', 'knowledge and concepts' and 'skills'; for mathematics the taxonomy is 'facts', 'skills', 'conceptual structures', 'general strategies' and 'personal qualities' (DES 1985); and the divisions of objectives for English are 'listening', 'speaking', 'reading', 'writing' and 'about language' (DES 1984). Even Benjamin Bloom would find such taxonomies primitive and unsatisfactory.

Many subjects are missing as yet, but the accumulated impact of those that have appeared presents the Primary class teacher with a bewildering array of requirements in a very short time. This in itself places a barrier against these teachers making a constructive response to the debate, but, as was noted above, the difficulties are compounded if their value stance is different and calls for a completely different approach to the curriculum and hence to its planning. The only discussion paper to consider the comments which have been made does so within 'the aims and objectives for English' model (DES 1986b), and ignores comments which both question this approach and challenge the strategy which would impose one approach to the exclusion of all others.

Perhaps the worst feature of this initiative – to achieve general agreement on curricular aims and objectives – is that it assumes that such agreement, although difficult, is possible. It assumes, in other words, the existence of only one approach, as if no others existed (as, indeed, is no doubt true in respect of the consciousness of its authors). As we have seen in earlier chapters, however, other options do exist and the advocates of these have for some time displayed the intellectual honesty of basing their advocacy on a careful analysis of the inadequacies of the alternatives. In particular, as we have seen they have highlighted the serious limitations of the 'aims and objectives' model of planning. Kieran Egan (1985), for example, argues that this approach, by encouraging them to concentrate on the organization of content and specified material (the agreed aims and objectives), causes teachers to ignore or even displace the most crucial factor in their curricular plans – the meaning that the child will attach to the experience of the planned curriculum. It could be argued that this first initiative is also displacing the meaning that teachers themselves, and especially Primary teachers, can find in curriculum planning.

The second policy initiative that central government has taken is to find more effective means of monitoring the performance of pupils, thus ensuring that these standards of performance are maintained in schools and, if possible, improved. As we noted earlier, the first widely publicized discussion of how this could be achieved on a national scale appears in the Bullock Report (DES 1975), which addresses itself to standards of literacy.

The members of the committee discuss the fact that a good deal of public attention is given to this area of the school's work and that disquiet has been expressed at the supposed fall of standards. They also show that on the existing evidence, national sample surveys carried out by the NFER (NFER 1955, 1960, 1970), reading standards have improved, although gains tended to level out over the decade 1960–1970. They argue that, although the results from surveys are not disturbing, they leave no room for complacency. In addition, they argue that both the tests and methods employed for measuring the movement in reading standards are inadequate. They strongly recommend, therefore, that a new system of monitoring these standards should be devised and introduced.

In their discussion of the form that monitoring should take, one important point emerges and this is that the scope of assessment should be extended to encompass a more demanding definition of literacy than simple reading performance. They argue, for example, that

> the existing criterion is determined by the reading standards of seven and nine year old children of many years ago on tests whose limitations are acknowledged. It should be replaced by a criterion capable of showing whether the reading and writing abilities of children are adequate to the demands made upon them in school and likely to face them in adult life. What we are proposing, then, is an entirely new approach. We are suggesting that monitoring should be extended beyond the limit of a single dimension to give more information than has ever been available before (DES 1975, p.36).

They go on to suggest that 'adequate research and development work should precede the introduction of such a system of monitoring' (op. cit., p.43).

These ideas of monitoring, discussed here in relation to literacy, are fundamental to the work of the Assessment of Performance Unit (APU) which was established in 1975 within the DES to provide information about general levels of performance of children at school. Although standards in literacy are one component of the work of the unit, its scope extends to cover most aspects of the school curriculum. Each team is investigating means of testing that will give a broader indication of achievement than is possible when only one type of test is used.

It should be noted, however, that the teams concerned to investigate mathematical and scientific understanding are far in advance of other teams in producing and implementing assessment procedures. Indeed, some areas seem to be presenting particularly difficult problems. Before it was disbanded, a paper was prepared for the exploratory group on aesthetic development, for example, and in it it is noted that 'many people experienced in this field are convinced that no comprehensive or adequate conceptual model for aesthetic experience yet exists. Nor has any real insight been gained into aesthetic development during childhood and adolescence. Nothing, for instance, exists in the field to compare with Piaget's work on conceptual development.' The paper goes on to argue, however, that 'the whole assessment exercise might, in drawing attention to the need for serious research in this area, prompt new initiatives.'

This problem of devising tests for more elusive (and some would argue more important) aspects of development also occurs in other areas. The team concerned with science, for example, faced similar difficulties, and this caused it to experiment with tests that would monitor the procedures that pupils adopted rather than the end-products of their learning, an approach which is being taken further by the team currently responsible for monitoring pupil performance in the sphere of design and technology.

The influence of this second initiative – the national monitoring of standards – remains something of an enigma. For, on the one hand, it seems inevitable that, by concentrating on pupil performance, a narrow view of accountability is being promoted. On the other hand, the teams working within the APU are concentrating on performance processes rather than performance products. In short, they are increasingly taking pains to find ways of measuring processes that are developing rather than adopting a narrow view by emphasizing facts that have been learnt or skills acquired.

It is even more difficult to evaluate the impact that the third initiative taken by central government will have on the Primary curriculum. For this initiative concerns the education – or training – of teachers. Nevertheless, it is important to note that this initiative – and in particular the aspects of it which are concerned with initial courses – is the most overtly political of the three strategies we have considered. For, as we saw earlier, DES have stipulated, quite unequivocally, that all students – including those who are preparing to teach in Primary and Nursery schools – will spend two years of a four-year B.Ed. course studying a subject area (DES 1983b), and in the new accreditation procedure for such courses, which has been established in addition to existing validation procedures and is administered by the Council for the Accreditation of Teacher Education (CATE), all courses will be inspected to ensure that they comply with the criteria established by DES. The imposition of a subject-centred view of curriculum is at its most obvious in this initiative, since it reflects a government requirement that the role of teacher-training should be to prepare teachers to teach a subject, and we will consider the implications of this when we examine the promotion of subject-specialisms later in this chapter. At this point we must merely note that the criteria by which CATE is required to assess these courses undermine the process approach to teacher education which we have discussed elsewhere (Blenkin and Kelly 1983b), not least because the learner's development – in this instance, the learner being the student-teacher and the development his/her professional development – is considered as of secondary importance to the acquisition of knowledge-content.

In summary, these three major initiatives from central government have, during the 1980s, dominated and shaped the discussions and evaluations of the curriculum at all levels of the schooling system. Their potential impact, we have argued, causes particular concern to those who are responsible for the curriculum in the Primary school, and this concern becomes alarm to those who are committed to a process rather than an 'aims and objectives' or content approach.

The full impact of these initiatives will be felt even more in a few years' time when the new teachers who have undergone these subject-centred courses will enter the schools. There has been a more immediate impact, however, at the level of the local education authorities, and the responses there have created a different kind of pressure on teachers and on the curriculum. For local authorities have been required by central government to develop curriculum policies and to review their assessment procedures in schools. It is to a consideration of developments in this sphere that we turn next, and we will begin with a consideration of their revisions of the arrangements for the keeping of school records.

The response of the local authorities

Although formal examinations are largely absent from the Primary schools since the majority are no longer involved in the 11+ examination procedures, there are of course still internal assessments which children undergo before transferring to the Secondary schools. These are mainly tests to assess levels of performance in language and reasoning and are intended to provide the objective evidence which will partly support the appropriate choice of school, although they are not intended to be the sole instrument for making that choice. Similarly, it is common practice to give children standardized tests at the age of seven years in order to assess their reading ages before they transfer from the Infant to the Junior departments of the Primary schools. In addition, a small minority of disturbed or slow-learning children may undergo diagnostic tests under the supervision of the educational psychologist, in order to aid decisions on appropriate action in relation to special education.

Apart from these examples, however, it is unusual to find either standardized tests or external examinations playing a significant part in the work of the schools. This is one important reason why the keeping of records – including the formal procedures required by the l.e.a.s – holds a particularly vital place in the work of the Primary teacher, since these are the only records of a child's attainments.

The formal records are designed largely to indicate the performance (mainly in reading and mathematics) of the child and also to give, however crudely, a profile of his/her personality and aptitude for work. These records are required, in other words, to be used at terminal points in the child's school career – at the end of a year or on transfer to a new teacher or school, for example.

There are other forms of records that are also used commonly and may be required of the teacher formally (by the headteacher or even the l.e.a.). These are the records of the teacher's planning and his/her evaluations of the work that has been undertaken with the children.

It is these two kinds of formal record-keeping system that have come to the fore as a result of the pressures for teacher-accountability. It is clear that the teacher's records – whether they indicate the individual child's achievements or present an evaluation of the teacher's work – are the most direct means of checking on the success or otherwise of the teacher's work. Much of the recent work in this sphere, therefore, has been the result of l.e.a. revisions of these formal records, revisions that reflect their response to the requests for information from the DES.

Local authorities have begun to strengthen and extend their requirements of teachers with regard to the keeping of records and the local advisers have begun to adopt a more active supervisory role in order to ensure that the schools carry out these requirements. With such a flurry of activity from their employers, which has clearly been designed to measure their effectiveness, it is hardly surprising that teachers should be apparently eager to adopt approaches that promise clear indication of progress on the part of pupils. In a situation that demands proof of achievements, teachers can perhaps be forgiven for choosing to ignore whether or not the tangible results are educational in nature.

What is apparent, however, is that the local authority inspectors, who had the opportunity of ensuring that the schools received the best advice available in relation to the keeping of records (a supportive process considered crucial by Plowden), seemed themselves in many instances to be promoting planning styles which were instrumental and out of step with the more advanced educational work that had been developed in some schools. This was reflected in the record sheets produced by the l.e.a.s which tended to be simplistic and gave teachers little scope to indicate the broader aspects of the work that children undertook. The elements that were considered worth recording were narrow and easily assessed and the teacher's attention was directed at the child's achievements rather than emerging processes.

The main line of argument and action of the l.e.a.s hinged on the belief that, if aims could be expressed with clarity and, where possible, in operational terms, then it would be a simple matter to achieve them. This was certainly an argument expressed in the documents discussed above. It was also an idea that was central to the only large-scale national project that had been concerned with offering teachers a framework for recording in detail the work of the school.

This was the Schools Council's project Aims of Primary Education, whose work we have repeatedly noted. It is now worth examining this work in more detail for two main reasons. Firstly, it provides us with an example of work undertaken which typifies the response to the criticisms made of Plowden. For the intention is to place the teacher's planning on a more systematic footing. Secondly, it was one of the few pieces of work available from Primary education in the sphere of curriculum planning when the events of the late 1970s heralded a national interest in accountability. Although, like other national projects, it had little direct impact on the teachers in the schools, it did offer the local authorities a model for resolving their urgent problem and its influence can be traced, therefore, through the activities of the advisers in l.e.a.s.

The project team undertook this work in three main phases – they attempted firstly to clarify the constraints on teacher's planning, secondly, to survey the opinions of school teachers in order to help them to clarify what their aims were and, thirdly, to provide the teachers with a model in order to aid them in translating their aims into practice.

It should be noted that, contrary to the claims in Plowden that good teachers were unable to make explicit their aims, the survey found no such difficulty, and listed 2000 aims, collected from teachers in the full Primary range. Admittedly these were uneven in their levels of abstraction, and many would be better described as objectives. It was discovered, for example, that, in the teachers' minds, 'the child should be developing community responsibility is ranged alongside the child should be able to write legibly . . . In terms of curriculum theory, there is an inadmissable mixture of aims and objectives. But in the teachers' terms there is an equivalence of importance, of concern to them in their work with children' (Ashton, Kneen and Davies 1975, p.4).

It should also be noted that 'surveys of teachers' opinions on aims may have their uses, but they cannot settle what those aims ought to be' (Dearden 1976, p.29). The Schools Council survey did not set out to do this, but did suggest that it would be useful for much work to be done in this sphere. What the research team did attempt to do (and this element of their work has been one source of influence in subsequent work on assessment, evaluation and accountability) was to help teachers both to formulate their aims and, more significantly, to translate them into practice.

The project team has produced, as part of its material, a guide to assist teachers in this task. The practice of formulating aims is justified by claiming that aims clarify thinking about education, they give a sense of direction, they clarify the implications of apparent incompatibilities in the work undertaken, they clarify in the teacher's mind his/her own commitment, they enable the best use to be made of limited resources, they aid the selection of the best methods and resources and, finally, they aid evaluation. What strikes one immediately when reading the justification of stating aims in this project is that there is a marked similarity between these justifications and those of Hilda Taba that were discussed in Chapter 3 (Taba 1962). Although, as was noted above, the work of the project was not intended to be prescriptive, there is a strong flavour of a behavioural approach in the translation of aims into achievable objectives. In the examples of this approach to planning which were produced by teachers as a result of discussions with members of the team, it is clear that a more formal method is adopted in planning for the older children. For even the Infant age-groups, however, the immediate objective is also behavioural and the intention is to look for the end-product, although the method and grouping to be adopted are both expressed in more informal terms.

In all the examples given, planning is linked to one of the schedules or spheres that we noted in Chapter 3, and is then detailed sequentially under seven headings:

1 Assessment
2 Aims (broken into three levels of specificity)
3 Content
4 Teaching method
5 Time allocation
6 Organization (of materials and classroom)
7 Organization of the children (by age, ability and number)
(Ashton, Kneen and Davies 1975).

Most of the examples of planned work that are given are designed for the development of mathematical learning, but the strategy that is advocated by the project team for the translation of aims into practice (which is as unwieldy as many of the similar strategies attempted in America) is intended to be applied to all aspects of curriculum planning though it is admitted that 'when it came to qualities, the kinds of feelings and attitudes and dispositions that the child should have, the task was infinitely more problematic' (op. cit., p.5.).

The project team does, however, come out in strong support of the behavioural objectives approach. They argue, as we saw, that 'if the teacher's aims are to help to guide his practice, then they should 'be expressed in behavioural terms. That is to say that they should state what the child will actually be able to do when the aim is achieved . . . Concentrating on what the child is intended to know, to be able to do, and so on, also helps the teacher by preventing the intrusion of method into the statement of aims' (op. cit., p.15).

Another piece of research that was available to l.e.a. advisers and administrators at the time of the first request for a review of their record-keeping systems was the NFER research project, Record-Keeping in the Primary School (NFER 1977), and in this project the same approach is adopted. For example, the discussion documents provided for teachers recommend 'a need for aims and objectives' if work is to be assessed effectively. Teachers are advised to consider elements such as,

(a) Analysis of aims into more specific objectives which can be used as a basis for record-keeping.
(b) What aspects of behaviour, (cognitive, affective and psychomotor) need to be recorded, i.e., What significant events? (NFER 1977).

This team's approach to the problem is also clearly based on a behavioural objectives model. In fact their analysis is more directly derivative of Bloom's taxonomy than is that of the Aims of Primary Education project described above.

It is interesting to contrast this example with the extreme caution expressed in the Introduction to the parallel work on assessment in Nursery education, for here the stated intention is to serve the needs of teachers not to impose external standards on them. Teachers are warned, therefore, that the assessment procedures produced by this team 'have been designed as a resource to be used not a target at which to aim. It is a recognized danger that assessment instead of producing useful information about children's development and performance may come to determine what is taught' (Bate and Smith 1978, p.8). It is clear that, although both teams were working to produce materials for assessment, the materials produced for the youngest children were presented with more caution and attempted to support the developmental tradition which, it can be argued, is stronger in the Nursery schools.

It is as well to be reminded again, however, that the work has been undertaken in a climate of economic stringency, when considerable public pressure has been placed on teachers to make themselves accountable for their work with children, and to try to ensure value for money. It is, therefore, understandable that they should seek security in an apparently systematic approach which stresses measurable end-products. When they are presented with a large collection of tasks for children to use and a record sheet designed to record the performances on the tasks, as is the case in the Assessment in Nursery Education project mentioned above and in many l.e.a. record sheets, it is difficult to envisage how teachers can avoid the urge to teach for performance.

One further point needs to be added and this is the fact that the most difficult elements of the child's development to assess – his/her feelings, attitudes and aesthetic awareness – are set aside in each of the examples that we have examined so far. We noted the comments made by the team involved in the Schools Council's Aims in Primary Education project. The NFER team argue that 'the possibility of assessing aesthetics was considered but deemed to be almost unassessable at nursery age. It was thought undesirable that teachers should make value judgements of children's aesthetic sense' (Bate and Smith 1978, p.170). The implication is that the judgements made in other areas (social skills, for example) can be objective and thus are desirable.

It can be argued, then, that, as teachers are pressured into accountability by local and central government, there is 'a return to simple objectives, a reduced "say" for both teachers and pupils in determining the content of their work, a move away from "democratic" towards "autocratic" and "bureaucratic" styles of evaluation and a resultant slowing down or even arresting of the pace of curriculum development' (Kelly 1977, p.180).

Some of these effects have certainly been noted in the projects discussed above and in the formal records produced by the l.e.a.s, for what they are doing is to advocate that teachers' aims should be translated into behavioural objectives if they are to be of use in practice. It is in the process of doing this that teachers are being misled into a distortion of their aims through the unwitting acceptance of an unsuitable curriculum model.

It certainly seems to be the case that teachers are being encouraged to consider a particular approach which runs counter to the ideology that has in many cases shaped their practice. In adopting the instrumental approach, apparently without considering its serious limitations, they are setting aside, first of all, the strengths of the child-centred ideology – in Dearden's terms 'the relational aims' – rather than using these aims to advantage and, in addition, developing from them the unified approach that we described in Chapter 5. In doing so, they are losing the strengths of the informal approach to education, and adopting instead an approach which restricts the freedom of both the child and the teacher. At the very least, there is an unresolved tension and a fundamental contradiction between this newly adopted behavioural objectives approach and the mainstream ideology of the Primary school.

Before leaving this discussion of teachers' records, however, we must note that not all of the recent developments have been within an objectives model of planning. There is evidence that the teachers themselves have gone some way towards the complex problem of recording both their own planning and the children's development within the informal, unified approach that we described in earlier chapters, as the example noted in Chapter 4 illustrates (Bierley 1983).

It must also be noted that some attempt has been made by a few l.e.a.s to extend this school-based approach to record-keeping. This is usually done by offering discussion documents or guidelines so that the staff of a school can develop records of observations to include examples of the child's achievements in addition to his/her 'experience' in certain areas. It is stated, for example, by one group of mathematics inspectors that 'an item by item assessment is of immediate value to the class teacher in maintaining success for each child. A record of specific achievements, rather than experiences, is also of long term value' (ILEA 1978, p.1). They go on to argue that records of this kind are more useful as they can be passed on to other teachers, can be used as diagnostic checks when little is known of a child's abilities and can provide a basis for comparing a child's ability with others for grouping purposes.

Schemes of this kind which give focus to school-based discussions are generally to be applauded as they avoid prescription from outside and place stress on support for the teacher, who, in the end, is the one to make the decisions.

From these last examples it can be seen that record-keeping can not only help the teacher to give an account of his/her work but also can enable him/her to develop his/her professional skills – to 'match' rather than 'mismatch' his/her planning to the child's level of development. The need to give an account of work thus becomes merely one of many professional reasons for keeping records and assessing pupil performance.

This is by no means true of all the examples of teachers' records that have been devised as we saw earlier. Many of them seem to have been designed to respond only to the demands for accountability and, in doing so, they serve to undermine both the teachers' judgements and the unified view of the curriculum that we have argued should be developed in the Primary school.

To a great extent, the development of assessment procedures has been a form of structure for the teacher's work that has either been imposed from outside the school or been encouraged to develop within it in the ways we have described above. This is one important area in which l.e.a.s. have made the impact of central government's active interest in the curriculum felt in their schools. The desire for a clearer structure, however, goes beyond record-keeping. A more general interest in structuring the curriculum has been a further way in which local authority demands for accountability have influenced developments in schools.

One practical way in which some teachers have been faced by this general question of structure, for example, is through the policy statements which they have been required to make to their local education authorities and to school governors. As we saw in our earlier discussion of government documents, not only have the l.e.a.s been urged to tighten their school record systems but also they have been advised to collect annually information from their schools about the curriculum that is offered. The need to understand the structure of the work they plan, then, has become a reality to the staff of the schools because of requests to express this structure in a coherent school policy.

The first observation that needs to be made here is that again the structure can take many forms. We have discussed in earlier chapters that it can be described in a linear and hierarchical form or it can be seen to be modular. We showed that the practical outcomes of adopting a particular structure have a direct impact on the work that is undertaken with children.

The differences in approaches are underlined, for example, in this extract from a discussion of the formulation of a school or classroom language policy which was produced by one local education authority's teachers' centre.

> Teachers will always disagree about what a 'language policy statement' should consist of. The statements that we see at C.L.P.E. vary enormously in their range of attitudes towards language and the types of language activities that they examine. . . . Their purpose is to help teachers to clarify and perhaps also justify the sort of language activities that go on in their schools. If they don't help teachers to think through more clearly the policy of their schools . . . then they might just as well not be written. . . . I personally prefer to begin with a description of what actually happens and follow this with a statement of why; others prefer to start with a list of aims and objectives and go on to say how they fulfil them (Warlow 1978).

Although it is implicit in this statement, what is not made clear to the teachers by this l.e.a. adviser is that the approach that they choose to adopt will influence directly all aspects of their work. No such choice is given to the teachers in most local authorities, however, for schools have, in general, been asked not for their school policies, but for a statement of their 'aims and objectives' within particular subject areas. Kent Local Education Authority, for example, initiated an 'aims and objectives' exercise in 1978 – referred to by two observers as the 'As and Os exercise' in an abbreviated style that is typical not of educational debate but of that of the managers of industry – and, in a report of their investigation into the impact that this exercise had on schools, Parsons and Steadman note that 'Kent's initiative may be viewed as one of the earliest moves in a national trend, a trend towards a greater supervision of, and influence upon, the school curriculum. Indeed, schemes like Kent's probably go some way to satisfying the DES, on a general administrative level, that the LEA is maintaining proper oversight of the curriculum' (1984, p.14). They go on to argue that the exercise certainly made teachers think – so much so that they adopt this as the title of their report. Unfortunately, they do not clarify whether, by this, they mean that the 'As and Os' exercise encouraged teachers to reflect critically on the planning of their work or to think in a particular way, for, although it is stressed that flexibility was encouraged by the authority, this flexibility was always within the same narrow 'aims and objectives' structure.

It is clear, then, that teachers need first of all to be alerted to the dangers of adopting a model uncritically when they are planning their policies. They also need to he helped to clarify what a policy is – which aspects of structure, in other words, they are to be concerned with. Unfortunately, few local authorities have supported teachers in their attempts to resolve these issues. Most have, presumably in their haste to document the policies, made the simplistic assumption that an educational policy – like an administrative policy – requires no more than the stating of 'aims and objectives'.

It is an attempt to provide teachers with some clarification in this sphere that underlies the work of the Schools Council's Learning Through Science project. The members of the project team attempt to spell out the aspects of planning that need to be considered when formulating a school policy and they offer guidance on the compilation of the policy document.

Although they sometimes appear to take on the rhetoric of an objectives model, it is clear that they are wishing to help teachers to give coherence to a process model. Attention is given to the place of science in the overall work of the school, stress is on school-based development, where teachers are encouraged and guided to increase their own expertise, and importance is attached to constant revision of the policy. All of these elements are included in the summary of this aspect of the team's work, and we can do no better than to quote this in full.

The following table is a suggested strategy for forming a school policy for science.

The Policy
An intention on the part of a school staff to agree areas of knowledge and experience, enumerate appropriate attitudes, skills and concepts, decide upon methods of evaluation and place these within an organisational framework which will give sufficient guidance to ensure effective and consistent teaching of science throughout the school.

The strategy
1   Discuss and decide upon what is meant by science.

2   Discuss and decide on the reasons for carrying out science with children in the age range appropriate to your school.

Make a brief written statement of these reasons.

3   Discuss and decide what experiences are most suitable for the children in your school.

Give full consideration to:
Use of source books.
Thinking about starting points from everyday situations that arise, or can be engineered, in school.
Use of the school, school grounds and local environment.
Science from interdisciplinary studies.

Make a comprehensive, written documentation of such experience.

4   Discuss and decide on ways to organise the work. Give full consideration to:
The amount of time needed.
Different methods of organisation.
Resources.

General Discussion of:
How to arrange the classroom.
Finding starting points.
How to plan investigations or projects.
The best ways to develop children's enquiries

5   Discuss ways of evaluating children's progress.

Try and use the findings from this discussion to agree on a form of record-keeping for science.

The outcome
A written document that gives all members of staff a clear idea of why they should be presenting scientific experiences to children, and how they should go about presenting such experiences.

Such a document should be subject to periodic review and frequently updated. Then the policy becomes a resource that maintains the school as a dynamic place of learning.

(Schools Council 1980, p.29)

We can see that the intention of this approach is to encourage curriculum development within the school as well as to assist teachers in giving an account of their policies. It is also clear that it is endeavouring to do these things within the context of the informal, enquiry-based approach of the Primary school.

We have shown, through the above examples, that there has been an increasing interest on the part of local authorities in defining the structures of both the teacher's planning of the curriculum and the child's learning, and that a main feature of this interest has been the need to give some account of the work undertaken in school, often in a form prescribed by the authority and not the school. We have also revealed, however, that this interest has not always been pursued with complete clarity concerning precisely what it entails. It is crucial that efforts be directed at achieving such clarity in what is a very important aspect of this approach to education.

In summary, we have indicated that an increase in political involvement in education has influenced many of the recent developments in Primary education. We have examined these developments in some detail and have argued that, although it is right that teachers should be called to account and this process can be of positive value in clarifying and developing their understanding of their work, in most cases the means by which accountability and political control are being sought are undermining the more advanced work of the schools. In other words, in reality, the demand for accountability in some cases is promoting instrumentalism and detracting from the processes of education.

Throughout our discussion of the effects on the Primary curriculum of the increased political involvement in education, we have made constant reference to a strong demand for subject specialisms. This also has the effect of undermining the unified approach, and, indeed, the process approach, to curriculum which has been developed in the Primary school. It is to a closer examination of this influence that we now turn.

The influence of subject specialists

The usual approach in the Primary school, unlike that of the Secondary school, is to adopt a one-teacher system – that is, an arrangement that assigns to one teacher the responsibility for most of the work of one class. Exceptions may be made in the case of music, physical education, modern languages or religious education, but, even with these exceptions, the majority of the child's programme is planned by one teacher. Indeed, as we argued in Chapter 5, this complete responsibility has been an important reason for the advancement of a unified curriculum.

This class-teaching model is, as Robin Alexander (1984) rightly points out, an historical accident in the sense that it derives from the form in which state elementary schools were established in the nineteenth century. It can be seen, however, as a happy accident as, in its twentieth century form, it provides an organizational structure in which the young child can form a close relationship with his/her teacher and this can provide a secure base from which his/her learning and development can be promoted.

The importance of this close relationship between child and adult is asserted with particular force in relation to the education of very young children (Wells 1981). It could be argued, however, that it is a vital component of teaching and learning at all stages, and not just in the sense that it provides emotional and social stability for the learner. For, if one's theory of instruction is of the kind proposed by Bruner and Eisner which we considered in Chapter 1, in order to extend the understanding of the learner, the teacher and the learner must negotiate and share meanings, and this presupposes, at the very least, that they work within an organizational structure which enables them to get to know each other well.

Recently, however, as we saw at the start of this chapter, this one-teacher system has become a source of concern, particularly in government circles, for it has been argued that, as the scope of the curriculum widens, many teachers are finding difficulty in coping and are reducing the quality of their work as they increase the quantity. This is the first source, therefore, of an interest in the introduction of subject specialisms into the Primary school.

This argument takes broadly two forms. The first claims that the range of work that remains to be covered, even if the above exceptions are made, places heavy demands on the teacher's knowledge and skills and many teachers are not able to meet these demands. As we saw earlier, this was a reason given by the HMIs in their survey (DES 1978) for the general neglect or poor teaching in certain important areas of human experience. Subjects such as science, history, geography and craft were all cited by them as generally suffering from this neglect.

Within their recommendations, therefore, the inspectors argue that subject specialists should be employed in Primary schools. They also argue that the existing teachers should be encouraged to develop their particular strengths for the purpose of extending the experiences of all the children in the schools by teaching certain aspects of content to classes other than their own.

They take note of the strengths of the 'one class to one teacher' system (op.cit., p.117) and acknowledge the dangers of undermining these advantages by introducing measures that will fragment the child's experience at school. They argue, however, as we saw in Chapter 5, that

> when a teacher is unable to deal satisfactorily with an important aspect of the curriculum, other ways of making this provision have to be found. If a teacher is only a little unsure, advice and guidance from a specialist, probably another member of staff, may be enough. In other cases, more often with older than with younger children, and much more often in Junior that in Infant schools, it may be necessary for the specialist to teach either the whole class or a group of children for particular topics . . . perhaps more subjects, in particular science, should be added to the curriculum list, at least for the older children (op.cit., p.118).

Some attempt to combat such weaknesses in a school's facilities has been made, of course, by establishing posts of special responsibility. The inspectors express disappointment at the fact that, in the great majority of cases, teachers holding such posts have made very little impact on either the school's work in general or on the work of individual teachers.

The HMIs, then, were in the late 1970s tentatively advancing the cause of subject teaching as one way of combating the weaknesses of the school curriculum. In the context of their overall recommendations, and in the light of their warnings about fragmenting the curriculum, however, it is obvious that they did so somewhat reluctantly.

We also saw earlier, however, that the politicians at the DES in general have shown no such reluctance in trying to advance subject teaching, and that the HMI have switched course and joined them in their determination to introduce subject specialisms into both teacher education and curriculum planning. Their reasons for doing so, however, are somewhat different and provide the second administrative argument for introducing subject-based teaching.

It was made obvious in the first part of this chapter that both of these groups are seeking national agreement on a common core of subjects and skills that will form the substance of the school's work. In the Primary school, in their view, the core should include the 'basic skills', science and religious education, and a large proportion of the child's time at school should be devoted to learning these common elements. Their main arguments for establishing agreement on the common core are those to do with accountability and national consistency which we have already discussed. In addition, however, a concentration on the core areas (the basic minimum of schooling) is seen as a means of ensuring that children who have weaker teachers will be at less of a disadvantage, as the scope of work of these teachers could be reduced to cover only the core areas.

Although this latter argument is not in itself concerned with the educational reasons for establishing a common core (those educational arguments to do with the nature and status of knowledge that we discussed in Chapter 2), since it stems from a concern to preserve and promote at the centre of the school's work the knowledge and skills whose importance derives from their social and economic utility, it does restrict educational discussions. It is clear that the DES is determined to establish agreement on the 'framework of the curriculum' or the 'common core' so that discussion can only focus on the content which is to be included. Unlike the approach that we argued was distinctive of the Primary curriculum, which stresses those processes that develop from the unity of the child's experience, this desire for national consensus is placing the stress on separate bodies of knowledge and skills which must be promoted in all schools and acquired by all children.

The view of both the HMIs and the DES assume that the widening scope of the curriculum is the result of an increase in content. As we also showed in Chapter 2, however, curriculum development does not inevitably mean an increase of or change in content. It is the process that underlies the content that is important.

The second way in which an interest in subject specialisms is influencing the curriculum is also partly administrative and based on the same assumptions. This time, however, it is linked to administrative and organizational factors that are internal to the teaching profession. Most of the recent large-scale attempts at curriculum enrichment, as we noted in our Introduction, have taken as their points of reference the curriculum theory that has been generated by those whose interests lie in Secondary education.

In the Schools Council, for example, most of the committees were linked to a subject or discipline. Admittedly there was one committee responsible for developments in Primary education and some of the projects therefore were able to explore more general curriculum issues. (The Aims of Primary Education project that we have already discussed is one example of work dealing with wider issues than those of content.) In general, however, the projects of the Schools Council were limited to curriculum development within subjects and, in the later stages of its work at least, relied heavily on subject specialists (usually from university departments) for advice and guidance. This, in turn, has led Primary teachers to see curriculum development in terms of content only and has encouraged them to 'look to subject programmes, again usually constructed in behavioural terms, in order to develop work in content areas' (Blenkin 1980, p.63).

These subject areas have not only been given prominence by national bodies like the Schools Council. They have also proved to be a lucrative source for publishers who have had considerable success in promoting commercially produced programmes in particular subject areas.

The two subjects which have had most attention in this respect, as we have constantly pointed out, are, of course, science and mathematics. We have already noted that these two areas are likely to be the weak points in the work of most Primary schools and this view has been reinforced – in science, at least – by the findings of the HMIs' survey. Indeed, most Primary teachers would admit to finding the teaching of mathematics and science difficult. We will begin, therefore, by examining two programmes that have been produced for the teaching of mathematics.

The first is a commercially produced programme called Mathematics for Schools which has had such an impact on the work of the schools that the author's name has become synonymous with mathematics for many teachers. It is not uncommon, for example, to hear the children in many schools being asked by their teachers to work at their 'Fletcher books' rather than at mathematics or number.

The authors claim to be concerned with 'more than the results of mathematics. . . . Rather, we have stressed th∋ thorough understanding of concepts and then the application of those concepts to new situations.' They go on to claim that their series is concerned with 'the course of all mathematical experiences, and the logical and psychological processes involved, from the reception class upward in all types of schools' (Fletcher 1970, p.2).

The workbooks for children which they offer are designed to build on and extend the existing practice in informal schools. They depend, therefore, on the teacher's first arranging activities for the children with real materials and then discussing these activities with the children. The books are intended to be used to practise the concepts which the teacher judges have been newly acquired by the children as a result of the activities.

In reality, however, this is rarely the case, as teachers tend to rely entirely on the children's workbooks supported by a small amount of practical materials, such as counters. The same problem of misuse applies to this material as that we noted earlier when we discussed the practical tests produced by the NFER. As we argued then, placing sequenced material of this kind in schools is unlikely to improve the teacher's practice. The evidence of those who have tried to do so suggests that good teachers become inhibited by the sequence and weak teachers become over-dependent on the materials. It would be a comfort if the activities asked of children by these books were at least a substitute for poor teaching, but many children (and adults!) quite rightly become confused by the instructions which are given, because they depend largely on two-dimensional sketches, a very difficult medium for expressing with clarity what is expected.

It is claimed by the authors, however, that the books fulfil five purposes. They 'aim to provide learning situations, use stimulating methods of presentation of the pages, show the structural development of mathematics, provide practice and consolidation and make evaluation possible' (Fletcher 1970, p.4). And so teachers who do not read beyond this will gain the impression that the series of books constitutes a full course of mathematics. However, the teacher's guide goes on to give detailed suggestions for practical work to supplement and reinforce that required by the workbooks. Thus teachers often fall between the two stools of, on the one hand, using the scheme to support their own informal teaching of mathematics and, on the other, relying on the children's books to provide a complete and sequentially structured programme of learning. In this, they are reflecting an ambivalence that can be observed in the scheme itself.

For, although it is said in the teacher's manual that the children's books are intended to assist in the learning of concepts when such learning has been sparked off by other activities or experiences the children have been having, they are arranged so that the mathematical concepts to be learned are sequential. Each book is sectioned so that various concepts at a certain level can be practised and the sections within one book are all linked to a discussion of the objectives of the work which appears in the teacher's guide. 'The objectives for each section,' the authors explain, 'are stated for the most part in terms of child behaviour. We have used this form of statement so that you can determine by discussion and observation when the children are familiar with the concepts detailed in each section and are ready to move on or, conversely, when they are not ready and are in need of further activities and discussion' (Fletcher 1970, p.4).

'Fletcher' mathematics, then, is an attempt to introduce a sequenced programme of mathematics into an informal setting. The materials are devised in such a way that the logical structure of the subject forms the sequence of learning for the child. It becomes, in other words, the blueprint for practice. Before each level is attempted, objectives are prespecified in behavioural terms and these form the basis of assessing the child's success. There is, however, some attempt to encourage teachers to use this programme in conjunction with a more integrated approach based on the child's exploration of the environment.

No such concession is made, however, in our second example, the Kent Mathematics Project. For it aims to present an independent programme in the form of the kind of 'teacher-proof' material that is a typical product of the objectives model as used by specialists to plan a system based on the demands of a subject, despite the claim that it is teacher-produced in all aspects of material, system and classroom organization. It is, therefore, a mathematics programme in its purest form and is packaged in such a way as to enable it to be used quite separately from other aspects of the school's work. It is not surprising that this approach to planning should be adopted within an authority which advanced, as we saw earlier, an 'aims and objectives' exercise.

The project is designed for children between nine and sixteen years of age, so that its main impact is on work at the later Primary stage. The build-up to acquire the necessary 'entry concepts and skills', however, has some inevitable influence on the work undertaken by younger childen in the schools that are using the project.

The tasks are presented (mainly in workcard form) in 'a material bank' and this includes work at nine mathematical levels which form a 'hierarchy of concept development'. The authors argue that concepts are developed through linear sequences of tasks, although these sequences interweave in a highly complex way. They claim that their 'material bank' takes full account of all these interrelationships and they try to illustrate this by using as an example the position in 'the grand framework' of 'the Pythagoras task'.

'This [the Pythagoras task] assumes understanding of area and requires the pupil to calculate squares and square roots. Also, the pupils have been introduced to Pythagoras through a concrete stage involving construction, cutting out and fitting triangles' (Kent County Council 1978, p.10). They then go on to indicate the number of concept lines in Level 2 in flow-plan form:

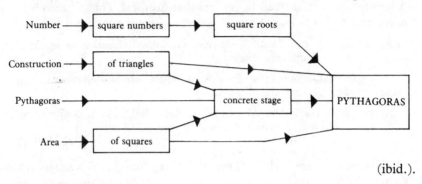

(ibid.).

The tasks themselves are derived from the 'concept hierarchy'. Each task is preceded by the task objective and it is explained that these usually describe briefly what the pupil should be able to do after working through the task. They go on to argue that it is not always possible to describe precise changes in pupil behaviour, and so some objectives describe the intention of the task in terms which do not describe the end-state 'but what should happen to the pupil during the task' (op.cit., p.11). 'Objectives have been designed in a form intended to be the most helpful to the teacher' (ibid.), that is, by expressing them in terms of the mathematics rather than in terms of the children's learning.

The project team has, of course, devised a system which provides a record of the pupil's work – 'the network' – which is based on the concept framework and incorporates codes to indicate the successful completion of tasks. The team explains that 'the position of a task in the framework is therefore an identification of the level of mathematics learning in an objectively designed structure of concept development and can be used for monitoring a pupil's progress and, if needed, for assessment purposes' (op. cit., p.13).

We can see, from the above evidence, that this project's approach is even more strictly behavioural than that of the Mathematics for Schools programme. Taken together, however, they constitute examples of materials produced by specialist mathematicians and in use at both ends of the Primary school. The first is widely used in work with young children and the second with older children. They also typify both in approach and content a wealth of other material that has been produced recently by mathematicians. This is despite the supposed success of the child-centred 'new mathematics' which many thought would transform the teaching in this sphere of the work of the Primary school.

One reason for the popularity of these programmes is, of course, that teachers feel more inadequate in this area than in others. This certainly was one finding of a recent Schools Council survey, where it was found that

> some teachers would favour a stronger centralized direction to mathematics teaching. For example, one suggested:

> . . . a manual, nationally accepted, showing the step-by-step procedure in the teaching of each phase of mathematics.

> Although few teachers would want to go as far as this . . . such views are evidence of a widespread feeling of uncertainty in the present situation

> (Ward 1979, p.57).

This survey also showed, however, that a large number of teachers are not looking to experts to pre-package material for them, but are anxious to develop their own expertise and improve their own teaching. It was found that 'understanding' was a key-word which constantly recurred in the replies to the questionnaires and it was sought for both teachers and pupils.

The government's solution is, of course, to turn some of the teachers themselves into mathematicians who will operate within the schools. It should be noted, however, that projects like the ones discussed above are unlikely to offer teachers an opportunity for developing their understanding for the reasons we discussed in Chapter 3. It is also unlikely that they will enable children to become mathematically educated in the widest sense, even if the mathematician is their teacher, for concept attainment is stressed at the expense of the process of concept development and the pupil is passively guided through the logical structure of the subject rather than to the logical structuring of his/her own understanding.

Finally, we must draw attention to the fact that the designing of materials that are to be learned strictly in accordance with the logical structure of the subject is likely to undermine or neglect other important elements. Mathematics, of course, being the most logical of the areas of human understanding, lends itself well to treatment of this kind. If teachers are encouraged to emphasize only the cognitive component as it manifests itself in the structure of the subject, however, they are unlikely to generate a commitment to mathematical understanding in their pupils, for, as the Cockcroft Report (DES 1982b) has pointed out, a mathematical education is not only a matter of the achievement of understanding of abstract concepts. It is also, for example, a matter of social and emotional development, the development of competence and self-image. This point about the learning of mathematics has been highlighted in studies of the sex-role stereotyping that occurs through the hidden curriculum of the Primary school. For in the sphere of mathematics the impact of stereotyping has been revealed in its starkest form. Many teachers view boys as ideal learners of mathematics, regardless of the evidence of the children's approaches to problems and the achievements of individual children, and many girls see themselves as less good at mathematics than boys, regardless of their personal performance (Walden and Walkerdine 1982).

It has also been shown, through studies of child development and not mathematics, that, far from being defeated by the concepts of number, children have, from a very early age – even as young as three and four years – a coherent set of principles for reasoning about numbers (Gelman and Gallistel 1978). They have the ability, for example, to perform simple additions and subtractions if the numbers involved are small. It is the formal codes of mathematics, not the concepts, that cause children confusion and difficulty – the language of learning not its structure. In a fascinating research study, 'What is difficult about learning arithmetic?', Martin Hughes (1983) devises games which enable young children to move in their thinking about, and in their performance of, arithmetical operations, back and forth between modes of representation that take a real form and those that use the formal code of mathematics. He argues that it is the 'translation procedures' – the strategies that the child can develop for translating concrete expressions to expressions in code and vice versa – that are crucial to success in understanding arithmetic. He argues that the teachers should concentrate on providing children with experiences that will demonstrate to them 'that there are situations where numbers – and operator signs – do indeed make life easier, where there is a rationale for using them, and where there is a purpose for making translations between symbols on the one hand and concrete objects and events on the other. If we can continue to keep this principle at the forefront of our teaching throughout school, then we may be able to make learning arithmetic a much easier process' (op.cit., p.221).

As can be seen from the above examples, it is important that, as with all learning in the Primary school, we keep in mind the meaning that the child is attaching to mathematical experiences, the processes and competencies that s/he is developing and the contribution that the learning of mathematics can make to his/her overall development. It must be added that teachers too need to be encouraged to understand the meaning and the usefulness of these processes to the development of human understanding. And this must mean all teachers, not just those who devote a large proportion of their time in training to a study of the subject itself. Indeed, it is by no means self-evident that an extended study of mathematics in itself will highlight the crucial nature of these processes to those teachers who opt to become mathematics consultants. There is no evidence, for example, that those mathematicians who have produced schemes and courses for teachers have considered this themselves, for all have focused on the structure of the subject first and the child's learning of it second, rather than seeing both as significant in relation to their contribution to the learner's overall development.

This concentration on subject structure has indeed led eminent mathematicians, both here and in the United States, to produce schemes which not only bewilder and alienate the young children for whom they are designed but also have engendered the same response in mature and intelligent teachers. There is no reason to suppose that a specialist mathematics teacher in each school will significantly change this situation – certainly not if their mathematical expertise derives primarily – or even exclusively – from their knowledge of the subject itself.

It is important, therefore, that all teachers should begin by developing an understanding of the importance of educational processes that will support the child's development and will lead to an increase in his/her powers of reflective thinking. This is particularly true in the sphere of mathematics, as, at present, most teachers see mathematics, more than any other sphere, as the domain of specialists.

This is not an argument for discouraging teachers from developing a special flair or expertise within one sphere of human endeavour – quite the reverse. For, as Eisner (1982) points out, human beings vary in the cognitive and representational styles that they favour, and this means that individual teachers will have developed different aptitudes before they embark upon their professional education. In short, their special interests and abilities will vary. And it is important that these strengths should be nurtured in their initial courses – indeed, throughout their careers – since teachers, above all other members of the adult community, need to demonstrate that they are good learners. We have stressed the importance of this point in earlier chapters when we noted the impact that it has on the children themselves. This disposition to be a good learner and to be inspired by and expert in a particular sphere, however, has other pay-offs for the community of the school. For such expertise can be both a rich resource for other colleagues and a support in the teacher's own professional as well as educational development. It must be stressed, however, that this particular interest and expertise, which enhances the abilities of the teacher in the eyes of the children and provides other colleagues with such valuable resource, is not necessarily prescribed in narrow school-subject terms. Nor can it be manufactured in their training by nominating the subjects which may be taught to teachers in training. For, although the teacher may have an abiding interest in and aptitude for mathematics, it may equally be expertise that derives from ornithology, photography, astronomy, horticulture or, as was the case with Seymour Papert (1980), an abiding interest in gears and machinery.

Although the teaching of mathematics, then, has been of major concern to teachers as well as to politicians in recent years, the opposite is claimed to be true of science. We noted earlier that it was constantly referred to by the inspectors in their recent report (DES 1978) as an area of human experience that is neglected in Primary education. As a result of the findings of that report, there has been considerable interest in the teaching of science recently, although, as yet, there has not been the proliferation of programmes that has occurred in mathematics. For those involved in developing the Primary science curriculum have approached their task as a complex one, which is closely interlinked with curriculum development in general, rather than attempting to find a quick solution by passing on to teachers packages devised by scientists.

We have already referred in earlier section of this chapter to aspects of the work in this sphere undertaken by the Schools Council and it is our intention now briefly to review the three projects together as they form an interesting picture of the development of ideas about curriculum within one area, and they span the life of this agency for curriculum development.

The team working on the first project, Science 5–13, began with the belief that science 'could contribute to educational ends which transcend subject boundaries, e.g. "self-realisation", "broadening experience", "educating the whole child" ' (Elliott 1980, p.98). They recognized, however, that these loosely expressed aims offered little guidance in planning day-to-day experiences. Their solution, as we noted in Chapter 3, was to adopt an objectives model of planning and to combine this with a Piagetian framework for matching appropriate objectives to the child's stage of development.

From the start, however, their objectives approach was somewhat different to the strict behavioural model. This is explained by one member of the team as due to disagreements among team members about the value of objectives. She tells us, for example, that 'one objection was that "they destroy everything we are trying to do in the classroom", that "one was making precise what was not precise", that "where you were making statements about objectives you were fitting on a veneer of structure which was inappropriate in the classroom situation" ' (Elliott 1980, p.105).

It was also found, especially in the courses that were conducted by the team for practising teachers, that the response to the use of the objectives of science as a starting-point for planning was disappointing, whereas their use as a guide for open-ended work with children brought enthusiastic responses from the teachers. Indeed, the project director acknowledges that this put objectives in perspective, for they were unlikely to be used in a mechanistic form by teachers who were seeking guidance rather than an externally imposed structure. By way of contrast, however, the team was under considerable pressure from teachers to produce pupil material, a contradiction that again draws attention to the confused thinking on the part of some teachers in the area of curriculum planning.

The project team resisted this pressure, however, and produced, in addition to its guide, 26 source books for teachers. These were intended to support teachers' planning of work, to give them ideas for extending topics which children were already enthusiastic about and to provide them with information. They were intended, in other words, as resources to enrich the scientific aspects of the work of teachers who were developing interests in the way that we described in Chapter 4.

The evaluation of the project revealed, however, that 'the project's books do not on their own give as much help as many teachers need in starting children learning science activity for the first time', and that they 'did not significantly change teachers' willingness to adopt methods for enabling children to learn more active inquiry' (Harlen 1975, p.89). It was, in fact, generally agreed that the dissemination of the project's ideas had been minimal.

The attempt at resolving this lack of impact, however, has not so far led to the employment of science specialists to package science programmes for teachers. Rather, the Schools Council placed emphasis on two quite different ways of solving the problem – first on finding ways of developing the class teacher's expertise and second on offering advice for school-based development. In an attempt to pursue these lines of development, therefore, the Schools Council sponsored two further projects, Progress in Learning Science and Learning Through Science, which we discussed earlier in this chapter.

In these two ensuing projects, it is worth noting that in both cases the teams support a unified approach to the curriculum. The evaluation of the Science 5–13 project had led to the belief that there is a close relation between mathematical and scientific activities for young children and that, in the view of the project evaluator at least, it makes little sense to continue to develop curriculum materials for these areas separately. And so neither of these subsequent projects seeks to promote science as a discrete area of knowledge or subject specialism. Both are concerned, however, to promote first the processes upon which scientific development depends and, second, the contribution that experiences of a scientific kind can make to the child's overall development. They are moving, in fact, from a concern with the objectives of science to a study of how the scientific process is advanced and how educational processes in general can be forwarded.

By using examples from the two areas of mathematics and science, we have tried to show the impact that can be made on the curriculum by an over-emphasis on the particular needs of one subject. We have also indicated what is likely to occur when the demands of the subject are dealt with in isolation from both the child's needs and the teacher's understanding. Finally we have shown that in one subject area, that of science, there are clear indications that the considerable experience of attempting to develop the curriculum is causing some specialists in this field to shift attention from the demands of the subject to the processes essential to educational development.

This, we would argue, is to be applauded, as it is our contention that, when special expertise in an area of human understanding (regardless of which area this is) is used to support and guide the understanding of teachers and to reveal the means by which children develop, then the unified approach to curriculum planning can be considerably advanced and the practical implications of the process of education are clarified. If this special expertise is used, however, to plan and structure the work for the teacher and prespecify the experiences to be undertaken by the children, or, worse, if teachers are given the impression that a deep understanding of a subject is the sole, or even the main, requirement of a teacher, then both the unified curriculum and the process of education itself are undermined.

This leads us finally, then, to a discussion of some developments by which a process model of curriculum is being promoted.

Planning for process

We argued in our previous section that, when teachers feel that their own understanding is particularly weak (as is the case with mathematics), then this aspect of work is likely to be vulnerable to the kind of external influence and isolated treatment that we described earlier. It is not unreasonable to assume, therefore, that the converse is likely to occur in areas where the teachers feel that they themselves have a degree of expertise and as a result feel more confident.

This certainly appears to be true, in theory and, quite often, in practice, of the work that has been undertaken in the area of language and literacy. Consequently, it is in this aspect of work that the understanding of processes is advancing most rapidly. In addition, the practice of schools changes more often in this sphere than in any other.

It was clear, for example, that, when the Bullock Report was published in 1975, a healthy and informed debate was being conducted within the profession concerning the best approaches to adopt in this important area of education. This was reflected in the report which, far from being concerned narrowly with 'basic skills' or subjects such as English Literature, used, as its terms of reference, all the aspects of language and argued that the development of oracy, literacy and study skills was the responsibility of all teachers, and that an additional responsibility for Primary teachers was to provide children with an experience of literature in a manner that would promote both their personal development and their understanding. Although the discussions within the report indicated that there was by no means agreement on how improvements could be achieved (particularly in the area of the teaching of reading), it was clear that many changes had been achieved already and this was apparent not just in the theoretical background but also in the work of teachers, publishers of children's books and so on.

It is also clear that Primary teachers, unlike many of their Secondary colleagues, recognize the importance of a wider view of language and are concerned to encourage children to talk as well as to read and write. It is unusual, in fact, to find a silent Primary school class, as the teachers now see the various forms of communication as important, however incompetently they themselves may set about communicating with children.

Since the publication of the Bullock Report (DES 1975), interest and research in the sphere of language has continued at an even more rapid rate and the resultant professional debate and practical experimentation has meant that, in many Primary schools, it is in the area of language that curriculum development is at its most advanced. Part of the reason for this is that, in a number of instances, the research has been initiated and developed by teachers themselves – both class-teachers and those concerned with teacher education within local authorities, universities and polytechnics. This has meant that a focus has been placed in many studies on adults and children at work in classrooms. Important pieces of research are, in this sense, school-based and the activities of class-teachers, who are participating in such research or who are initiating it, are becoming innovative and contributing to our general understanding of curriculum theory. It is an area, in short, where research is not being seen as the province of the academics in other related disciplines but also of the teachers themselves. The insights that linguists, psychologists, sociologists and others have offered are certainly acknowledged as making an important contribution, but, increasingly, educationists themselves are taking on the research role in the sphere of language. Indeed, this is one of the reasons why many Primary teachers were perturbed by the low level of discussion and the narrow concerns of the HMI's curriculum document, *English from 5 to 16* (DES 1984), which we discussed earlier. One adviser, for example, who was excited at the developments that are under way in the teaching of language at the school level, described this document as 'the truly mind-bendingly boring and intellectually stultifying "English from 5 to 16" ' (Bower 1985).

The confidence that many – though by no means all – teachers feel in the area of language and the curriculum is one explanation of their willingness to take on a research role in this sphere. Another reason is that the principles that underlie their confidence and understanding relate to processes of development in education, which include a concern for content but are not defined by it. These teachers do not see themselves, in other words, as subject specialists, but as experts in the processes of teaching and learning.

In a companion to this book, *The Primary Curriculum in Action* (Blenkin and Kelly 1983a), Marian Whitehead outlines in detail the recent developments in our understanding of the role of language in education and argues that 'theories and research suggest implications for language policies in the Primary curriculum which may be expressed as three main insights. Firstly, the child's role in language learning is an active one. Secondly, this learning is a creative process and exhibits innovatory and exploratory features. Thirdly, this process is most typically an interaction between partners in a conversation and is strongly affected by feelings and relationships' (op. cit., p.60). She goes on to put forward three principles upon which the language policy of a school should be based. First, it must enrich the language development of the individual pupils, bearing in mind that this process is well under way before formal schooling begins. Second, literacy should be seen as a crucial extension and enhancement of the child's language development. Third, the school should generate its own research about language procedures and activities that are adopted and these 'projects' should involve teachers, pupils and parents.

Many teachers have approached their school language policy in this way and indeed, have been encouraged to do so by some local authorities. This has led teachers to revise the assumptions they have made about the teaching of language and literacy and the ideas that they once held about their role in children's learning. In some instances, this process of rethinking has led to radical changes in their practice.

It has changed, for example, some teachers' views about the involvement of parents in education and has led many teachers to work in close co-operation with the parents of the children in their class, especially in relation to the teaching of reading. Projects of this kind, which were pioneered in the London Borough of Harringey (Tizard, Schofield and Hewison 1982), are not without difficulties, of course. To work so closely with parents does demand a degree of professional confidence, understanding and organizational ability on the part of the teachers within a school, and many teachers, while seeing the worth of such developments, may not be in a position, for a variety of reasons, to practise such innovations themselves. It is encouraging to note, however, that even teachers who were anxious about, and therefore discouraged from involving themselves in such projects have become involved as a result of enlisting the help and support of a more impartial professional agent – an advisory teacher, for example, or an educational psychologist – outside of the immediate school community (Miller, Robson and Bushell 1985).

It is in the area of language, therefore, that some teachers have shown considerable confidence in taking their place among those who are concerned to research into and develop the school curriculum, and this has led them to be involved, with other researchers, at the forefront of those discussions. It was Jill Bennett (1979, 1981), for example, who helped to convince many of her colleagues that children's reading ability is enhanced considerably if they read 'real' books rather than those produced as part of a reading scheme. Accounts such as hers, where the 'reading for meaning' movement (Spencer 1980) is analysed and matched against her own classroom practice, offer other teachers both a valid theoretical framework for reflecting on their work and one which is authentic, in so far as such theorizing stems from and is concerned about professional practice itself.

There is an increasing number of such case studies in the educational literature, and most of these, at present, relate to investigations into and evaluations of current practice in the sphere of language teaching. Marian Whitehead (1985, 1986), for example, to whose work we referred above, is furnishing teachers with considerable insights into the process of learning to write through her analytical accounts of both her own work with young writers and that of other researchers in the field. She argues that 'in language learning, as in other forms of learning, the young child practises and exploits new skills with a persistence which can appear monotonous and even infuriating to the adult. We might compare the repetition of "I like my . . ." sentences to the baby's repeated dropping of objects from a pram. Or to the occurrence of frame-like structures in early talk: "all gone juice", "all gone baby". Or even to the repeated figures and letter-like forms in early drawings. . . . Childen are only going to fail to progress beyond these demonstrated achievements if the risks and experiments involved in all learning become too punitive, or if the stimulus to try something else is weak or non-existent. Ill-considered teaching strategies may also trap children in rigid, simplistic procedures' (1986, p.30).

It can be argued that when teachers are professionally confident, as is true of those who are researching into language, and are also committed to advancing the processes of education, to making professional evaluations of their work, and to increasing the scope and range of the professional theory that is available, they can show considerable research ability. And this is so despite the fact that many hailed the notion of 'teacher as researcher' (Stenhouse 1975) as unattainable idealism. It should be noted too that when Lawrence Stenhouse proposed this research role for teachers he argued that it was the main ingredient in curriculum development. These signs of teacher participation in educational research must be greeted, then, with optimism, as they are the most promising developments that have occurred during the last decade in what has been a gloomy and constraining time for education in general, and the Primary curriculum in particular. For such studies are not only adding to the corpus of professional knowledge and understanding itself, but they are also calling into question the role that research can play in education and the form that educational research should take if it is to promote educational change and development (Downey and Kelly 1986).

Such research, however, must be of an intellectually honest and rigorous kind. It must, in other words, lead teachers to evaluate the values and theories that underpin their practice as well as that practice itself, in a manner that is illustrated by the examples given above. Anything less would reflect that same failure to question and challenge, or even to recognize and acknowledge, the underlying assumptions of one's approach to education that we have noted as a salient feature of the official documents we discussed earlier and of many of the other assertions about education we have tried to challenge throughout this book. It is for this reason that teachers in their initial education need to be provided with an adequate intellectual base from which to pursue this kind of questioning and analysis both of their own theory and practice and of the theoretical perspectives offered to them, too often without this level of intellectual rigour, by others. No amount of study of subject-content will provide such a base, as the naive assumptions and assertions of those who advocate a subject-based approach make abundantly clear.

In summary, research in the sphere of language has informed educational theory in a number of ways. From the work of those outside the field of education have come insights into the role language and literacy play in the development and cognition, as we saw in earlier chapters when we considered the work of Margaret Donaldson and her colleagues. From within the profession have also come classroom-based studies which have challenged many of our past practices in schools and the theories upon which these practices were based. And many of these insights have application beyond the sphere of language itself.

There is one area of human experience, however, to which a study of language development provides very little explanation – that of visual imagery and artistic development.

This is an area of human experience which, up to now, has been afforded no obvious utilitarian value, although the increasing importance given to Craft, Design and Technology may alter the circumstances in this respect. It is also an area that has held a prominent place in the work of the Primary school. Recently, however, it has become threatened for, as a result of demands for accountability, it is tending to be regarded as unimportant and teachers are being encouraged to feel that an interest in graphic work is not completely academically respectable but is a 'frill' rather than a critical skill (Goodnow 1977).

In addition, it is an area that is threatened by the attitudes of many teachers to art as a subject. It is not unusual for children who are not talented artists to become quickly self-conscious and modest about drawing and painting so that, as a result, many become reluctant to engage in work of this kind even in the early years of schooling. In other words, many teachers do not recognize the importance of artistic experience to the development of every child.

For these reasons, therefore, it is interesting to look in more detail at the views of Eliott Eisner (1979) that we noted in Chapter 5. For he explains the role of visual communication in human development in a similar way to those whose main interest and concern is with language. He does so by considering why art is important before concerning himself with how it should be taught. Eisner begins, therefore, by asking what it is that children learn when they make visual images, and proceeds to discuss nine aspects of learning that can occur. These can be summarized as:

1   Children learn that they can create images and that this provides intrinsic satisfaction.
2   Children learn that the images that they create can function as symbols, both as public images and as personal symbols.
3   Childen learn that symbolic images can be used as a vehicle for symbolic play so that symbols become one means of imagining and empathizing.
4   Children learn that the process of image-making requires them to make personal judgements in an area where external and rigid standards do not exist.
5   Children learn that images can be related to other images to form a whole and so

are encouraged to consider spatial relationships.

6 Children learn that they can develop skills which will enable them to create illusion and form images that are visually persuasive which will in turn provide a vehicle for transforming ideas, images and feelings into a public form.

7 Children learn from making images that ideas and emotions that are not physically present can be symbolized.

8 Children learn from making images that there are ideas, images and feelings that can only be expressed through visual form.

9 Children learn that the world itself can be regarded as a source of aesthetic experience and as a pool of expressive form.

(Eisner 1979).

Eisner argues, therefore, that, far from being a 'fringe' activity or trivial hobby, visual representation can not only make its own unique contribution to the process of education but can also have significance in the child's more general cognitive development.

This was a central theme pursued by the Gulbenkian enquiry (Calouste Gulbenkian Foundation 1982), which investigated the role of the arts in education. Perhaps it is not insignificant that this enquiry was sponsored privately, unlike the similar enquiries into language (DES 1975) and mathematics (DES 1982b). In the report of this enquiry, it is argued that 'a well-informed pursuit of all kinds of creativity will enable us not only to cope more positively with the economic necessities of the world, but also to increase the potential for discovery and progress on the many fronts of human interest and activity that they offer us' (op. cit., p.141), and it goes on to list six areas of educational responsibility where the arts have an important contribution to make:

(a) Developing the full variety of human intelligence.
(b) Developing the capacity for creative thought and action.
(c) The education of feelings and sensibility.
(d) Developing physical and perceptual skills.
(e) The exploration of values.
(f) Understanding the changing social culture. (ibid.)

Although a research interest in this aspect of the curriculum seems, at present, to be minimal by comparison with that shown in the sphere of language, the research that is being undertaken seems to confirm Eisner's claims that this form of representation has great significance in cognitive development. For example, John Matthews' (1984) longitudinal studies of his own children's 'scribblings', from collections of drawings which cover a period from babyhood to their adolescence, together with his studies of the drawings made by young children he has worked with in schools, seem to suggest that, far from being meaningless doodles, there is an interaction occurring between the marks that the child makes and the symbolization of thought that is suggested by these marks, an interaction which is by no means frivolous and may be significant to the development of concepts far beyond those normally associated with drawing and art. Work such as this has called into question, for example, our practice of concentrating on Euclidean rather than topological shape in our teaching of early geometry.

The contribution that graphic symbolism makes to human development remains as something of an enigma, although there are clear suggestions that it provides the learner with powerful systems for conceptualization. Before moving on, however, it is worth noting the work of one teacher who uses creative work – that is drama, music, dance, writing as well as art – as a starting-point for all learning. From this wider perspective, Harriet Proudfoot (1983) shows, in her case studies of four children in her class who are unable, for various reasons, to put their full energies into their work, how she enables children to be actively involved in their learning through encouraging them to participate in a wide range of creative arts. She argues that

> the processes of creative work demand an active involvement. You have actually to *do* them – to look ('Till your eyes ache,' one child said) and use the pencil or paintbrush; to move in response to the music and the feelings it calls up; to *be* someone else and think and talk and move like them, and in response to other characters. Unlike learning bare facts, you can't escape participating, and the demand is on the whole self – mind, body, sensitivity, intellect and feelings. While they make this demand, the arts are at the same time training these faculties, so that they offer something like a total education (op.cit., p.156).

One final aspect of recent change, where the potential for promoting children's development has already been made manifest, is that brought about by the advent of the microcomputer. Again, as in all areas, the possibilities exist for a mundane and even stultifying use of this new technology, and one can, not unexpectedly, see many examples of this kind of pedestrianism in both theory and practice. Again too, however, one can see heartening examples of its use to promote the kind of process approach to education and curriculum we have been advocating here, and, again, equally hearteningly, one can see these not only in some of the theoretical discussions of the educational potential of the microcomputer, such as that of Seymour Papert (1980), but also in the realities of the practice of some committed teachers (Dodds 1984; Ross 1984; Maxwell 1984).

It has been argued (Kelly 1984, p.xiv) that 'the major advantage of the microcomputer is not that it can think for one but that it can make one think, so that its potential for promoting the development of children's thought processes is enormous'. It has also been claimed, perhaps somewhat optimistically and certainly in a manner which reflects too confident and broad a generalization, that 'software programs of today . . . teach process; not new skills *per se* but how to learn new skills, even how to think. Indeed, modern Piagetians believe that computers allow children to conduct their research about the world on a scale never before possible in a sandbox or a playground' (Rheingold 1983, p.38). Howard Rheingold in the same paper describes this as 'in effect, bringing the seminal thinking of John Dewey and Jean Piaget into the age of the silicon chip' (ibid.) – a clear indication of its potential in relation to the approach to education we are advocating. Finally, Seymour Papert (1980, p.8) sums up the same view of the potential of the microcomputer by outlining the two themes of his approach, 'that children can learn to use computers in a masterful way, and that learning to use computers can change the way they learn everything else'.

Perhaps more significant, and certainly more convincing, than these somewhat abstract assertions, are the concrete examples of how some teachers have been able to translate this theoretical perspective into practice, and thus not only to reinforce these assertions but also to contribute to our developing understanding of the possibilities offered by this new technology. Alistair Ross (1985, p.66), for example, argues on the basis of his own experience of using the data processing facility of the microcomputer with his Junior children:

> The processes of hypothesis-making and hypothesis-testing enable children to develop skills that help them better explain their world in other, non-classroom contexts. . . . My argument here is that . . . data processing techniques with a microcomputer enable childen to use their imaginations to make connections between items of information – to suggest correlations and to guess at causal relationships – *and then to test and justify them*. . . . If childen become adept at the hypothetico-deductive method, they then will also begin to understand a range of abstract concepts concerned with their focus of study, because these concepts are built up slowly as testable generalizations based on real information. Again, it is the *process* of concept formation that is ultimately of importance in the curriculum, not the actual concepts themselves.

Here again, then, we have an example of a development within a particular area which represents an attempt not to promote that area as a body of knowledge but to explore its potential as a contributor to the educational development of children. This is of course by no means the approach everyone has adopted to the use of microcomputers in education, but then the same is true, as we have seen, in all other areas of the curriculum. It does, however, indicate what is possible if one does adopt this approach, and suggests further ways in which one can translate the notion of education as process into the realities of classroom practice.

It also illustrates the other theme which has reappeared constantly throughout this discussion, the contribution that some confident and committed teachers are making to research in education, and thus to our corpus of knowledge and understanding of its many dimensions. For not the least significant comment made by Alistair Ross of his work is that the analysis from which we quoted just now 'was not complete when I began work with my class. . . . It has been worked out – is still being worked out – as I attempt different data processing techniques with childen' (ibid.). It is this kind of research and continuous self-evaluation by teachers which will not only advance their own competence but which can, when appropriately documented, contribute to a wide understanding of teaching and learning. It also represents a very different concept of teacher evaluation or appraisal than that encapsulated in most of the usages of that term by politicians and educational administrators.

We have shown in this last section that there is evidence that progress is being made in clarifying the processes that underlie education. It has been argued in this recent work that the educational process is complex and subtle, and the principles upon which it is based cannot be adhered to if a straightforward application of learning sequences to direct and deliberate shaping of behaviour is made. When this is attempted, as happens when the objectives model is adopted, the educational process is reduced to a form of training, the curriculum is fragmented, and important principles are set aside in order to achieve measurable results.

It has also been shown through these examples that it is by no means necessary – or even desirable – to start curriculum planning with a statement of long-term aims and a selection of content to secure those aims, in other words to adopt a content model, as this will also lead to fragmentation and will detract from a concentration on the child's experiences and the contribution that these are making to his/her development. It is clear that, in all of the examples we have given, we have found teachers who are working with educational principles at the forefront of their minds and that the subject matter of education has featured as a vital dimension in their planning. However, these principles have been there to guide day-to-day interactions with children and have served as a theoretical structure within which to make evaluations of this work. And the subject matter has been dependent on the contribution it might make to the child's educational development and has not been seen as a prerequisite of that development. In these examples, therefore, the objectives and content models of planning have been deliberately rejected and a process model adopted.

Finally, this work has been based on the view that progress in the Primary school is more likely to be made if attention is given to the processes to be pursued in teaching. The mainstream Primary school tradition has already developed some practical expertise in this respect, but in the past teachers have failed to make explicit their approach to education, and have relied too much on intuitive understanding. The work that we have described in this last section attempts to help teachers to achieve more clarity in their planning for process development.

At a time when demands for accountability are being made on them, it is encouraging to find that teachers are being warned against the excesses of instrumentalism, and helped to find other approaches which are more deman-ding but more likely to promote education. It is even more encouraging to find some teachers who are undertaking this task for themselves. This work has, therefore, placed much stress on the teacher's developing expertise as it has shown that it is upon the skill and understanding of the teacher that education depends.

Summary and conclusions

In this chapter, we have examined the changing context of the Primary curriculum, and have attempted, in the light of the theoretical discussions of our earlier chapters, to make an evaluation of some recent constraints and developments which have occurred.

We began by drawing attention to the fact that curriculum development in the Primary sector of education is not a recent phenomenon. Nevertheless, recent years have witnessed a number of attempts to accelerate or to constrain that process for a variety of reasons, and it is these attempts that we have been concerned to examine here.

It seemed to us that these developments could best be viewed under three headings: first, those that appear to have been prompted by the increased political involvement in education which recent years have witnessed; second-ly, those that appear to be prompted by a desire to emphasize a subject specialist approach to the Primary curriculum (a development which is of course by no means unconnected with the first); and, thirdly, those develop-ments which appear to have acknowledged the kind of concern with the processes of education which we have attempted to argue in earlier chapters is an essential ingredient of the Primary curriculum.

Under the first of these headings we looked in particular at the recent publications which have emerged both from Her Majesty's Inspectorate and from the Department of Education and Science, and the policy initiatives that both have taken, since these seemed to us to be prompted by demands for increased public control of schooling. However, we also felt it appropriate under the same heading to examine the responses of local education authorities to these demands and the impact that their resultant policies were having on the school curriculum. We noted the influence that some of the projects that have set out to encourage teachers to adopt a more structured approach both to planning and the keeping of records have had on l.e.a. policies. These seemed to be motivated by the same desire to increase external control of the curriculum and to make possible greater external monitoring of standards, and they seemed likely too, if not handled properly, to result in the same kind of limitation on the freedom of the teacher and the school to attend to what seem from the inside to be the educational needs of their pupils.

We found ourselves looking again at official publications and policies when we came to examine recent developments under our second heading, pressures for the introduction of subject specialisms. Here in particular we noted the ambivalence of those publications which while recommending an increased emphasis on teaching in certain traditional subject areas also from time to time were to be noted extolling the merits of a unified approach to learning. We also here devoted attention to some recent projects in specfic areas such as science and mathematics. Again we noted some internal inconsistencies not only between the ideas of, on the one hand, teaching these subjects as subjects and, on the other, attempting to see them as part of a unified curriculum but also between an approach to the teaching of them which emphasizes subject-content and one that views them from the standpoint of what they can contribute to the overall development of the individual child. Those that seemed to have most to offer and to fit most naturally with the established ethos of the Primary school were those, like the Learning Through Science project, which have come to acknowledge the primacy of the second of these two possible roles.

This, we argued, was the main source of the strength of those projects we saw as falling appropriately into our third and final category which embraced those developments that have recognized the centrality to Primary education of a process model of curriculum. We found it interesting to note that developments under this heading have been more commonly found in those areas of the curriculum where, unlike in mathematics and science, Primary teachers have for a long time felt more confident of their abilities, in the Humanities, for example, and especially in the area of language development. Developments such as those that followed the publication of the Bullock Report (DES 1975) have, in our view, been free of the major inconsistencies of some of the other developments that we have considered, in so far as they have started from a recognition that education is concerned with development and that planning a curriculum for such education must begin from a consideration of processes rather than intended behavioural outcomes. They thus have the merit of internal consistency and, in our view, the added merit of being in harmony with the basic principles of Primary education.

Any such attempt at categorization of these recent developments, however, is bound to bring its own difficulties, not least in that there will inevitably be a good deal of overlap whatever categories one chooses. This overlap we have tried to draw attention to as and when it has occurred.

It is also inevitable that, when attention has been devoted to the curriculum of the Primary school by different groups of people viewing it from different standpoints, there will be conflict between the views offered. This too we have tried to highlight.

What is more serious and less excusable is the conflict we have detected within some of the views expressed. We hope we have been able to show both that this conflict exists and some of the forms that it takes. We have also endeavoured to demonstrate that to a large extent it stems from a failure to appreciate the fundamental principles which our earlier chapters have been designed to pick out, for example, a failure to recognize the implications of adopting an instrumental view of the curriculum and a corresponding failure to distinguish between the ideas of education as the promotion of certain kinds of development and as the acquisition of certain bodies of knowledge, a failure which in turn leads to certain confusions about the role of subject-content in education.

This confusion and conflict within and between recent developments in the Primary curriculum can only lead to a similar lack of clarity in the minds of teachers themselves as they attempt to respond to the demands made of them. What is required, therefore, is a good deal of rethinking about both the theory and the practice of Primary education not only by the teachers themselves but also, and perhaps even more importantly, by those who have become increasingly concerned in recent years to advise those teachers on what they should be doing. Greater accountability and external control over education can only be effective if those who are demanding the former and exercising the latter have a clear view of what it is they are demanding.

Suggested further reading

It is suggested that teachers and student-teachers might attempt a critical analysis of documentation on the curriculum emanating either from their local authority or HMI/DES or both in the light of what has been offered in this book and especially in Chapter 6.

CHAPTER 7

IN CONCLUSION

The earlier chapters of this book have covered a good deal of ground. We hope they have done so in a coherent manner and that the progression of our argument has been clear. In case this is not so or, if it is, in order to drive it home firmly, we will attempt in this final short chapter to highlight the thread of that argument, to pick out the main points from our earlier discussions and to draw some conclusions from them.

We began by exploring some of the major influences on the development of Primary education in the hope that in this way we might achieve a clearer view of its theoretical bases. We attempted to show that a major influence on the Primary curriculum has been that 'developmental' tradition (Blyth 1965) which has derived from what is often called the 'progressive' movement and that its guiding principles are those of that movement. We tried to establish that that assumption is justified by showing that the view of Primary education expressed first by the Hadow Report (1931) and, more recently, by the Plowden Report (1967), and thus given a degree of official sanction, is at root the view that has developed over many years as a result of the theorizing of thinkers such as Rousseau, Froebel and Dewey, and has been reinforced by researchers in developmental psychology, in particular by the work of Jean Piaget and Jerome Bruner.

We also wished to demonstrate, however, that what is now being called a process view of curriculum is far more than a mere restatement of 'progressivism', and reflects the kind of rigorous work that has been done in the areas of Curriculum Studies and Child Development in the two decades since the publication of the Plowden Report (1967). In particular, we have been at pains to show that it owes much to a clearer view of its epistemological base, the different, non-rationalist, theory of knowledge which is one of its important elements, and to the increased knowledge and understanding we have of how children develop as a result of the extensive recent studies of those working in the field of developmental psychology.

More important than the origins of that view, however, are its main tenets and these we tried to identify. We suggested that it is rooted in an empiricist epistemology which regards knowledge as a human creation and therefore devotes more attention to the knower than to the knowledge itself. This represents a major shift of emphasis which is crucial for education and it is this shift that has to be appreciated and understood if one is to develop a clear and proper concept of what it means for education to be 'child-centred'.

A number of further principles follow from the acceptance of this major premise. It follows, for example, that one cannot from this position justify the imposition of knowledge on children. That can only be justified if one regards knowledge itself as possessing an independent status and sanctity. Rather education has to be viewed as the promotion of the developing experience of the educand. If further follows, then, that education has to be seen as growth, as the development of the intellectual capacities of each individual pupil, rather than as the acquisition of bodies of knowledge – a point which explains both the role and the support of developmental psychology in the advance of this view and which leads to the claim that education has to be defined in terms of the processes that are integral to it rather than by reference to bodies of subject-content that are to be assimilated. This has in turn led to the recognition that education is a dynamic process in which the pupil him/herself must be an active participant rather than a passive recipient.

Such a view of education, although supported by the work of a large number of distinguished theorists and practitioners, is not, of course, without its critics. And it was to an examination of some of their criticisms that we next turned. We stressed first of all the need to evaluate it on its own terms, to base criticisms of it on a proper appreciation of its basic principles rather than to attack it from a totally different standpoint and to condemn it for not doing what it does not set out to do. That, we suggested, has been a serious weakness of many of its critics. We noted, too, that criticisms have often been directed at the practice rather than the theory of this approach to education and we pointed out that, while such criticisms may well be often justified, the existence of incompetent practitioners does not invalidate the theories they are failing to act upon.

We suggested that the criticisms that needed to be taken seriously were those that have been directed at the philosophical or epistemological bases of this theory and at certain aspects of the theory of education that has been built upon them. As far as the former are concerned, there can be little argument, since there are no grounds upon which one can decide between conflicting theories of knowledge. The latter, however, did throw up some interesting questions, like those about the validity and meaning of concepts such as 'growth', 'interests', 'needs', 'activity' and 'discovery' in the planning and practice of education and our examination of these was designed both to respond to the criticisms and to advance our efforts to reveal the basic principles of this theory of education.

We found that much of the criticism offered of this view, or of what has been conceived as being the 'progressive' view of education, has been confused by the, unwarranted, assumption that the prime concern of education, and thus curriculum planning, should be the knowledge-content to which children are to be exposed. This, we suggested, is a feature not only of those theories which explicitly advocate a curriculum based on knowledge-content but even some of those who purport to adopt a developmental stance. For this reason, we felt that the issue of content-based planning warranted some wider discussion and this we attempted to give it. Our conclusions were that such a position can only be adopted by those who are able to accept the rationalist view of the superior value of some knowledge or of certain bodies of knowledge, and that, in any case, even those who have advocated this kind of view, seem to have done so on the unquestioned assumption that certain forms of development would auto- matically follow from the child's exposure to this superior knowledge. Since this is palpably not the case, we suggested that we ought to give further attention, as is our basic intent, to the questions of what kinds of knowledge will promote this development and how such development can be advanced without pre-empting decisions about the kinds of knowledge-content which might be most effective in achieving this. Again our view was that the prime concern of education is the child to be educated and not the knowledge to be transmitted.

A second major feature of this view and one that we felt merited separate and dealied attention is its rejection of an instrumental approach to education and its corresponding stress on the intrinsic value of educational activities. This had been the starting-point for the development of this view, since the main source of Rousseau's dissatisfaction with the dominant educational theory of his time was the fact that, since the time of Plato, education has been seen as a means to an end, as a device for producing certain results, as a blueprint for the manufacture of certain kinds of people, and had thus been defined in terms of the qualities these people should display and, especially, the knowledge they should possess. The main force of Rousseau's revolt, therefore, had been the demand that attention should be switched from the 'man' to the child, from the product to the process.

This issue is fundamental to the choice of appropriate models for curriculum planning and we devoted some time to a consideration of this problem. We first examined the main features and the main difficulties of an instrumental approach to curriculum planning through the prespecification of curriculum objectives. Our conclusion was that, in addition to presenting many problems in itself, the main source of its unsuitability for use in the Primary school is that its basic principles are in conflict with those we have picked out as central to the view of education we have examined. One cannot use an instrumental planning model in a context whose major feature is a commitment to intrinsic values.

Another planning model, therefore, had to be found and we proceeded to consider some of the implications of viewing education as process, of adopting a process rather than a product ideology. We tried to demonstrate first of all that this is the essence of that view of education we have claimed is endemic to the Primary school and we then went on to pick out its main features and implications for educational practice. Pre-eminent among these, we suggested, is that concern with the development of skills, knowledge and understanding, with intellectual development generally, that we had stressed earlier. The emphasis is on how children learn rather than on what they learn and thus their own explorations and the context created for them by their teachers become the key features of educational practice. The nature and the timing of the teachers' interventions are also crucial.

If the child's growth and development become central, then the demands of knowledge itself must move to the periphery. And this is true whether we are concerned with that knowledge which might be regarded as in some way intrinsically valuable or with that whose importance derives from its utilitarian value to society. This we saw earlier is the major shift of emphasis that this view of education requires. It becomes important, therefore, to consider what this entails for the subject-content of education and it was to this we turned in Chapter 5. The main requirement of this kind of education is that the child's learning should be coherent, that his/her knowledge should be a unity and thus that there should be a unified curriculum. There were two particular aspects of this that we felt it necessary to discuss at some length. The first of these was the need to try to attend to the learning of skills *pari passu* with other kinds of learning. This we stressed not only because of the difficulty of defining skills sufficiently clearly to enable them to be separated out, but also, and primarily, because if we attempt to teach them separately we put at risk that unity and coherence of learning that we have claimed is crucial and we may find that, in attempting to teach skills whose point and relevance is not clear, we have inhibited rather than advanced the pupil's intellectual growth. Secondly, we noted that this approach has implications for the practice of dividing the curriculum into separate areas or subjects. Such subdivisions can only be justified if they make sense to the pupil in the organization of his/her own learning and knowledge and, since his/her subdivisions may not be ours and in order to be true to our epistemological bases, we must avoid imposing these categories too positively upon him/her.

The emphasis of our discussion had thus slowly moved from theoretical towards practical considerations and, against the backcloth we had tried to paint of principles of both theory and practice, we turned in Chapter 6 to a detailed examination of the changing context of Primary education, proposals, recommendations even demands that have emerged from surveys, from researches and, especially, from recent political initiatives.

Some of these reinforce the views we have expressed, others are contradictory to them. What concerns us about the second group is not that they disagree with us, but that they seem to do so for the wrong reasons. For, in the first place, the fact that they run counter to the main principles of Primary education appears often to result from a lack of clarity of thinking rather than from positive disagreement, and such lack of clarity must lead to confused forms of practice. Secondly, some are clearly influenced by or are even direct responses to external pressures. For those external constraints, whose absence we suggested in our Introduction has enabled the curriculum of some Primary schools to develop so rapidly and in such an interesting way, are now emerging, and teachers are subject to increasing demands and pressures from outside.

The first developments we considered, then, were those that appear to have been prompted largely by such external pressures. Demands that teachers be more directly accountable to outside agencies can only encourage an emphasis on those aspects of their work that these agencies can best understand, so that pressures for the teaching of the 'basic skills', for the return of traditional subject specialisms and, in general, for the adoption of an instrumental approach to education have increased perceptibly in the last ten years. This is reflected in the approach and in the recommendations of some of the projects, as we have tried to show, and particularly in those attempts to re-establish subject specialisms in the Primary curriculum which formed the second group of developments we examined. However, other proposals that have been made for advances in the Primary curriculum have attempted to remain true to the basic principles of Primary education and to avoid the inevitable contradictions involved in trying to impose an incompatible approach on what has become in some places a highly developed tradition. It was these that formed the last group of developments that we considered.

It is in part to strengthen the claims of these that this book has been written, although it is also the case that when faced with pressures to change one's ways, everyone needs a clear understanding of what those ways are based on. There is thus a need for a clear statement of the basic principles of this approach to education both to discourage contradictory practices and to give clarity to those practices that are consonant with these principles. And there is a particular need for teachers to be assisted towards a clear picture of them at a time when they are subject to pressures to reject them and to return to something different.

Our second main intention in attempting to produce a clear statement of the underlying principles of a process approach to the Primary curriculum was to recommend it to teachers in other sectors of the education system. For there are elements in this approach which seem to us to have much to offer at all stages of education, elements which it could be argued are essential ingredients of any transaction between teacher and pupil worthy of being called education.

This seems to be particularly important in the present climate. For if there are pressures on Primary teachers to adopt different approaches to their work, approaches which are less justifiable educationally than those we have advocated in this book, these pressures can be seen to be at work even more directly and with far greater force in our Secondary schools. Vocationalism is a particularly insidious form of instrumentalism, and is thus diametrically opposed to that idea of education as human development which we have been at pains to explore. Yet vocationalism is rife in the Secondary school curriculum (much of which is now funded by the Department of Trade and Industry rather than the Department of Education and Science), and even in that of our universities, so that for this reason too an attempt to state the basic principles of a developmental approach to education is not inappropriate at the present time.

In attempting to unpick these principles, the question we have found it most difficult to tackle, or at least to articulate our response to, has been that of the role of subject-content or knowledge in a process curriculum. And we would not want to claim to have answered that question to our own satisfaction, let alone that of the reader.

It is clear to us that there has to be a content to education, and that knowledge is necessary to support pupil enquiry and thus pupil development. It is also clear that there is knowledge which is worth having – not in the instrumental sense but in the intrinsic, or perhaps rather the developmental, sense. It has to be the case, however, that the judgement as to whether it is worth having must in the end be made by the individual. If it is to be made by someone else on his/her behalf, the decision must be based on a judgement not about the value of the knowledge but about its contribution to that individual's development.

Our commitment, then, is not to the intrinsic value of certain identifiable bodies of knowledge, and certainly not to particular aspects of them, but to certain qualities of mind, and of personality generally, those which, as we said earlier in the book, represent enhanced powers and capabilities in the individual, increased control over his/her world and a heightened awareness of features of that world which might otherwise go unnoticed. It is our view, as we said earlier, that too many people's lives are unduly, even unfairly limited because they have not been given the opportunity to develop these capacities, this control, this level of awareness, and that education, properly conceived, can and should attempt to put this right. Our value position is thus essentially that of John Stuart Mill when he asserted that 'it is better to be a human being dissatisfied than a pig satisfied; better to be a Socrates dissatisfied than a fool satisfied', although we would, of course, repudiate the content-based interpretation which has usually been placed on that assertion.

We believe that this kind of development will be forwarded if children are exposed to the right kinds of knowledge. What constitutes the right kinds of knowledge, however, must be determined by reference to the individual child him/herself as well as, and ahead of, and not merely to the knowledge itself. The trick to providing a proper education is, in our view, to be found by solving this equation, getting the balance right, between the development of the child and the kinds of knowledge which will best promote that development. Our concerns spring from the facts that considerations of knowledge alone have been allowed to dominate curriculum planning, that the place of knowledge has superseded all concern for the development of the child (exactly Rousseau's concern), that somehow it has been too readily assumed that the right kind of development must follow exposure to certain kinds of knowledge and, worse, that, if it does not, this is due to some deficiency in the child and not to the educational recipe for his/her diet.

Much work still remains to be done on this issue. The equation remains to be worked out both at the general theoretical level and at the particular level of teachers' practice. But it needs work of the right kind. We have surely had enough of attempts to criticize, or even to commend, aspects of the Primary curriculum from positions of ignorance of its nature, from mistaken, misunderstood or misguided perspectives, whose main characteristic has been a failure to appreciate the nuances of what we have been attempting to outline. The Primary school does have its own canons of excellence; it should only be criticized or evaluated by those who understand what these are.

There is much work to be done. This book is offered as a contribution to that work. It is an offering which is intended not to be definitive but, in accordance with its basic tenets, developmental.

BIBLIOGRAPHY

Alexander, R.J. (1984) *Primary Teaching*. London: Holt, Rinehart & Winston.

Allen, D. (ed.) (1973) *Early Years at School*. London: BBC Publications.

Archambault, R.D. (ed.) (1965) *Philosophical Analysis and Education*. London: Routledge & Kegan Paul.

Armstrong, M. (1980) *Closely Observed Children: the Diary of a Primary Classroom*. London: Writers & Readers Publishing Co-operative, in association with the Chameleon Editorial Group.

Ashton, P., Kneen, P. and Davies, F. (1975) *Aims into Practice in the Primary School*. London: University of London Press.

Ayer, A.J. (1964) *Man as a Subject for Science*. London: Athlone Press.

Barnes, D. (1976) *From Communication to Curriculum*. Harmondsworth: Penguin.

Barnes, D. (1982) *Practical Curriculum Study*. London: Routledge & Kegan Paul.

Bate, M. and Smith, M. (1978) *Manual for Assessment in Nursery Education*. Windsor: National Foundation for Educational Research.

Beard, R.M. (1969) *An Outline of Piaget's Developmental Psychology*. London: Routledge & Kegan Paul.

Bennett, J. (1979) *Learning to Read with Picture Books*. Stroud: The Thimble Press for Signal.

Bennett, J. (1981) *Reaching Out*. Stroud: The Thimble Press for Signal.

Bennett, N. (1976) *Teaching Styles and Pupil Progress*. London: Open Books.

Bierley, M. (1983) The development of a record-keeping system, 162–182 in Blenkin and Kelly (1983).

216   The Primary Curriculum

8

Blenkin, G. (1980) The influence of initial styles of curriculum development, 45–64 in Kelly (1980).
Blenkin, G. (1983) The basic skills, 29–55 in Blenkin and Kelly (1983).
Blenkin, G.M. and Kelly, A.V. (eds.) (1983a) *The Primary Curriculum in Action: A Process Approach to Educational Practice*. London: Harper & Row.
Blenkin, G. and Kelly, V. (1983b) The education of teachers, 218–243 in Blenkin and Kelly (1983a).
Bloom, B.S. *et al.* (1956) *Taxonomy of Eductional Objectives I: Cognitive Domain*. London: Longmans.
Blyth, W.A.L. (1965) *English Primary Education: A Sociological Description: Volume II: Background*. London: Routledge & Kegan Paul.
Blyth, W.A.L. (1974) One development project's awkward thinking about objectives. *Journal of Curriculum Studies* 6, 99–111.
Blyth, W.A.L. (1984) *Development, Experience and Curriculum in Primary Education*. London: Croom Helm.
Bobbitt, F. (1918) *The Curriculum*. Boston: Houghton Mifflin.
Bobbitt, F. (1924) *How to Make a Curriculum*. Boston: Houghton Mifflin.
Bower, E. (1985) Ten years after Bullock. *Primary Education Review* No. 23, Summer 1985, 13–15.
Bruner, J.S. (1960) *The Process of Education*. New York: Vintage Books.
Bruner, J.S. (1968) *Toward a Theory of Instruction*. New York: Norton.
Bruner, J.S. (1974) *The Relevance of Education* (3rd edn). Harmondsworth: Penguin Education.
Bruner, J.S. (1978) Introduction to Lock (1978).
Calouste Gulbenkian Foundation (1982) *The Arts in Schools: Principles, Practice and Provision*. London: Calouste Gulbenkian Foundation.
Campbell, R.J. (1985) *Developing the Primary School Curriculum*. London: Holt, Rinehart & Winston.
Carey, S. (1974) Cognitive competence, 169–193 in Connolly and Bruner (1974).
Charters, W. (1924) *Curriculum Construction*. New York: Macmillan.
Childs, J.L. (1956) *American Pragmatism and Education*. New York: Holt, Rinehart & Winston.
Clark, M.M. *Young Fluent Readers*. London: Heinemann.
Connolly, K. and Bruner, J.S. (eds.) (1974) *The Growth of Competence*. London: Academic Press.
Darling, J. (1978) Progressive, traditional and radical: a realignment. *Journal of Philosophy of Education* 12, 157–166.
Davies, I.K. (1976) *Objectives in Curriculum Design*. Maidenhead: McGraw-Hill.

Dearden, R.F. (1967) Instruction and learning by discovery, 135–155 in Peters (1967).

Dearden, R.F. (1968) *The Philosophy of Primary Education*. London: Routledge & Kegan Paul.

Dearden, R.F. (1971) What is the integrated day?, 45–56 in Walton (1971).

Dearden, R.F. (1976) *Problems in Primary Education*. London: Routledge & Kegan Paul.

Dewey, J. (1916) *Democracy and Education*. New York: Collier-Macmillan (1966 edition).

Dewey, J. (1938) *Experience and Education*. New York: Macmillan (first Collier Books edition 1963).

Dodds, D. (1984) Computers in the Primary classroom, 36–63 in Kelly (1984).

Donaldson, M. (1978) *Children's Minds*. Glasgow: Fontana, Collins.

Donaldson, M., Grieve, R. and Pratt, C. (eds.) (1983) *Early Childhood Development and Education: Readings in Psychology*. Oxford: Blackwell.

Downey, M. and Kelly, A.V. (1979) *Theory and Practice of Education*. London: Harper & Row (third edition 1986).

Egan, K. (1979) *Educational Development*. New York: Oxford University Press.

Egan, K. (1985) Teaching as story-telling: a non-mechanistic approach to planning teaching. *Journal of Curriculum Studies* 17, 4, 397–406.

Eisner, E.W. (1969) Instructional and expressive objectives: their formulation and use in curriculum, 1–8 in Popham *et al.* (1969).

Eisner, E.W. (1979) The contribution of painting to children's cognitive development. *Journal of Curriculum Studies* 11, 109–116.

Eisner, E.W. (1982) *Cognition and Curriculum: A Basis for Deciding What to Teach*. New York and London: Longman.

Elliot, J. (1980) Science 5–13, 96–114 in Stenhouse (1980).

Elliot, J. and Connolly, K. (1974) Hierarchical structure in skill development, 135–168 in Connolly and Bruner (1974).

Flavell, J.H. (1963) *The Developmental Psychology of Jean Piaget*. New York: Van Nostrand Reinhold.

Fletcher, H. (1970) *Mathematics for Schools: Teacher's Resource Book*. London: Addison-Wesley.

Fontana, D. (ed.) (1978) *The Education of the Young Child*. London: Open Books.

Foss, B. (1969) Other aspects of child psychology, 42–54 in Peters (1969).

Furth, H.G. (1970) *Piaget for Teachers*. Englewood Cliffs, N.J.: Prentice-Hall.

Galton, M., Simon, B. and Croll, P. (1980) *Inside the Primary Classroom*. London: Routledge & Kegan Paul.

Gelman, R. and Gallistel, C.R. (1978) *The Child's Understanding of Number.* Cambridge, Mass.: Harvard University Press.

Goodnow, J. (1977) *Children's Drawings.* Glasgow: Fontana, Open Books.

Gordon, P. and Lawton, D. (1978) *Curriculum Change in the Nineteenth and Twentieth Centuries.* London: Hodder & Stoughton.

Gray, J. and Satterley, D. (1981) Formal or informal? A reassessment of the British evidence. *British Journal of Educational Psychology* 51.

Gribble, J.H. (1970) Pandora's box: the affective domain of educational objectives. *Journal of Curriculum Studies* 2, 11–24.

Grugeon, D. (1973) Organization for openness, 46–60 in Allen (1973).

Halliday, M.A.K. (1965) *Learning How to Mean: Explorations in the Development of Language.* London: Edward Arnold.

Hamilton, D. (1976) *Curriculum Evaluation.* London: Open Books.

Harlen, W. (1975) *Science 5–13: A Formative Evaluation.* Schools Council Research Studies. London: Macmillan Education for the Schools Council.

Harlen, W. (1979) Accountability that is of benefit to schools. *Journal of Curriculum Studies* 11, 287–297.

Hirst, P.H. (1965) Liberal education and the nature of knowledge, 113–138 in Archambault (1965); also 87–111 in Peters (1973).

Hirst, P.H. (1969) The logic of the curriculum. *Journal of Curriculum Studies* 1, 142–158; also 232–250 in Hooper (1971).

Hirst, P.H. (1974) *Knowledge and the Curriculum.* London: Routledge & Kegan Paul.

Hirst, P.H. (1975) The curriculum and its objectives – a defence of piecemeal rational planning. *Studies in Education* 2, *The Curriculum*, 9–21. The Doris Lee Lectures. London: University of London, Institute of Education.

Hodgkin, R.A. (1976) *Born Curious: New Perspectives in Educational Theory*, London: John Wiley.

Hogben, D. (1972) The behavioural objectives approach: some problems and some dangers. *Journal of Curriculum Studies* 4, 42–50.

Hollins, T.H.B. (1964) The problem of values and John Dewey, 91–108 in Hollins (1964).

Hollins, T.H.B. (ed.) (1964) *Aims in Eduction: The Philosophic Approach.* Manchester: Manchester University Press.

Hooper, R. (ed.) (1971) *The Curriculum: Context, Design and Development.* Edinburgh: Oliver & Boyd in association with the Open University Press.

Hughes, M. (1983) What is difficult about learning arithmetic?, 204–221 in Donaldson *et al.* (1983).

Hughes, M. and Grieve, R. (1983) On asking children bizarre questions, 104–114 in Donaldson *et al.* (1983).

Inner London Education Authority (1978) *Primary School Mathematics 2: Checkpoints.* ILEA Curriculum Guidelines. London: ILEA Inspectorate.

Inner London Education Authority (1985) *Improving Primary Schools* (The Thomas Report). London: ILEA.

Jackson, A. and Hannon, P. (1981) *The Belfield Reading Project.* Rochdale: Belfield Community College.

James, C.M. (1968) *Young Lives at Stake.* London: Collins.

Katz, L.G. (1977) *Talks with Teachers.* Washington, D.C.: National Association for the Education of Young Children.

Keddie, N. (1971) Classroom Knowledge, 131–160 in Young (1971).

Kelly, A.V. (1977) *The Curriculum: Theory and Practice.* London: Harper & Row (second edition 1982).

Kelly, A.V. (ed.) (1980) *Curriculum Context.* London: Harper & Row.

Kelley, A.V. (ed.) (1984a) *Microcomputers and the Curriculum.* London: Harper & Row.

Kelly, A.V. (1984b) Microcomputers and the curriculum – uses and abuses, 1–19 in Kelly (1984a)

Kelly, A.V. (1986) *Knowledge and Curriculum Planning.* London: Harper & Row.

Kelly, P.J. (1973) Nuffield 'A' level biological science project, 91–109 in Schools Council (1973).

Kent County Council (1978) *Kent Mathematics Project: Teachers' Guide: Level 1–4.* London: Ward Lock Educational.

Kilpatrick, W.H. (1951) *Philosophy of Education.* New York: Macmillan.

King, R. (1978) *All Things Bright and Beautiful, A Sociological Study of Infant's Classrooms.* Chichester: John Wiley.

Kohlberg, L. and Mayer, R. (1972) Development as the aim of education. *Harvard Educational Review* 4, 449–496.

Kratwohl, D.R. (ed.) (1964) *Taxonomy of Educational Objectives II: Affective Domain.* London: Longmans.

Kratwohl, D.R. (1965) Stating objectives appropriately for program, for curriculum and for instructional materials development. *Journal of Teacher Education* 16, 83–92.

Lawton, D. (1975) *Class Culture and the Curriculum.* London: Routledge & Kegan Paul.

Lester-Smith, W.O. (1958) *Education: An Introductory Survey.* Harmondsworth: Penguin.

Lock, A. (ed.) (1978) *Action, Gesture and Symbol: The Emergence of Language.* London: Academic Press.

Lunzer, E.A. and Morris, J.F. (eds.) (1968) *Development in Human Learning*. London: Staples Press.

MacDonald, B. (1973) Humanities curriculum project, 80–90 in Schools Council (1973).

McKenzie, M. (1975) Learning to read and the reading process, 20–27 in Rosen (1975).

Mager, R.F. (1962) *Preparing Instructional Objectives*. Palo Alto, California: Fearon.

Matthews, G. (1978) Mathematics, 167–183 in Fontana (1978).

Matthews, J. (1984) Children drawing: are young children really scribbling? *Early Child Development and Care* 18, 1 and 2, 1–39.

Maxwell, B. (1984) Why LOGO? 84–106 in Kelly (1984).

Miller, A., Robson, D. and Bushell, R. (1985) The development of paired reading in Derbyshire, in Topping and Wolfendale (1985).

National Foundation for Educational Research (1955, 1960 and 1970). *Reading Surveys Using National Survey Form Six (NS6)* Test reported in Start and Wells (1972).

National Foundation for Educational Research (1977) *Areas of Discussion for Teacher Groups, Record-Keeping in the Primary School* (unpublished). Slough: NFER.

National Foundation for Educational Research (1978) *L.E.A.S. and Schools Item Banking Project – General Brochure*. NFER, December 1978 (mimeo).

Papert, S. (1980) *Mindstorms: Children, Computers and Powerful Ideas*. Brighton: Harvester.

Parsons, C. and Steadman, S. (1984) *It Makes You Think! Stating Aims and Objectives in the Primary School*. Schools Council Programme 1. Purpose and Planning in Schools. York: Longman for the Schools Council.

Patterson, C.H. (1977) *Foundations for a Theory of Instruction and Educational Psychology*. New York: Harper & Row.

Peters, R.S. (1965) Education as initiation, 87–111 in Archambault (1965).

Peters, R.S. (1966) *Ethics and Education*. London: Allen & Unwin.

Peters, R.S. (1967) What is an educational process?, 1–23 in Peters (1967).

Peters, R.S. (ed.) (1967) *The Concept of Education*. London: Routledge & Kegan Paul.

Peters, R.S. (1969) A recognizable philosophy of education: a constructive criticism, 1–20 in Peters (1969).

Peters, R.S. (ed.) (1969) *Perspectives on Plowden*. London: Routledge & Kegan Paul.

Peters, R.S. (ed.) (1973) *The Philosophy of Education*. Oxford: Oxford University Press.

Phenix, P.H. (1964) *Realms of Meaning*. New York: McGraw-Hill.

Piaget, J. (1969) *Science of Education and the Psychology of the Child*. First published in Great Britain 1971. London: Longman.

Piaget, J. (1973) *To Understand is to Invent*. New York: Grossman.

Popham, W.J. (1969) Objectives and instruction, 32–52 in Popham *et al.* (1969).

Popham, W.J., Eisner, E.W., Sullivan, H.J. and Tyler, L.L. (1969) *Instructional Objectives*, American Educational Research Association Monograph Series on Curriculum Evaluation No. 3. Chicago: Rand McNally.

Pring, R.A. (1971) Bloom's taxonomy: a philosophical critique (2). *Cambridge Journal of Education* 2, 83–91.

Proudfoot, H. (1983) Development throught the creative arts, 115–156 in Blenkin and Kelly (1983a).

Reed, G.F. (1968) Skill. 104–143 in Lunzer and Morris (1968).

Rheingold, H. (1983) Video games go to school. *Psychology Today* 17, 9, 37–46.

Richards, C. (1980) Demythologizing primary education. *Journal of Curriculum Studies*, 77–78.

Richards, R. (1979) *Learning through science*. Schools Council Newsletter No. 30, 5–7.

Richards, R. (1983) Learning through science, 96–114 in Blenkin and Kelly (1983a).

Rosen, H. (ed.) (1975) *Language and Literacy in our Schools: Some Appraisals of the Bullock Report*. Studies in Education 1. London: University of London, Institute of Education.

Ross, A. (1984) Learning why to hypothesize: a case study of data processing in a Primary school, 64–83 in Kelly (1984a).

Rowland, S. (1984) *The Enquiring Classroom: An Introduction to Children's Learning*. Lewes: Falmer.

Rusk, R.R. (1957) *The Doctrines of the Great Educators*. London: Macmillan.

Ryle, G. (1967) *The Concept of Mind*. London: Hutchinson.

Sadler, J.E. (1974) *Concepts in Primary Education*. London: Allen & Unwin.

Salmon, P. (ed.) (1980) *Coming to Know*. London: Routledge & Kegan Paul.

Scheffler, I. (1960) *The Language of Education*. Springfield, Illinois: C.C. Thomas.

Schools Council (1972) *Exploration Man: An Introduction to Integrated Studies*. Oxford: Oxford University Press for the Schools Council.

Schools Council (1973) *Evaluation in Curriculum Development: Twelve Case Studies*. Schools Council Research Studies. London: Macmillan Education for the Schools Council.

Schools Council (1980) *Learning Through Science: Formulating a School Policy.* London: Macdonald Educational for the Schools Council.

Shields, M.M. (1978) The child as psychologist; construing the social world, 529–556 in Lock (1978).

Skilbeck, M. (1984) *School-based Curriculum Development.* London: Harper & Row.

Smith, F. (1971) *Understanding Reading.* New York: Holt, Rinehart & Winston.

Sockett, H. (1976) *Designing the Curriculum.* London: Open Books.

Southgate, V., Arnold, H. and Johnson, S. (1981) *Extending Beginning Reading.* London: Heinemann Educational for the Schools Council.

Spencer, M. (1980) Handing down the magic, 46–62 in Salmon (1980).

Start, K.B. and Wells, B.K. (1972) *The Trend of Reading Standards.* Slough: National Foundation for Educational Research.

Stenhouse, L. (1970) Some limitations of the use of objectives in curriculum research and planning. *Pedagogica Europaea* 6, 73–83.

Stenhouse, L. (1975) *An Introduction to Curriculum Research and Development.* London: Heinemann.

Stenhouse, L. (ed.) (1980) *Curriculum Research and Development in Action.* London: Heinemann.

Stewart, W.A.C. and MaCann, W.P. (1967–1968) *The Educational Innovators* (Vols. 1 and 2). London: Macmillan.

Taba, H. (1962) *Curriculum Development: Theory and Practice.* New York: Harcourt, Brace & World.

Taylor J. (1971) *Organising and Integrating the Infant Day.* Unwin Education Books: 5. London: Allen & Unwin.

Thomas, N. (1980) The national primary survey: methods and findings. *Journal of Curriculum Studies* 12, 75–81.

Tinbergen, N. (1976) *The Importance of Being Playful.* London: British Association for Early Childhood Education Pamphlet No.1.

Tizard, B., Mortimore, J. and Burchell, B. (1981) *Involving Parents in Nursery and First Schools: A Source Book for Teachers.* London: Grant McIntyre.

Tizard, B. and Hughes, M. (1984) *Young Childen Learning, Talking and Thinking at Home and at School.* London: Fontana.

Tizard, J., Schofield, W.N. and Hewison, J. (1982) Collaboration between teachers and parents in assisting children's reading. *British Journal of Educational Psychology* 52, 1–15.

Topping, K. and Wolfendale, S. (eds.) (1985) *Parental Involvement in Children's Reading.* London: Croom Helm.

Turner, J. (1975) *Cognitive Development.* London: Methuen.

Tyler, R.W. (1932) *The Construction of Examinations in Botany and Zoology*. Service Studies in Higher Education. Ohio State University, Bureau of Educational Research Monographs, No. 15, 49–50.

Tyler, R.W. (1949) *Basic Principles of Curriculum and Instruction*. Chicago: University of Chicago Press.

Walden, R. and Walkerdine, V. (1982) *Girls and Mathematics: The Early Years*. Bedford Way Papers No. 8. London: Heinemann.

Walton, J. (ed.) (1971) *The Integrated Day in Theory and Practice*. London: Ward Lock Educational.

Ward, M. (1979) *Mathematics and the 10-year-old: Schools Council Working Paper 61*. London: Evans/Methuen Educational for the Schools Council.

Warlow, A. (1978) *Some thoughts about formulating a school or classroom language policy*. Unpublished paper from ILEA Centre for Language in Primary Education, Ebury Teachers' Centre, London.

Wells, G. (1981) *Learning through Interaction: The Study of Language Development*. Cambridge: Cambridge Unversity Press.

Wheeler, D.K. (1967) *Curriculum Process*. London: University of London Press.

Whitbread, N. (1972) *The Evolution of the Nursery-Infant School: A History of Infant and Nursery Education in Britain, 1800–1970*. London: Routledge & Kegan Paul.

White, J.P. (1968) Education in obedience. *New Society*, 2 May.

White, J.P. (1973) *Towards a Compulsory Curriculum*. London: Routledge & Kegan Paul.

Whitehead, A.N. (1932) *The Aims of Education*. London: Williams & Norgate.

Whitehead, M. (1983) Language development and the Primary curriculum, 57–80 in Blenkin and Kelly (1983a).

Whitehead, M. (1985) On learning to write – recent research and developmental writing. *Curriculum* 6, 2, 12–19.

Whitehead, M. (1986) "Breakthrough" revisited. Some thoughts on "Breakthrough to Literacy" and developmental writing. *Curriculum* 7, 26–32.

Willes, M.J. (1983) *Children into Pupils: a Study of Language in Early Schooling*. London: Routledge & Kegan Paul.

Williams, R. (1961, 1965) *The Long Revolution*. London: Chatto & Windus (1961); also Harmondsworth: Penguin Pelican (1965).

Wilson, P.S. (1971) *Interest and Discipline in Education*. London: Routledge & Kegan Paul.

Woodhead, M. (1976) *Intervening in Disadvantage: A Challenge for Nursery Education*. Windsor: National Foundation for Education Research.

Young, M.F.D. (ed.) (1971) *Knowledge and Control*. London: Collier-Macmillan.

Government reports and other official publications referred to in the text – listed in chronological order

Board of Education (1931) *Primary Education* (the Hadow Report on Primary Education). London: HMSO.

Central Advisory Council for Education (1967) *Children and Their Primary Schools*. (The Plowden Report.) London: HMSO.

Department of Education and Science (1975) *A Language for Life* (The Bullock Report). London: HMSO.

Department of Education and Science (1977) *Education in Schools: A Consultative Document* (Green Paper). Cmnd 6869. London: HMSO.

Department of Education and Science (1978) *Primary Education in England: A Survey by HM Inspectors of Schools*. London: HMSO.

Department of Education and Science (1979) *Aspects of Secondary Education in England: A Survey by HM Inspectors of Schools*. London. HMSO.

Department of Education and Science (1980a) *A View of the Curriculum: HMI Series: Matters for Discussion No. 11*. London: HMSO.

Department of Education and Science (1980b) *A Framework for the School Curriculum*. Document BES/7980/20. London: DES/Welsh Office.

Department of Education and Science (1982a) *Education 5–9: An Illustrative Survey of 80 First Schools in England*. London: HMSO.

Department of Education and Science (1982b) *Mathematics Counts* (The Cockcroft Report). London: HMSO.

Department of Education and Science (1983a) *Teaching Quality* (White Paper). Cmnd 8836. London: HMSO.

Department of Education and Science (1983b) *Initial Teacher Training: Approval of Courses*. London: DES (mimeo)

Department of Education and Science (1984) *English from 5 to 16. Curriculum Matters 1. An HMI Series*. London: HMSO.

Department of Education and Science (1985a) *The Curriculum from 5 to 16. Curriculum Matters 2. An HMI Series*. London: HMSO.

Department of Education and Science (1985b) *Mathematics from 5 to 16. Curriculum Matters 3. An HMI Series*. London: HMSO.

Department of Education and Science (1985c) *Music from 5 to 16. Curriculum Matters 4. An HMI Series*. London: HMSO.

Department of Education and Science (1985d) *Home Economics from 5 to 16.*

Curriculum Matters 5. An HMI Series. London: HMSO.

Department of Education and Science (1985e) *Better Schools* (White Paper). Cmnd 9469. London: HMSO.

Department of Education and Science (1986a) *Health Education from 5 to 16. Curriculum Matters 6. An HMI Series.* London: HMSO.

Department of Education and Science (1986b) *English from 5 to 16. The Responses to Curriculum Matters 1. An HMI Report.* London: DES.

INDEX OF AUTHORS

INDEX OF SUBJECTS